Text Editor Navigation Keys

PRESS	TO MOVE
Right arrow	Right one space or character
Left arrow	Left one space or character
Up arrow	Up one line
Down arrow	Down one line
PgUp	Up 21 lines (one screen)
PgDn	Down 21 lines (one screen)
Home	To left end of current line
End	To right end of current line
Control-Right arrow	One word to the right
Control-Left arrow	One word to the left
Control-Home	To beginning of file
Control-End	To end of file

Key Combinations for Selecting Text

PRESS	TO SELECT
Shift-Right arrow	Character at cursor; extends block one character at a time to the right
Shift-Left arrow	Character to left of cursor; extends block one character at a time to the left
Shift-Up arrow	Current line, from the left of the cursor to the line above the cursor; extends block up one line at a time
Shift-Down arrow	Current line, from the cursor to the right end; extends block down one line at a time
Shift-Control-Home	Everything from cursor to beginning of file
Shift-Control-End	Everything from cursor to end of file
Control-A	Entire file (selects All)

Computer users are not all alike.
Neither are SYBEX books.

We know our customers have a variety of needs. They've told us so. And because we've listened, we've developed several distinct types of books to meet the needs of each of our customers. What are you looking for in computer help?

If you're looking for the basics, try the **ABC's** series. You'll find short, unintimidating tutorials and helpful illustrations. For a more visual approach, select **Teach Yourself**, featuring screen-by-screen illustrations of how to use your latest software purchase.

Mastering and **Understanding** titles offer you a step-by-step introduction, plus an in-depth examination of intermediate-level features, to use as you progress.

Our **Up & Running** series is designed for computer-literate consumers who want a no-nonsense overview of new programs. Just 20 basic lessons, and you're on your way.

We also publish two types of reference books. Our **Instant References** provide quick access to each of a program's commands and functions. SYBEX **Encyclopedias** provide a *comprehensive reference* and explanation of all of the commands, features and functions of the subject software.

Sometimes a subject requires a special treatment that our standard series doesn't provide. So you'll find we have titles like **Advanced Techniques, Handbooks, Tips & Tricks**, and others that are specifically tailored to satisfy a unique need.

We carefully select our authors for their in-depth understanding of the software they're writing about, as well as their ability to write clearly and communicate effectively. Each manuscript is thoroughly reviewed by our technical staff to ensure its complete accuracy. Our production department makes sure it's easy to use. All of this adds up to the highest quality books available, consistently appearing on best-seller charts worldwide.

You'll find SYBEX publishes a variety of books on every popular software package. Looking for computer help? Help Yourself to SYBEX.

For a complete catalog of our publications:

SYBEX Inc.
2021 Challenger Drive, Alameda, CA 94501
Tel: (415) 523-8233/(800) 227-2346 Telex: 336311
Fax: (415) 523-2373

SYBEX is committed to using natural resources wisely to preserve and improve our environment. As a leader in the computer book publishing industry, we are aware that over 40% of America's solid waste is paper. This is why we have been printing the text of books like this one on recycled paper since 1982.

This year our use of recycled paper will result in the saving of more than 15,300 trees. We will lower air pollution effluents by 54,000 pounds, save 6,300,000 gallons of water, and reduce landfill by 2,700 cubic yards.

In choosing a SYBEX book you are not only making a choice for the best in skills and information, you are also choosing to enhance the quality of life for all of us.

The ABC's of FoxPro 2

The ABC's of FoxPro® 2

Second Edition

Scott D. Palmer

San Francisco • Paris • Düsseldorf • Soest

Acquisitions Editors: Dianne King and David Clark
Editors: Doug Robert and Jeff Kapellas
Technical Editors: Sheldon Dunn and Lin Beacom
Word Processors: Ann Dunn and Susan Trybull
Book Designers: Suzanne Albertson
Chapter Art: Charlotte Carter
Layout: Lucie Živny
Screen Graphics: Delia Brown and Cuong Le
Typesetter: Elizabeth Newman
Proofreaders: Elizabeth G. Chuan and R. M. Holmes
Indexer: Ted Laux
Cover Designer: Ingalls + Associates
Cover Photographer: Mark Johann
Screen reproductions produced by XenoFont.

XenoFont is a trademark of XenoSoft.

SYBEX is a registered trademark of SYBEX, Inc.

TRADEMARKS: SYBEX has attempted throughout this book to distinguish proprietary trademarks from descriptive terms by following the capitalization style used by the manufacturer.

SYBEX is not affiliated with any manufacturer.

Every effort has been made to supply complete and accurate information. However, SYBEX assumes no responsibility for its use, nor for any infringement of the intellectual property rights of third parties which would result from such use.

First edition copyright ©1990 SYBEX Inc.

Copyright ©1991 SYBEX Inc., 2021 Challenger Drive, Alameda, CA 94501. World rights reserved. No part of this publication may be stored in a retrieval system, transmitted, or reproduced in any way, including but not limited to photocopy, photograph, magnetic or other record, without the prior agreement and written permission of the publisher.

Library of Congress Card Number: 91-65869
ISBN: 0-89588-877-7
Manufactured in the United States of America
10 9 8 7 6 5 4 3 2

*Dedicated to my father, who taught me courage;
to my mother, who taught me compassion;
and to Brand Blanshard, who taught me why life is important.*

ACKNOWLEDGMENTS

MANY PEOPLE'S HARD WORK AND IDEAS GO INTO THE creation of any good book. Like most such books, this was very much a team effort.

Foremost among those who helped were Doug Robert and Jeff Kapellas, my editors at SYBEX, who lent both their editorial and managerial talents to the project. I also owe thanks to Dianne King and David Clark, acquisitions editors at SYBEX, for thinking of me in connection with this project. Lin Beacom and Sheldon Dunn, the technical reviewers, also made many helpful suggestions.

Gloria Pfeif and Susan Russell at Fox Software were a tremendous help in providing information about the new features of FoxPro 2 and the philosophy behind them.

Last but not least, I depended on my family's patience and support, without which this would just be a computer book.

◊ CONTENTS AT A GLANCE ◊

Introduction   xviii

PART I   Preliminaries
Lesson 1	Getting to Know Your PC	2
Lesson 2	Creating Your First Database	10

PART II   The Basics
Lesson 3	Putting Records into Your Database	22
Lesson 4	Customizing the Way FoxPro Displays Your Data	34
Lesson 5	Changing Your Client Data	42
Lesson 6	Taking a Shortcut with the View Window	50
Lesson 7	Modifying Your Client File Structure	56
Lesson 8	Viewing Your Client Data	66
Lesson 9	Creating Simple Reports	76

PART III   Intermediate-Level Skills
Lesson 10	Sorting a Database File	90
Lesson 11	Indexing Your Client File	100
Lesson 12	Finding Specific Records	114
Lesson 13	Creating Sophisticated Reports	126

PART IV   Advanced-Level Skills
Lesson 14	Creating Your Own Data-Entry Screens	144
Lesson 15	Linking Files	162
Lesson 16	Creating Multifile Reports	174
Lesson 17	Creating Your Own Menu System	188

PART V   Specific Skills
Lesson 18	Advanced Field Techniques	210
Lesson 19	Using FoxPro's Command Window	226
Lesson 20	Using FoxPro's Text Editor	242
Lesson 21	Creating Form Letters	252
Lesson 22	Creating Mailing Labels	260
Lesson 23	Using Macros to Speed Up Your Work	270
Lesson 24	Using FoxPro's Desk Accessories	278
Lesson 25	Introducing FoxPro 2's Advanced Features	290
Appendix	Installing FoxPro	298
Index		301

TABLE OF CONTENTS

Introduction		xviii
	How to Use This Book	xix

PART I Preliminaries

Lesson 1	Getting to Know Your PC	2
	Your PC Is Simpler Than You Think	3
	Parts of Your PC	4
	The Keyboard	4
	The Mouse	8
	Saving Your Work	8
Lesson 2	Creating Your First Database	10
	What's a Computer Database?	11
	How to Create a Database File	11
	Lesson Summary	16
	Hot Tips	18

PART II The Basics

Lesson 3	Putting Records into Your Database	22
	Opening a File	23
	Displaying Your Records	27
	Changing to Table View	27
	Viewing Your Table	29
	Dealing with Larger Tables	29
	Closing a Database File	30
	Lesson Summary	30
	Hot Tips	32
Lesson 4	Customizing the Way FoxPro Displays Your Data	34
	Moving a Screen Window	35
	Using the Keyboard to Move a Window	35

	Using the Mouse to Move a Window	35
	Resizing a Screen Window	35
	Using the Keyboard to Resize a Window	37
	Using the Mouse to Resize a Window	37
	Moving the Window Before Resizing	37
	Splitting the Browse Window	38
	Using the Keyboard to Split a Window	38
	Using the Mouse to Split a Window	39
	Restoring the "Default" Window	39
	Lesson Summary	40
Lesson 5	Changing Your Client Data	42
	How to Add New Records to a Database	43
	Editing the Data in Your Records	44
	Editing Records in a Multicolumn Table	44
	Editing Records in Form View	45
	How to Delete Records	46
	Marking Records for Deletion	46
	Packing the Database	48
	Lesson Summary	48
	Hot Tips	49
Lesson 6	Taking a Shortcut with the View Window	50
	Using the View Window	51
	Database Action Buttons	51
	The Setup Window	53
	Work Areas and Relations	54
	Hot Tips	54
Lesson 7	Modifying Your Client File Structure	56
	Different Field Types	57
	Changing the Structure of Your Database File	58
	Displaying Your Database Structure	59
	Adding Fields	59
	Deleting Fields	62
	Changing a Field Definition	63

	Lesson Summary	63
	Hot Tips	64
Lesson 8	Viewing Your Client Data	66
	Entering Data into Memo Fields	67
	Rearranging the Browse Window	68
	How to Move a Column	68
	How to Resize a Column	70
	Selecting Columns to Display	71
	Lesson Summary	73
	Hot Tips	74
Lesson 9	Creating Simple Reports	76
	Creating a Quick Report	77
	The Layout Window	78
	Modifying Your Quick Report	80
	Adding a Title to Your Report	80
	Saving and Printing Your Report	82
	Creating a Form Report	83
	Modifying a Form Report	84
	Lesson Summary	86
	Hot Tip	86

PART III   Intermediate-Level Skills

Lesson 10	Sorting a Database File	90
	Getting Ready to Sort Your Client File	91
	Sorting on a Single Field	92
	Sorting on Multiple Fields	94
	Sorting on Letters and Numbers	96
	Lesson Summary	97
	Hot Tips	98
Lesson 11	Indexing Your Client File	100
	How to Index a Database File	101
	Keeping Index Files Up-to-Date	105

	Working with Multiple Index Files	107
	Setting the Index Order	108
	Simplifying Your Work by Using View Files	109
	Lesson Summary	110
	Hot Tips	111
Lesson 12	Finding Specific Records	114
	Search Conditions	115
	The Idea of Search Conditions	115
	A Simple Search with LIST	115
	Multiple Search Conditions	117
	Logical Operators	117
	Doing a Multiple-Conditions Search	118
	Printing Your Search Resuts	115
	Using LOCATE and SEEK	119
	LOCATE with Non-Indexed Databases	119
	SEEK with Indexed Databases	121
	Using SET FILTER	123
	Lesson Summary	124
	Hot Tips	125
Lesson 13	Creating Sophisticated Reports	126
	Laying Out Your Report	127
	Using the Page Layout Dialog Box	127
	Entering Title Information	128
	Date Stamping and Page Numbering	129
	Grouping Records	134
	Formatting Report Fields	136
	Filtering Records in Your Report	137
	Lesson Summary	138
	Hot Tips	139

PART IV   Advanced-Level Skills

Lesson 14	Creating Your Own Data-Entry Screens	144
	Using FoxPro's Screen Painter	145

	Starting the Screen Painter	146
	Adding Boxes to Your Screen	150
	Adding Formats and Data Validation	151
	Adding Field Attributes	152
	Using the Screen Format	157
	Pushing Ahead with the Screen Painter	158
	Lesson Summary	161
Lesson 15	Linking Files	162
	Setting Up a Transaction File	163
	The Non-Linking Approach	163
	The Linked-File Approach	164
	Creating a Linked-File Database	164
	Creating the Transaction File	164
	How to Link the Client and Sales Files	170
	Saving Your Link Setup as a View File	172
	Lesson Summary	172
	Hot Tip	173
Lesson 16	Creating Multifile Reports	174
	Creating Linked-File Reports	175
	Creating a Simple Linked Report with LIST	176
	How to Create a Linked Quick Report	178
	Creating a Linked Custom Report	181
	Using Advanced Report Functions	184
	Lesson Summary	186
Lesson 17	Creating Your Own Menu System	188
	Creating a Menu System	189
	Starting FoxApp	190
	Running Your FoxApp Menu System	192
	A More Sophisticated Menu System	195
	Basic Programming Concepts	195
	Creating a "dBASE-Compatible" Menu	197
	Creating FoxPro Drop-Down Menus	204
	Lesson Summary	206

PART V	**Specific Skills**	
Lesson 18	Advanced Field Techniques	210
	Using Field Options	211
	Formatting with PICTURE	214
	Data Validation with RANGE and VALID	216
	Appending Records with Formats and Data Validation	217
	Using Field Functions in FoxPro	218
	Report Formatting with Functions	219
	Sorting and Indexing with Field Functions	222
	Using FoxPro's On/Off Panel	224
	Lesson Summary	225
Lesson 19	Using FoxPro's Command Window	226
	Creating and Using Database Files	227
	Creating a Database	228
	Operations within Your Database Files	231
	Using SET Commands	238
	Important SET Commands	239
Lesson 20	Using FoxPro's Text Editor	242
	Starting the Text Editor	243
	Using the Menus	243
	The Edit Menu	244
	Saving and Closing Your File	246
	Moving Around in Your File	247
	Selecting Text	247
	Copying Text between Files	249
	Lesson Summary	250
Lesson 21	Creating Form Letters	252
	Form Letters in FoxPro	253
	Creating a Form Letter	254
	Inserting Name and Address Fields	255
	Final Formatting	258
	Printing Your Form Letters	259

Lesson 22	Creating Mailing Labels	260
	Creating a Label Format	261
	Setting Up Your Database	261
	Setting Up a Label Format	262
	Creating an Envelope Format	263
	Printing Labels and Envelopes	267
Lesson 23	Using Macros to Speed Up Your Work	270
	Creating Some Useful Macros	271
	Testing the Macro	273
	Saving Your New Macro	273
	Creating a More Sophisticated Macro	274
	Testing the Macro	274
Lesson 24	Using FoxPro's Desk Accessories	278
	FoxPro's Filer	279
	Filer Operations	280
	FoxPro's Calculator	286
	FoxPro's Calendar/Diary	287
Lesson 25	Introducing FoxPro 2's Advanced Features	290
	Different Versions of FoxPro	291
	Relational Query-By-Example	292
	New Index File Types	296
	Projects	296
	External Routine API	297
	Rushmore Technology	297
Appendix	Installing FoxPro	298
	The Installation Process	299
	Modifying FoxPro's Start-up with CONFIG.FP	300
Index		301

INTRODUCTION

IF YOU NEED TO SET UP A PC DATABASE BUT DON'T HAVE time to become a computer expert first, then this book is for you. In plain English, it gives you a fast-track way to learn FoxPro's most useful features, with a step-by-step approach and plenty of simple, hands-on examples.

You learn by doing: everything from simple record keeping to sophisticated reports, form letters, and multifile databases. And it will be easier than you expect. With FoxPro, you'll be able to create:

- Personnel databases
- Customer and inventory databases
- Sales reports
- Personalized billing and direct-mail pieces
- Split-screen views of your data
- Sophisticated databases for scientific research

This is first and foremost a practical manual. Database concepts are explained when they are relevant, but the main focus is on *doing*. Just as you can't learn to drive a car by reading a Driver's Ed book, you can't learn to set up a database by reading a database book. *The ABCs of FoxPro 2* is designed to get you out "on the road" right away, as you learn new techniques quickly and remember them easily. Lessons are kept short so that you can see your progress at each new milestone.

After a brief introduction to your PC, you'll set up a customer database for a small business. In the lessons after that, you'll learn how to enter and edit customer records using FoxPro's drop-down menus and speed keys. You'll also learn to display your customer data on-screen in a variety of ways; to put it in any order you like; to preview and print out quick reports, form letters, and mailing labels; and to use FoxPro's handy utility features.

Finally, you'll learn how to speed up your work by creating multi-file databases with links between different files. If you wanted to do this with most other database packages, you would almost have to be a programmer, but with FoxPro, it's as easy as clicking the mouse or pressing the Enter key.

This book will be your guide to gaining a productive business skill. Unlike most books about database management, which are aimed at programmers and computer specialists, *The ABCs of FoxPro 2* was written with you in mind: the beginning user who needs to acquire practical skills that you can put to work right away.

How to Use This Book

Before you can start using this book, of course, you have to have FoxPro installed on your PC. If you've already done that, then congratulations, you're ahead of the game! If not, don't despair: the appendix will help you with the installation. (It's also very important to read the "Release Notes" that are included with your FoxPro manuals. These provide last-minute information about changes in the program.

This book is designed for use with the latest version of FoxPro. FoxPro 2 has many amazing new features, but most of them are in advanced areas (such as SQL support) that you won't need to worry about unless you need to become a serious database programmer or FoxPro "power user."

Most of this book, therefore, cannot only be used with FoxPro 2 but also with earlier versions of FoxPro. The single major exception is in generating screen formats, which—at least for the average user—was easier in earlier versions of FoxPro. Virtually everything else in this book will work equally well regardless of which version of FoxPro you use.

The best way to use this book is while sitting at your PC. Each lesson has several hands-on examples that let you actually *do* database work in FoxPro while you read along in the book. The explanations in the book will give you the knowledge you need, but it's by working through the examples that you'll acquire practical skills.

To make your time even more productive, you can modify the book's examples to fit your own database needs. That way, before you've even finished the book, you'll have a working database that is ready to use!

FoxPro can be used either with or without a mouse. It works fine with just a keyboard, but its window displays are designed to take advantage of a mouse if you have one. Because of this, there are at least two ways to do most things: with the keyboard or with the mouse.

If you've used other PC programs, FoxPro will seem quite different. Its screen displays (what computer people call its "user interface") are based on ideas from FoxBase+Mac, a version of FoxPro that runs on the Apple Macintosh. Because the Macintosh has proven so easy for many people, FoxPro incorporates Mac-style screen windows that are best handled with a mouse. I *strongly recommend* that you use a mouse.

As you work through the early lessons, you'll find instructions both for using the mouse and for using the keyboard. To select from a FoxPro menu, for example, you'll be told to either click on a menu option with your mouse or highlight the option with your keyboard arrow keys and press Enter. At the end of these first lessons, you'll also find a summary of the main skills you've acquired in the lesson. The summaries contain side-by-side instructions for mouse and keyboard, as well as "speed key" combinations to bypass FoxPro's drop-down menus. In later chapters, when you've had plenty of practice using the mouse and the keyboard, summaries will appear only after the longer lessons, to refresh your memory concerning the key points.

So if you want to learn how to create your databases in FoxPro *today*, let's get started! Turn on your PC, settle into your chair, and prepare for an enjoyable and profitable learning adventure!

PART I

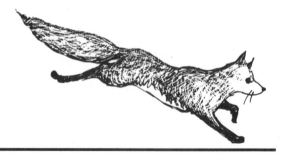

Preliminaries

LESSON 1
Getting to Know Your PC

LESSON 2
Creating Your First Database

LESSON 1
Getting to Know Your PC

Featuring

- How your PC works
- Parts of your PC
- Saving your work

BEFORE YOU START USING FOXPRO, IT WOULD BE AN excellent idea for us to take a quick guided tour of your PC. That way, you'll know how your PC works with FoxPro and what you should do to create and work with databases.

If you're already an experienced PC user, then you can skip this lesson and go directly to Lesson 2, where you'll learn to set up your first database. If you're in any doubt about your PC knowledge, however, you should at least glance through this lesson.

Your PC Is Simpler Than You Think

Let's dispel one myth at the very beginning. A lot of smart people are intimidated by PCs because they think that computers are hard to understand. However, the basic idea that makes computers work is very simple, even if things can get really complicated when we put that idea into action.

Did you ever walk into a room and turn on the lights? You just flipped the wall switch, and—presto!—the lights were on. What you used was an on/off switch. And that's the basic idea on which a computer is built: the on/off switch. In fact, you can think of a computer as nothing more than a large number of on/off switches hooked together.

The trick that turns simple on/off switches into a computer is that a computer uses sequences of ONs and OFFs to represent information. In your PC's internal lingo, for example, the sequence OFF-ON-OFF-OFF-OFF-OFF-OFF-ON represents the capital letter A, while the sequence OFF-ON-OFF-OFF-OFF-OFF-ON-OFF represents a capital B, and OFF-OFF-ON-OFF-ON-ON-ON-OFF represents a period. Usually, these sequences are written as combinations of 1s and 0s, with 1 meaning ON and 0 meaning OFF.

Your PC's microprocessor (its "brain," probably an Intel 8086, 80286, or 80386 computer chip) reads these sequences from other computer chips inside the PC and makes decisions based on the information that they contain.

Even though it's simple in concept, designing a computer is complicated in practice. Until the late 1970s, computer users themselves had to bear the brunt of that complexity, and therefore needed to be highly trained specialists. Programs had to be wired into the machines themselves or written in code that was hard even for the specialists to follow.

Things today are different. Just as you no longer need to be a mechanic to drive an automobile, you don't need to be an expert to use a computer. Computer programs are designed to be easy for non-experts to understand. If you don't know how to do something, there's almost always a "help" key that you can press to get an on-screen explanation of how to solve your problem.

It's also practically impossible to hurt your computer by pressing the wrong key, so don't be afraid to experiment if you're not sure what to do. You should, however, avoid experimenting with vital business files unless you've made copies—just in case something does go wrong.

Parts of Your PC

Now that you understand the essential ideas behind how computers work, let's look at the different parts of your PC that are involved in setting all those tiny on/off switches.

The Keyboard

All PCs use the same basic keyboard, but there are a few minor variations. Standard PCs often use a keyboard with the function keys on the left, while newer model PCs and IBM PS/2s use an "enhanced" keyboard with the function keys on top and a separate keypad for moving around on the PC's screen.

Figure 1.1 shows a standard PC/XT keyboard along with the enhanced keyboard used by PC/ATs and the IBM PS/2 series of PCs. The standard keyboard has the function keys on the left side and a numeric keypad on the right; the keypad keys are also used as "arrow keys" to move the on-screen cursor. The PC/AT and PS/2 keyboards are essentially identical: both have the function keys in a row across the top, with dedicated arrow keys between the letter keys and the numeric keypad on the right.

No matter which keyboard you're using, there are certain keys that you need to know about, whether you're working with FoxPro or any other software package.

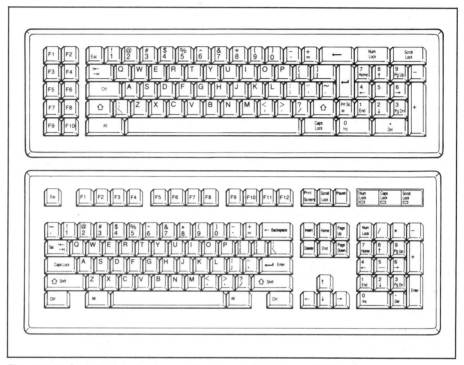

Figure 1.1: Standard and enhanced keyboards for PCs and PS/2s

The Enter Key

The Enter key, also called the Return key (a name left over from typewriter keyboards), is a key that you will often use to tell your PC to do something. When you type a command or highlight a menu option on one of FoxPro's drop-down menus, you press the Enter key to make FoxPro carry out the action you've chosen. (Usually, you can also do it by clicking the mouse, but we'll get to that in a minute.)

The Enter key is on the right side of your keyboard, and it probably has the symbol ⏎ on it. Apart from selecting menu options and typing in commands, you can use the Enter key to put data into your customer records and to "push" (select) various "buttons" that Fox-Pro displays on the screen. We'll discuss the specific buttons when they come up in learning to use FoxPro.

The Tab Key

The Tab key, located to the left of the letter Q on your keyboard, is identified by its two arrows pointing in opposite directions, ⇆. Some keyboards also show the word *TAB* next to the arrows.

The Tab key is particularly important in FoxPro. First, you will use the Tab key to move from one data item to another in your database records—for example, from the "first name" part of a customer record to the "last name" part. To move backward, you hold down either of the Shift keys (the keys that change letters to uppercase) while you press the Tab key. This use of the Tab key is common to almost all database packages.

In FoxPro, you can also use the Tab key to move from one part of an on-screen window to another. For example, many of FoxPro's windows come with on-screen "radio buttons" (which you can highlight and "push" by pressing the Enter key). You move from one of these buttons to the next (or backward to the previous one) by pressing the Tab key, just as you do when moving around the data items in a database record.

The Escape Key

The Escape key is the opposite of the Enter key. Instead of telling FoxPro to "go ahead," the Escape key tells FoxPro to stop whatever it's currently doing and "back out." Depending on when you press it, then, the Escape key will get you out of FoxPro's drop-down menus, close on-screen windows, or cancel a database operation you've started. The Escape key is located at either the top left or the top right of your keyboard and is probably labeled Esc.

The Control Key

The Control key (often abbreviated as Ctrl) is located above the left Shift key on a standard keyboard and below the left Shift key on an enhanced keyboard. You can use the Control key in combination with other keys to bypass FoxPro's menus for greater speed. These combinations are called *speed keys*.

For example, if you have several windows open on the screen, you can jump from one to another by pressing Ctrl-F1 (holding down the Control key and pressing the F1 function key). This is faster than opening FoxPro's Window menu and choosing the "Cycle" menu option. Control-key combinations are often written with a caret: for example, Ctrl-A would be written as ^A.

The Alt Key

The Alt Key is located to the left of the space bar on both standard and enhanced keyboards. In FoxPro, you'll use the Alt key primarily to open menus from FoxPro's menu bar. For example, Alt-R opens the Record menu, and Alt-W opens the Window menu.

The Function Keys

The function keys, alone or in combination with other keys, perform a variety of special tasks. We've already noted how the F1 function key, when pressed together with the Control key, takes you from one screen window to the next.

Pressing the F1 key by itself, on the other hand, brings up FoxPro's on-screen Help window. When you aren't sure what to do next, pressing F1 gets you information about how to accomplish your task. The F2 through F9 keys type FoxPro commands for you, such as **LIST**, while the F10 key activates drop-down menus.

The Cursor Keys

The cursor keys, located in a group on the right side of your keyboard, also help you move around the screen. If you're using a standard PC keyboard, the cursor keys are part of your numeric keypad: the keys for 2, 4, 6, and 8 are marked with arrows that show the direction in which they move the on-screen cursor. If you have an enhanced keyboard, the cursor keys will also be by themselves between the letter keys and the numeric keypad.

Also on the numeric keypad are the *Home*, *End*, *PgUp* (Page Up), and *PgDn* (Page Down) keys. These provide faster ways of moving the cursor around the screen.

If you're using keys in the numeric keypad and they don't seem to work right, check to see if you've accidentally pressed the *NumLock* key. This key changes all the keys on the numeric keypad into number keys instead of cursor keys. Pressing it again changes them back to cursor keys.

The Mouse

The mouse is a device that connects by a cable to the back of your PC and puts an extra cursor on your screen. By rolling the mouse around your desk and clicking or holding down the mouse buttons, you can move quickly from one screen window to another, move and resize windows, make menu choices, select files, and "push" on-screen buttons. Although you can do the same things just by using the keyboard, a mouse often lets you do them more quickly and easily. It's a worthwhile investment.

In the early parts of this book, we'll give separate step-by-step instructions for performing each task with the keyboard and the mouse. Later on, when you have a good feel for using either of them, we'll omit the dual-instructions approach unless it's really important or illuminating.

Saving Your Work

Your PC is like an electronic desk. Its random-access memory (RAM) is like the desktop: that's where the PC keeps everything it is currently working on. The PC's disk drives are like desk drawers: that's where it puts things it doesn't need right now, but which it will need again later on. Its processor is like a person sitting at the desk: that's the "brain" that manipulates jobs on the desktop, stores them in desk drawers (disk drives), and retrieves them when they are needed again.

This analogy can also be used to show why it's important to save your work. Turning off your PC is like opening a window next to your desk: everything that's on the desktop will blow away and be lost. However, if you've stored copies of your work in the desk drawers (on disk), you can get everything back again whenever you need it.

Most of the time, FoxPro will save your work automatically when you close a file window. For text and report files, however, FoxPro will ask if you want to save the file when you close it. To save the file, you would simply "push" the Yes button on the screen by pressing Enter or clicking on it with the mouse.

LESSON 2
Creating Your First Database

Featuring

- What is a computer database?
- How to create a database file

ONCE YOU'VE INSTALLED FOXPRO AND YOU KNOW HOW to work with your PC, you're almost ready to create your first database. But before we do that, let's take a quick look at what a database actually is.

In general terms, a database is just a collection of information that's organized so you can find what you need. It doesn't need to be on a computer. Thus, the phone book is a database; so is your filing cabinet, the latest issue of *TV Guide*, or the menu at your favorite restaurant.

What's a Computer Database?

On a computer, a database consists of one or more *data files*, each of which contains a particular kind of information. Files on your computer are just electronic versions of the paper files in your filing cabinet. For example, a customer data file might contain the following information about each of your customers:

- Account number
- First name
- Last name
- Street address
- City
- State
- Zip code
- Account balance

Like a stack of preprinted paper forms that you fill out, FoxPro data files allow a fixed amount of space for each piece of information (account number, first name, etc.) and let you fill in the blanks. In computer jargon, each blank to be filled in is called a *field*, and each paper form corresponds to a *record*. Thus, "Account number," "First name," and "Zip code" are examples of fields in a customer record. A FoxPro data file can contain up to *one billion* records!

How To Create a Database File

Now that you know what a database file is, it's time to create one. Before we get started, however, remember that if at any point you feel you need further information about the features you will be using, you can always press F1 to bring up FoxPro's on-screen Help window.

If you haven't already started FoxPro, fire it up by doing the following:

① Change to your FoxPro directory by typing

   cd\foxpro

   Then press the Enter key.

② Start FoxPro by typing

   foxpro

   and again press Enter.

When FoxPro starts up, you'll see a *menu bar* across the top of the screen and the *Command window* in the lower right corner. (Don't worry about the Command window right now; we'll get to it later on.) For now, here's how to create your first database file:

① Open the File menu from the menu bar by holding down the Alt key and pressing the letter F. If you're using a mouse, move the on-screen mouse cursor to the word "File" in the menu bar and click the appropriate mouse button. (Which button to click varies from one brand of mouse to another.) The File menu drops down, as shown in Figure 2.1.

② When the menu is first opened, the highlight will be on the first menu option, "New." You pick this option by either pressing the Enter key or moving the mouse cursor to the word "New" and clicking the mouse button.

③ Now, you'll see a *dialog box* in the middle of the screen (Figure 2.2). It lets you choose the kind of file you want to create. We want to create a database file, which happens to be the type of file already selected, so for now just press Enter to select the

Creating Your First Database 13

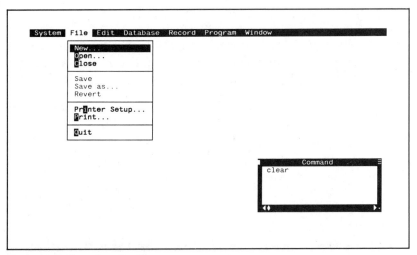

Figure 2.1: Opening the File menu

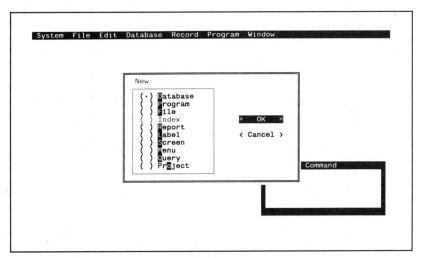

Figure 2.2: The dialog box for selecting a new file type

OK button. (If the highlight isn't on the OK button, move to it by pressing the Tab key; then press Enter to select it. With a mouse, just move the mouse cursor to OK and click the mouse button.)

④ A new dialog box, which has the word "Structure" in the upper left corner, should appear on the screen. This lets you define the database file structure, which is similar to setting up blanks and boxes on a paper form. On the first line, in the blank under "Name," type **ACCOUNT** and press Enter.

⑤ The highlight now moves to the second column, under "Type." Press Enter again and you'll see a list of the available data types, as shown in Figure 2.3. You can define this item as any type on the list, but for now, just press Enter to select "Character" type.

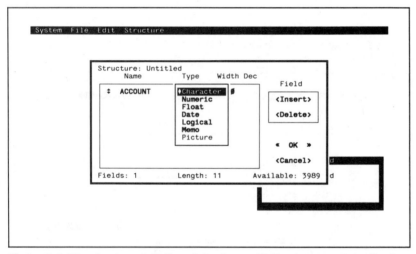

Figure 2.3: *The structure definition dialog box, with the data type selection box*

⑥ The highlight next moves to the "Width" column. Type **5** and press the Enter key.

⑦ The highlight moves automatically to the next line, skipping the "Dec" (decimal) column because character data does not use decimal places. You are now ready to define the next data item for this database file. By repeating the general method you used in steps 4 through 6, add the following fields to your database file:

Name	Type	Width	Dec
FIRSTNAME	Character	10	
LASTNAME	Character	10	
ADDRESS	Character	15	
CITY	Character	10	
STATE	Character	2	
ZIP	Character	5	

⑧ Now, let's add one more field that's just a little different. Instead of a character field this time, we'll enter a numeric field for the client's account balance. Type **BALANCE** and select the "Numeric" field type from the menu popup. Then enter **8** in the Width column (for a total field width of 8) and **2** in the Dec column to indicate two decimal places. Because the total width is 8, the maximum number that can be entered in the field is 99,999.99. (Remember, the decimal point takes a place as well.)

⑨ After you've entered the last item (the *2* in the Dec column), press the Tab key once to move the highlight to the OK button, and press Enter. (With a mouse, just move the mouse cursor to OK and click on it with the mouse button.)

⑩ A new dialog box will appear that prompts you to name your new database file. Let's name our file *clients,* as in Figure 2.4. You can enter a name of up to eight characters, including letters, numbers, hyphens, and underscores, but no other characters like periods, asterisks, or dollar signs. Don't press Enter after typing the name.

⑪ Above the file name you've just typed, you'll see a box that lists the *directories* in which you can put your new file. If you want to put the file in a directory other than the current directory

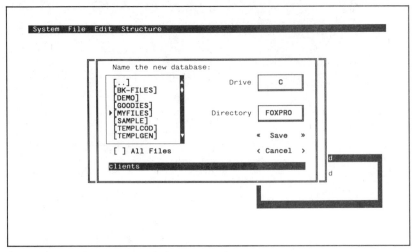

Figure 2.4: *Naming a file and choosing a directory*

(you'll see the name of the current directory on the right side of the dialog box—at this point it should be FOXPRO), press Tab until the highlight is in the box with the directory list. Then use the arrow keys to highlight the directory you want, and press Enter. (With a mouse, just double-click on the directory you want.)

 Next, use the Tab key to move to the Save button on-screen and press Enter (or click on the on-screen Save button with the mouse). FoxPro will ask

Input data records now?

Since we've already done plenty for a first database lesson, just move to the on-screen No button and select it by pressing the Enter key or clicking the mouse. The on-screen cursor will return to the Command window, at which point you should type **use** in the Command window and press Enter.

Lesson Summary

We've covered a lot of ground in a very short space, so let's review what we've learned. A *database* is an organized collection of information; on a computer, it consists of one or more *data files*. In these data files, there are *fields* defined by the user; each field is set up to hold a certain type of data, such as name, address, or account number. A data file is kept in a *directory* on one of the computer's disks. The operations involved in creating a data file in FoxPro are summarized in Table 2.1.

Table 2.1: Steps for Creating a Data File

OPERATION	USING THE KEYBOARD	USING A MOUSE
Start FoxPro	Type **foxpro** then press Enter	N/A
Open File menu	Press Alt-F	Click on "File" in menu bar
Define data file	Highlight "New" in File menu; press Enter	Click on "New" in File menu
Choose file type	Make sure "Database" is selected in dialog box; highlight OK button; press Enter	Make sure "Database" is selected; click on OK button
Define file	Enter name, type, and width for each field; highlight OK button; press Enter	After entering name, type, and width for each field, click on OK button
Name file	Enter name in dialog box	N/A
Choose directory (optional)	Tab to directory list; highlight desired directory; press Enter	Double-click on desired directory in directory list
Save file to disk	Tab to Save button; press Enter	Click on Save button

Hot Tips

- To have your PC always tell you what directory you're in, insert this line into your AUTOEXEC.BAT file or type it at the DOS prompt: **prompt pg**.

- Sometimes you need to press the mouse button twice instead of just once. If you click the mouse once and nothing happens, try "double-clicking" it. The two clicks can't be more than a second apart.

- If you haven't used a mouse before, your shoulder may get sore from the unaccustomed type of movement. Try resting your arm on something while you move the mouse around.

PART II

The Basics

LESSON 3
Putting Records
into Your Database

LESSON 4
Customizing the Way
FoxPro Displays Your Data

LESSON 5
Changing Your Client Data

LESSON 6
Taking a Shortcut
with the View Window

LESSON 7
Modifying Your
Client File Structure

LESSON 8
Viewing Your Client Data

LESSON 9
Creating Simple Reports

LESSON 3
Putting Records into Your Database

Featuring

- How to reopen a database file
- How to enter records
- How to display a single record
- How to display a table
- How to close a database file

AT THIS POINT THE DATABASE FILE WE'VE CREATED IS nothing more than a structured shell, patiently awaiting the information that will enable us to keep track of our clients: account number, name, address, and current balance. With these preliminaries taken care of, we are prepared to enter some of the records that we'll be using throughout the exercises in this book.

If you're continuing directly from Lesson 2, then you're already in the FoxPro Command window and your client file is open. Type **use** in the Command window and press Enter. (This closes the file that is open, because we're going to learn how to reopen a file.) If you took a break after Lesson 2, then simply restart FoxPro and you'll once again be in the Command window.

Opening a File

Before you can put records into a database file—or do anything else with it—you have to open it first. Here's how to reopen your client file:

① Open the File menu by holding down the Alt key and pressing *F;* with a mouse, just click on the word "File" in the menu bar.

② Use the arrow keys (or the mouse) to move the highlight to the second menu choice, "Open." Press Enter or click on "Open" with the mouse.

③ You'll see the "Open" dialog box on the screen. On the left side of the box, you'll see a list of files and disk directories, as shown in Figure 3.1. You can move the highlight up and down

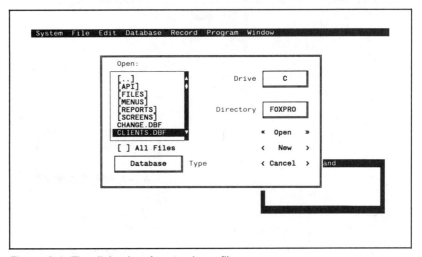

Figure 3.1: *The dialog box for opening a file*

in the list by using the PgDn, PgUp, and arrow keys; with a mouse, you can click on the up and down arrows that are in the right side of the box frame. Move the highlight down until you reach "CLIENTS.DBF" and press Enter, or double-click on it with the mouse.

④ Open the Record menu by holding down the Alt key and pressing *R*. (With a mouse, just click on the word "Record" in the menu bar.) Press Enter to select the first menu option, "Append," as shown in Figure 3.2.

⑤ Now a new window has popped open on the screen: the Append window, shown in Figure 3.3. This lets you add records to your database. (Later on, you'll learn how to create your own customized screens for adding records.) With the highlight in the Account field, type **00001**.

⑥ Entering the rest of your data records is just about as simple as it can get. At each field, you type in the information you want and press Enter to move to the next field. If you fill up a field, FoxPro will beep and automatically move the cursor to the next field or the next record. Here's what you should type as

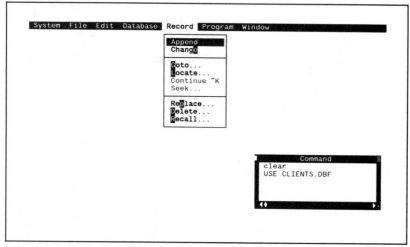

Figure 3.2: Choosing "Append" from the Record menu

the rest of your first client record:

Firstname: John

Lastname: Jones

Address: 123 City Place

City: New York

State: NY

Zip: 10016

Balance: 12.50

⑦ If you make a mistake typing, don't worry about it. If you're still in the field you need to correct, use the Backspace key to erase your mistake; then type in the correct information. If you've moved on to a different field or record, use the arrow keys to move back to the field with the mistake; then just type over the old information and use the Delete key to erase any extra characters on the right. Now, just enter a few more records:

Account: 00002

Firstname: Archibald

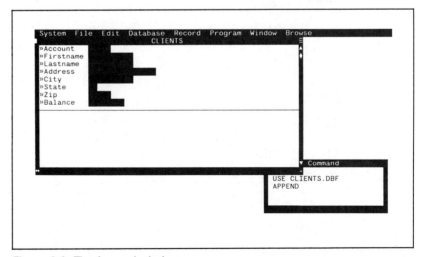

Figure 3.3: The Append window

Lastname: Leach
Address: 10 Downing St.
City: Hollywood
State: CA
Zip: 90069
Balance: 125.75

Account: 00003
Firstname: Walter
Lastname: Huston
Address: 25 Maple Ave.
City: Pittsburgh
State: PA
Zip: 15230
Balance: 95.50

Account: 00004
Firstname: Joe Bob
Lastname: Briggs
Address: P.O. Box 2002
City: Dallas
State: TX
Zip: 75221
Balance: 147.23

Account: 00005
Firstname: Michael
Lastname: Ende
Address: 501 Elm St.

City: **Chicago**

State: **IL**

Zip: **60646**

Balance: **49.95**

(8) When you've finished entering the last record, press the Escape key to close the Append window.

Displaying Your Records

The information you've typed in so far can be used to show quite a few of FoxPro's features. Let's start by displaying the information in various ways.

As usual, it's very easy. Just open the Database menu by pressing Alt-D or clicking on "Database" with the mouse. Select the second menu choice, "Browse."

Browsing a database file lets you display the records you've already entered. If you want to, you can even edit and change the records, but we'll get to that later.

Changing to Table View

Since you've just created a file and entered some records, the Browse window will show a single-record or "form" view of your data. Each record takes up several lines, with a different field on each line: Account on the first line, Firstname on the second, Lastname on the third, and so on, as shown in Figure 3.4.

Sometimes, of course, you'd rather see more than a simple two-column display of your data. You might want to see a table that can show more records. FoxPro makes this easy.

When you chose "Browse" from the Database menu, FoxPro added a new Browse menu on the right side of the menu bar, as you saw in Figure 3.4. Just press Alt-B to open this menu (or use the mouse to click on the word "Browse" in the menu bar), and pick the first menu choice, "Browse." This switches your Browse window from a form view to a multicolumn, multirecord table, as shown in

Figure 3.5. To change it back, you can reopen the Browse menu, at which time you will find that the first menu option is now "Change." Picking "Change" will change your table back to single-record form view.

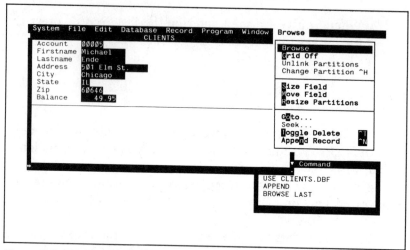

Figure 3.4: *The Browse Window, in "form" view, with the Browse menu open*

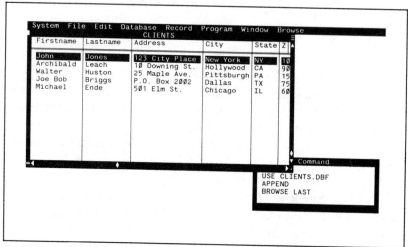

Figure 3.5: *The Browse window in multicolumn "table" view*

If you can't see as much of your database file as you'd like, you can "zoom" the Browse window to take up the whole screen by holding down the Control key and pressing the F10 function key. If you're using a mouse, you simply click on the zoom button, which occupies the top right corner of the Browse window. (The zoom button appears in Figure 3.5 as a stack of three short lines, but it might look different on your screen.) You can unzoom the window by repeating the action.

*V*iewing Your Table

Let's take a look at what's in your table. First, zoom the table to full-screen size by pressing Control-F10 or clicking the zoom button on the Browse window. That way, you can see everything.

Across the top line of your table are the names of your database fields—Account, Firstname, Lastname, and so on, in the same order as they appear in the database file itself. Notice that FoxPro makes the table column wide enough so that you can see the whole field name, even when the field itself has a narrower width. For example, the State field will accept no more than a two-letter entry, but the column is wide enough to display the name "State."

Each row of your table is a single record. You can move from one column to the next by pressing the Tab key; to move backward, just hold down the Shift key and press Tab. To move up or down one record at a time, use the up and down arrow keys; if you have a lot of records and want to go up or down a whole screen at a time, use the PgUp and PgDn keys.

If you're using a mouse, it's even easier: just click on the little arrows that you'll find in the frame of the Browse window. Clicking on an arrow moves you in the direction of the arrow. You should play around in the table for a little while until you can navigate it easily.

*D*ealing with Larger Tables

There's one other important thing to realize. Our customer database file is relatively small, so our Browse table shows everything in the file. Every field is listed across the top of the screen, and all five records are shown on the screen. Of course, it would be silly if database files were limited in size to what could be displayed on the screen at one time.

In fact, files can be a lot bigger. If your PC can handle it, a FoxPro database file can have up to 255 fields and as many as a billion records!

If your entire file can't be shown on-screen at once, you can move to off-screen columns by repeatedly pressing the Tab key to move right and Shift-Tab to move left. You can move to off-screen rows by pressing the PgUp and PgDn keys; with a mouse, you can click on the up and down arrows in the right side of the Browse window frame.

We'll come back to this point later on, when we add more fields to our clients file. If you want to get some practice right now, you should close the file we've created (instructions for closing a file are below) and open the FoxPro sample "customer" file (CUST.DBF) included with the package. It has 10 fields and 73 records, so that you can practice moving to off-screen rows and columns.

Closing a Database File

You can exit from the Browse window (or almost any other window in FoxPro) by pressing the Escape key or using the mouse to click on the button at the top left corner of the window (shown as a small white rectangle in the figures in this book). After you've closed the window, you can close the clients database file by typing **use** in the Command window and pressing Enter. (If you aren't already in the Command window, pressing Control-F2 will take you there.) You can also close a database file by using a button in the View window, but we'll cover that later.

Lesson Summary

In this lesson, we have seen how to open and close database files, how to add data to a database file, and how to display your data in both single-record and table format on the PC's screen. The key points to remember are summarized in Table 3.1.

Table 3.1: Key Points from Lesson 3

OPERATION	USING THE KEYBOARD	USING A MOUSE
Close a database file	Type **use** in the Command window; press Enter	Select "View" from Window menu; then select "Close" button
Open a database file	Select "Open" from the File menu; highlight file name; press Enter	Select "Open" from File menu; highlight file name; double-click with mouse
Enter data	Choose "Append" from Record menu; type data into fields	Same
Display data	Choose "Browse" from Database menu	Same
Change Browse window from form to table	Choose "Browse" from Browse menu	Same
Change Browse window from table to form	Choose "Change" from Browse menu	Same
Zoom current window to full-screen size	Press Control-F10	Click on zoom button in top right corner of window
Move right in table	Press Tab key	Click on right arrow in bottom border of Browse window
Move left in table	Press Shift-Tab	Click on left arrow in bottom border of Browse window

Table 3.1: Key Points from Lesson 3 (continued)

OPERATION	USING THE KEYBOARD	USING A MOUSE
Move up in table	Press the up arrow or PgUp key	Click on up arrow in right border of Browse window
Move down in table	Press the down arrow or PgDn key	Click on down arrow in right border of Browse window

Hot Tips

- Each menu choice has one letter highlighted. Another way to pick a menu choice is by pressing the key for the letter it has highlighted.

- When you see a button in a dialog box that has double angle brackets, such as << Save >>, you don't have to tab the highlight to the button: just hold down the Control key and press Enter. (The double brackets indicate that this is the *default button*.)

- If you want to learn FoxPro commands to bypass the menus, just watch the commands that appear in the Command box as you make your menu choices.

- You might think that since "Open" in the File menu opens a file, then "Close" in the File menu closes a file. However, "Close" in the File menu simply closes whatever window you're currently in—the same as pressing Escape or clicking on the window's close button. If you accidentally close the Command window, you can reopen it by pressing Control-F2.

LESSON 4
Customizing the Way FoxPro Displays Your Data

Featuring

- How to move and resize screen windows
- How to split the Browse window

◇ ◇ ◇ ◇

WE'VE ALREADY SEEN QUITE A BIT ABOUT HOW TO SET up a database file and put information into it. Now, let's take a quick look at some things we can do with the small database that we've already created.

Like any database management package, FoxPro lets you create databases and use them in a variety of ways. But unlike any other database management package, FoxPro gives you tremendous flexibility in displaying your data on the screen.

Moving a Screen Window

One of the first skills to master in displaying your data is the ability to move windows around the screen.

First, reopen the CLIENTS database file by selecting "Open" from the File menu, moving the highlight to CLIENTS.DBF in the "Open File" dialog box, and pressing Enter or double-clicking the mouse. Then, choose "Browse" from the Database menu to open a Browse window.

We've already seen (in Lesson 3) how you can zoom a window to fill up the whole screen by pressing Control-F10 or clicking on the "zoom" button at the top right of the window's frame. But did you realize that you can also move a window around the screen and make it any size you want?

Using the Keyboard to Move a Window

The simplest (but not the easiest) way to move a window is to open the Window menu and select the "Move" menu choice, as shown in Figure 4.1. You can then use the arrow keys on your keyboard to move the window around on the screen. Try it. When you've got the window right where you want it, just press Enter. The window's border will blink as long as it's "in motion," and will go back to normal as soon as you press the Enter key.

Although opening the Window menu only takes a couple of steps, FoxPro provides you with a speed key to do the same thing in just one step. If you look at the "Move" option on the Window menu, you'll see ^F7 right next to it (see Figure 4.1). Remembering that the Control key is often denoted by the caret (^), you can see that holding down the Control key and pressing the F7 function key has the same effect as opening the Window menu and selecting the "Move" menu choice. It's just faster.

Lesson 4

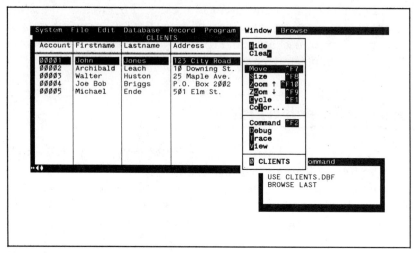

Figure 4.1: *Opening the Window menu*

Try moving the "CLIENTS" Browse window around the screen a bit until you're sure you have the hang of things.

Using the Mouse to Move a Window

Using the mouse to move a window is especially easy; if you've ever used an Apple Macintosh or a Commodore Amiga, you'll find that it works exactly the same way in FoxPro.

To move the window, just move the mouse cursor to the top (horizontal) border of the window and "grab" it by holding down the mouse button. Then, while holding down the mouse button, move the mouse to move the window. When the window is where you want it, just let go of the mouse button and the window will remain in its new location onscreen.

Try moving the "CLIENTS" Browse window around the screen a bit until it's second nature to you.

Resizing a Screen Window

Now that you've learned how to move a window around the screen, you'll find that resizing a window is a snap because it works the same way as moving a window.

Using the Keyboard to Resize a Window

To expand or shrink a window with the keyboard, you either select "Size" from the Window menu or press Control-F8. You then use the arrow keys to move the bottom and right borders of the window until the window is the size and shape that you want. It can be a perfect square, a flat rectangle, or any other rectangular dimension you choose.

Just the same as when you're moving a window, the borders will blink on and off as long as the window is in "resizing" mode. When it's the size and shape you want, press Enter and the window borders will go back to normal.

Try resizing the "CLIENTS" Browse window a few times for practice.

Using the Mouse to Resize a Window

Resizing a window with the mouse works the same in FoxPro as it does in programs on the Apple Macintosh. At the lower right corner of the window, next to the right-facing arrow, you'll see a "size" button, which looks like a white dot in the figures in this book. You simply move the mouse cursor onto this button and grab it by holding down your mouse button.

By moving your mouse while still holding down the button, you move the right and bottom borders of the window—expanding or contracting the window any way you like. As long as the window is in "resizing" mode, the window borders will blink on and off. When the window is the size and shape you want, simply release the mouse button and the window borders will go back to normal.

Try resizing the "CLIENTS" Browse window a few times until you get the hang of it.

Moving the Window Before Resizing

Whether you're expanding or contracting the window, the top left corner is sort of an anchor point that remains motionless while you move the bottom and right borders of the window. This means that a window will only expand down and to the right. If your window is in the middle of the screen, you might need to move it up and to the left before you can expand it as much as you want. You get maximum space to expand the window, of course, by moving it to the top left corner of the screen.

Splitting the Browse Window

Another feature that makes FoxPro unique is its ability to split the Browse window between two views of your data: the table view on one side, and the single-record "form" view on the other side, as shown in Figure 4.2.

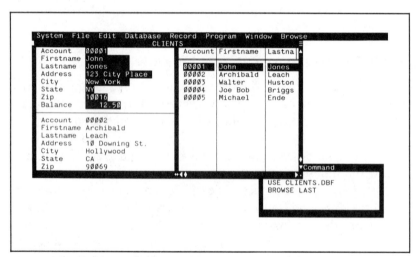

Figure 4.2: *Splitting the Browse window*

Using the Keyboard to Split a Window

To split the Browse window from the keyboard, open the Browse menu and choose "Resize Partitions." Then, tap the right arrow key a few times and you'll see that the Browse window is splitting into two parts.

When the split is where you want it, just press the Enter key. By selecting "Change" from the Browse menu, you can see your records in form view on one side and table view on the other. If you want to restore the Browse window to its original unsplit condition, just choose "Resize Partitions" again from the Browse menu. Use the left arrow key to move the right part of the window so that it completely covers the other part; then press Enter.

Using the Mouse to Split a Window

You're already familiar with several of the little gadgets in the frames of FoxPro's on-screen windows: the "close" button at the top left, the "zoom" button at the top right, and the "size" button at the lower right. In the lower left corner, however, is a button that we haven't talked about: the "splitter," which divides the Browse window into two parts. It appears as a very short arrow with an arrowhead at either end.

Move the mouse cursor onto the splitter and "grab" it by holding down your mouse button. Then, while still holding down the mouse button, move the mouse slowly to the right. As you move it, you'll see the Browse window splitting in two. By selecting "Change" from the Browse menu, you can see your records in form view on one side and table view on the other.

To restore the Browse window to its original condition, just grab the splitter button again; it's where you left it—under the vertical border in the middle of the Browse window. Move it to the left until the right part of the window completely covers the other part, and then let go of the mouse button.

Restoring the "Default" Window

One thing that may surprise you is that the next time you open your window, it will have the same size, shape, and location as it did when you closed it this time. If the window is split when you close it, then it will be split when you open it up again.

Every time you close a window in the normal way, FoxPro takes a "snapshot" of how it looks. Therefore, before you exit from the Browse window by pressing Escape or clicking on the close button at the top left of the frame, you should make sure you have the window the way you want it to look. This becomes the new "default view"—meaning that this is how the window will look unless you change it again.

To keep FoxPro from resetting the default view of your Browse window, close the window by pressing Control-Q instead of using the Escape key or clicking on the window's close button.

Lesson Summary

The key points from Lesson 4 are summarized in Table 4.1.

Table 4.1: Key Points from Lesson 4

OPERATION	USING THE KEYBOARD	USING A MOUSE
Zoom window to full screen	Press Control-F10	Click on zoom button at top right
Move window	Press Control-F7 and move with arrow keys	Grab top border with mouse cursor and drag
Resize window	Press Control-F8 and resize with arrow keys	Grab size button at lower right corner of border and drag it
Split Browse window	Choose "Resize Partitions" from the Browse menu, then use arrow keys	Grab "splitter" button in bottom frame border and drag horizontally

LESSON 5
Changing Your Client Data

> ### *Featuring*
> - How to add new records
> - How to edit data in your records
> - How to mark records for deletion
> - How to delete records with PACK

CHANGE IS A PART OF LIFE. NOTHING STANDS STILL, AND that includes the data in your client database. As you go along, you might get new clients and need to add records for them to your file. Information about current clients might change, and some of your other clients might move away and cease to be clients, in which case you would probably need to delete their records. And some clients might change only their names or their phone numbers, so you need to learn how to make such changes in your records.

Changing Your Client Data **43**

All these jobs are easy in FoxPro. Let's start with the simplest of all: adding new records to your database file.

How to Add New Records to a Database

The first thing to do is reopen CLIENTS.DBF. (If you aren't sure about how to open and close a file, this is a good time to review Lesson 3.)

① Open the Record menu and select the "Append" menu choice.

② The Append window will pop open on the screen, showing a blank record. The cursor will be in the first field of the blank record, so you can simply start typing in the new record. Don't forget that if you get to the end of a field when typing in data, FoxPro beeps and takes you down to the next field without you having to press Enter. Take a minute now to enter the following record:

Account: 00006

Firstname: Richard

Lastname: Feynman

Address: 100 QED Place

City: Menlo Park

State: CA

Zip: 94025

Balance: 41.25

Your screen should look like Figure 5.1.

③ Close the Append window by pressing Escape or clicking on the close button with the mouse. FoxPro automatically saves your new record, so you don't need to worry about it.

④ To verify that your new record is now in the database, open the Database menu and select "Browse." You can display all your

Lesson 5

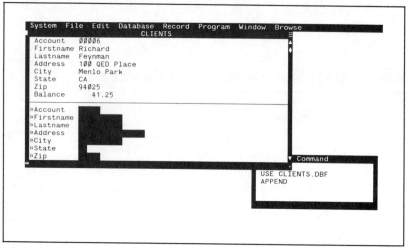

Figure 5.1: Adding a record to the "CLIENTS" Append window

records by pressing the PgUp key or by clicking on the up arrow in the right border of the window.

⑤ As before, you can switch between the table and form views of your data by picking either "Browse" or "Change" from the Browse menu.

Editing the Data in Your Records

FoxPro makes it easy to change the data in your records any time you need to. Let's look at two ways to do it.

Editing Records in a Multicolumn Table

① Display your data in table view in the Browse window.

② Move to the first record (John Jones) by using the arrow and PgUp/PgDn keys, or simply click on that line of the table.

③ Let's pretend that the address for Mr. Jones was entered incorrectly. Instead of 123 City Place, he lives at 123 City Road.

Press the Tab key three times to move to the Address column, or simply click on that column with the mouse.

④ Just like a word processor, FoxPro lets you move quickly around a field by using the arrow keys. You could move to the word *Place* by pressing the right arrow key nine times to skip the nine characters before the word, but it is simpler to just hold down the Control key and press the right arrow key twice, which skips two "words," landing the cursor on the *P* of *Place*.

⑤ Type **Road**. As you can see in Figure 5.2, after this you need to tap the Delete key twice to delete the first two letters in *Place*. (You may have noticed that the rest of the word was pushed off to the right and deleted automatically.) Press Enter to make the change permanent.

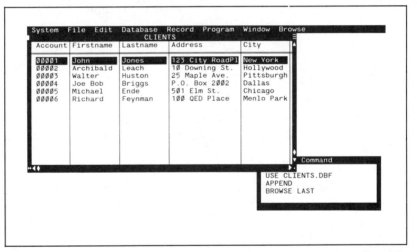

Figure 5.2: *Changing the address in Account 00001 from "Place" to "Road."*

Editing Records in Form View

You can edit records in form view just as easily as you can in table view.

① Select "Change" from the Browse menu to switch to a single-record view of your data.

② For this example, let's say that John Jones' account balance is not $12.50, but $125.00. Tap the down arrow key three times to move down to the Balance field, type **125.00**, then press Enter.

③ Notice that after you entered the new account balance, FoxPro automatically jumped down to the next record, because "Balance" was the last field in the record you were editing. However, now we want to edit record 5. Press the PgDn key three times to get there.

④ Tap the down arrow key three times to get to the Address field (or click on "Address" with the mouse). Press the Insert key at the lower right on your keyboard and type **510** to overwrite the original street number, 501. Then press Insert again, to go back to insert mode, and press Enter.

⑤ Close the Browse window by pressing Escape or clicking on the close button with the mouse.

How to Delete Records

Deleting records is serious business. If you accidentally wiped out even one of your records, reentering the lost data could be a real pain in the neck.

That's why FoxPro breaks the deletion process into two steps: to protect you against accidents. First, you mark the records for deletion; second, you "pack" the database to actually remove the marked records.

Marking Records for Deletion

To mark records for deletion:

① Reopen the Browse window and display your records in table view.

② Move the highlight bar to the last record, the one for Richard Feynman.

③ Open the Browse window and select the "Toggle Delete" menu choice. Doing this causes a little diamond or dot to appear to the left of the record, indicating that you've marked it for deletion. This is illustrated in Figure 5.3.

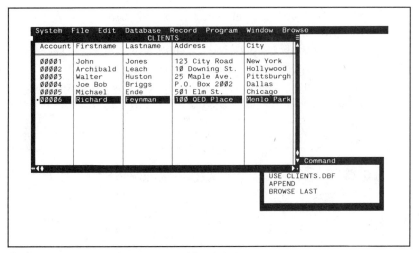

Figure 5.3: *Account 00006 marked for deletion*

④ Assuming for the sake of this example that it would be a mistake to delete the name of this eminent physicist, press Ctrl-T (hold down the Ctrl key and press *T*) to unmark the record. (Ctrl-T, or ^T, is the speed key displayed next to "Toggle Delete" on the Browse menu.)

⑤ Move the highlight bar up to the second record (Archibald Leach), and press Ctrl-T again to mark this record for deletion.

Marking records for deletion involves what's called a "toggle." A toggle is basically just like a light switch: press it once, and the light goes on; press it again, and the light goes off. If you press Ctrl-T once, a record is marked for deletion; press it again (with the highlight on the same record), and the record is unmarked.

Packing the Database

Now that we've marked a record we really mean to delete, we can go ahead and actually delete it.

① Open the Database menu and select the "Pack" menu choice, as shown in Figure 5.4. (Alternatively, you can go to the Command window by pressing Ctrl-F2, and type **pack**.) A dialog box will open, asking you to confirm that you want to pack the database. Press Enter or click on the "Yes" button with the mouse. Your PC will be occupied for a few moments and then the Browse window will disappear.

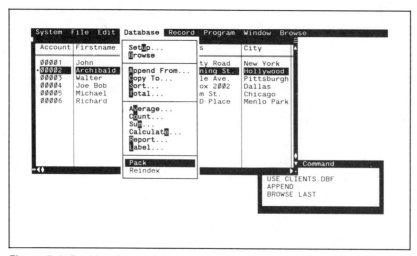

Figure 5.4: Packing the database

② Reopen the Browse window, and you'll see that the record for Archibald Leach has disappeared.

Lesson Summary

To add new records to a database file, open the file and choose "Append" from the Record menu. Alternatively, you can just type **append** in the Command window and press Enter. This opens up the Append window, where you can type in your new data.

To edit the information in already existing records, display the database file in either table or form view, then move to the part you want to change and simply type over the old information. The Insert key on your keyboard switches your PC between "insert" and "overwrite" modes.

To delete records from your database: First, display the database file in table view, then mark the records you want to delete by highlighting them and pressing Ctrl-T. (If you make a mistake, you can unmark a record by pressing Ctrl-T again.) Once you have the records marked, choose "Pack" from the Database menu or type **pack** in the Command window and press Enter. The records will be deleted.

Hot Tips

- When your database file is displayed on-screen, there are two simple ways to move up and down in the file. With the keyboard, you can use the PgUp and PgDn keys; with the mouse, you can click on the up and down arrows that appear in the right border of the Browse window. For this operation, using the keyboard is generally more efficient.

- Don't forget that when you're adding or editing records, FoxPro automatically jumps to the next field when you get to the end of the current field. If your data doesn't fill up the field, just press Enter to jump to the next field.

LESSON 6
Taking a Shortcut with the View Window

Featuring

- Opening and browsing files in the View window
- Why the Setup window is important
- How work areas keep several database files open
- Why links between database files are important

UP TO THIS POINT, WE'VE DONE EVERYTHING BY USING FoxPro's menus from the menu bar at the top of the screen. However, there's a faster way that not only lets you bypass a lot of the menus, but provides some key information about the data you're working with.

Using the View Window

Open the View window by choosing the "View" menu option from the Window menu.

The first thing you notice about the View window (shown in Figure 6.1) is that it's divided into four main areas. On the left side is a stack of text buttons that you can "push," or select, either by clicking on them with the mouse or by typing the letter that's highlighted. In the middle of the window there's a box labeled "Work Areas," with ten work areas listed: A through J. On the right, there's a box marked "Relations," which will be empty the first time you open it. (Next to the "Relations" button, there's a button labeled "1-to-Many," which we'll ignore right now.) Along the bottom of the window is a small, flat box. When you open a database file, it will display statistics on your file.

Database Action Buttons

Although all the buttons down the left side of the View window have important jobs, the four at the bottom are the most important

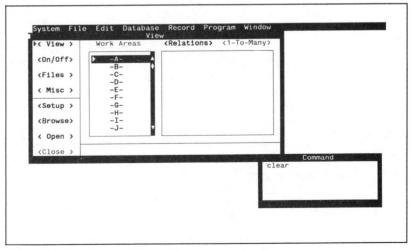

Figure 6.1: The View window when you first open it

for us right now. To get an idea of how these buttons work, do the following:

① Push the Open button by clicking on it with the mouse or pressing (on your keyboard) the highlighted letter (*P*).

② A dialog box opens up that looks very similar to the Open File dialog box you've seen before. Use the PgDn key to move the highlight down to your CLIENTS.DBF file and press Enter. Your client database file is now "open for business" in Work Area A, as you can see in Figure 6.2. Notice that the bottom of the View window now lists the name of your file and the number of records in it.

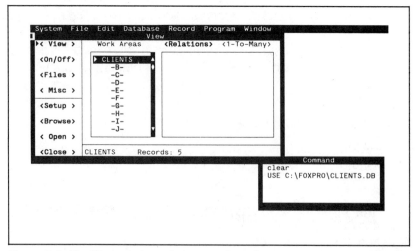

Figure 6.2: The View window after using "Open" to bring up your CLIENTS file

③ You can perform another familiar operation by pushing the Browse button that is just above the Open button. Try clicking on it with the mouse or pressing *B* on your keyboard. Your records are shown exactly as they were the last time you had the Browse window open.

④ Close the Browse window. You're back at the View window.

The Setup Window

Now we're going to look at something you haven't seen before. The Setup button takes you to a new window where you can do a tremendous number of things with your database, such as changing its structure, putting the records in a different order, and controlling which fields are shown in the Browse window. To get started, open the Setup window by clicking on the Setup button or pressing *S* on your keyboard. The Setup window is shown in Figure 6.3.

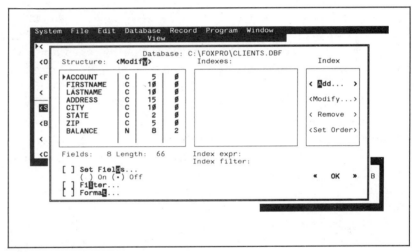

Figure 6.3: *The Setup window*

On the left is a box labeled "Structure" with its own Modify button. The Structure box displays a list of the fields in your current database file, along with the length and data type of each field.

In the middle, a box labeled "Indexes" lists the index files that are active for your database. Index files let you display your records in any order you want. For example, you can display your records in alphabetical order by last name or in numerical order by account balance without making any changes in the file itself. (We'll learn how to create index files in a later lesson.)

On the right, there are buttons to add, modify, remove, and change the order of index files themselves for a particular database.

At the bottom left, there are buttons that let you control how your data is displayed in the Browse window.

We'll come back to all of these features of the Setup window later on. For now, just press Escape to close the Setup window and return to the View window.

Work Areas and Relations

The View window has two boxes that show important information about your database files.

The middle box, "Work Areas," shows which files are open in FoxPro's work areas. When you open a database file, it goes into the current work area. Using the View window, you can open up to 10 database files at the same time, putting each one in a different work area. (Although there are 125 work areas, only 10 are shown in the View window.)

Having database files open in different work areas is important because it enables you to set up links between different files. For example, you can keep your client address information in one database file and keep specific sales transactions in another database file. Additionally, linking the files allows you to treat them as a single database file for purposes of entering data and producing reports.

When we set up multifile databases and reports in a later lesson, we'll see how useful the "Relations" box on the right can be, when it shows a tree diagram of the links between different database files.

As a last bit of practice in using the View window, close your client database file by selecting the Close button—the bottom one in the stack of buttons in the View window.

Hot Tips

- The letters that FoxPro uses to denote its work areas have nothing to do with the letters that denote your disk drives. Thus, a file that is open in work area A can be from your A:, B:, or C: drive. The same goes for any other work area.

- When you select the Browse button in the View window or "Browse" from the Database menu, FoxPro carries out the command **BROWSE LAST**. That means that when your Browse window opens, it will look the same as it did the last time you closed it. If you had zoomed it to take up the whole screen, or changed it to single-record form view, that's how it will look. If you prefer to start fresh, simply press Ctrl-F2 to go to the Command window, type **browse**, and press Enter.

LESSON 7
Modifying Your Client File Structure

Featuring

- Why field types are important
- How to display your file's structure
- How to add a new field
- How to delete an unwanted field
- How to change a field

IT SEEMS TO BE A PART OF HUMAN NATURE TO CLASSIFY everything and anything as being of one kind or another. Thus, we speak of Democrats and Republicans; plants and animals; and sitcoms, dramas, documentaries, and commercials.

One result of classifying things is that most things actually become easier to deal with. If we know that a thing fits into a certain category, we know what to expect from it and how to treat it.

Different Field Types

Database management systems such as FoxPro require you to classify the information you want it to use. Then, once the program knows what kind of data goes into a field, it knows how to treat that data to produce relevant results.

FoxPro recognizes six different data or field types:

① **Character:** This type includes all letters, numbers, and punctuation symbols, such as *A*, *m*, *80286*, and *!*. This is the data type you'll probably use most often. It is used for items such as account numbers, names, addresses, telephone numbers, and zip codes. Note that when you put a number in a character field, it's treated as just another kind of letter; so you can't do any arithmetic with it. A character field can hold up to 254 letters, digits, spaces, or other symbols.

② **Numeric:** This includes any numbers you'll be using for math calculations, such as order amount, number of units sold, or net income. The numbers in a numeric field can be either positive or negative; unless you put a hyphen or a minus sign in front of it, FoxPro assumes that it's positive. Therefore, you don't need to use a plus sign for positive numbers, but you may do so if you want. A numeric field can be up to 20 places long, including digits, plus or minus sign, and decimal point. Thus, 6.023 and 19000 are both five places long, as is −12.7.

③ **Float:** This is usually referred to as "floating point," meaning that the decimal point can move around. For most ordinary jobs, the data is treated the same as it would be in a numeric field. You probably won't use float data unless you're doing scientific calculations. Like the numeric type, it can be up to 20 places long, including digits, plus or minus sign, and decimal point.

④ **Date:** This type of field handles dates in month/day/year format. Although it's usually displayed with two digits for each, such as 05/17/91, a date field is actually stored with eight digits, so you can enter and display dates in the form 05/17/1991. You can also change the display format to European (day/month/year) or ANSI (year/month/day).

⑤ **Logical:** This type handles the answers to yes/no questions, such as "Is this person's account paid up?" or "Is this customer eligible for a discount?". There are only two values that can go into a logical field: true and false, denoted by T and F.

⑥ **Memo:** This type of field holds free-text data. Unlike other field types, where you must tell FoxPro how long the field is going to be, memo fields let you type in as little or as much information as you like. Thus, a memo field can contain a brief note, such as "Called to confirm order, 1/5/91," or can contain a long report. The content of memo fields is stored in a separate file from your main database file. For example, while your client database file is named clients.dbf, a memo file to go with it will be named clients.fpt.

When you're defining fields, as we'll do later in this lesson, you'll notice an extra data type at the bottom of the type selection box: the Picture type. This type of field is supported only by the Apple Macintosh version of FoxPro (FoxBase+ Mac), so you won't need to worry about it.

Changing the Structure of Your Database File

Now that you are familiar with the different field types, we can go ahead and learn how to define new fields for your database file, as well as get rid of old ones and redefine others.

Displaying Your Database Structure

First, of course, it's a good idea to review the structure you've already created in your database file. To do this, start by opening your client file through the View window:

① Open the Window menu and select "View."

② Select the Open button in the View window by clicking on it with the mouse or by pressing *P* on the keyboard. Select your clients database file.

③ Push the Setup button in the View window. The Setup dialog box opens, displaying the current structure of your file on the left, as you saw previously in Figure 6.3.

④ You can scroll up and down to see all your field definitions by using the up and down arrow keys. Notice that for each field, you are given the name of the field, the field type ("C" for character, "N" for numeric), the width, and the number of decimal places. For nonnumeric fields, of course, this last is always blank.

If you wish, you can skip opening the View window and just enter the command **display structure** in the Command window. Your database structure will be displayed (as shown in Figure 7.1), but there is a tradeoff to using this method: the extra help you can receive in the Setup dialog box is not accessible from the Command window.

*A*dding Fields

Next, we're going to add several fields to illustrate different field types. First, though, get back into the Setup dialog box if you aren't already there. Now, let's add a field:

① Select the Modify button (the one next to the word "Structure") by clicking on it with the mouse or by pressing the letter *Y* on your keyboard. The corresponding Structure dialog box will pop open on the screen, as shown in Figure 7.2.

Lesson 7

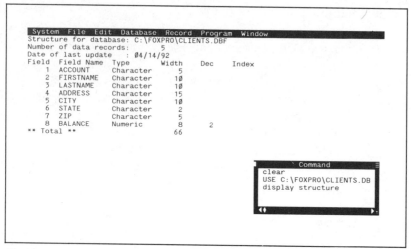

Figure 7.1: *The structure of a database file using the command* **display structure**

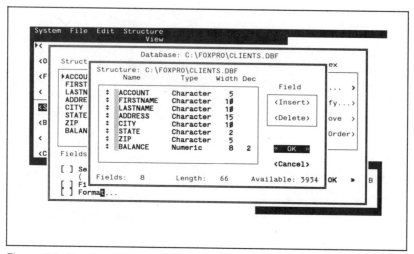

Figure 7.2: *The Structure dialog box*

② Go to the first field on the list (by pressing the Tab key or using the mouse) and press the down arrow key eight times. The cursor should now be in the Name column on the line under "BALANCE."

③ Type **PAID** and press the Enter key twice.

④ Highlight "Logical" in the type selection list that pops up, and press Enter. The width of a logical field is necessarily 1, so Fox-Pro automatically enters 1 in the Width column and moves down to the Name column on the next line.

⑤ Type **BIRTHDAY** and press the Enter key twice. Select the "Date" field type, which automatically receives a width of 8.

⑥ Type **NOTES** and press the Enter key twice. Select the "Memo" field type. Your screen should look like the one in Figure 7.3.

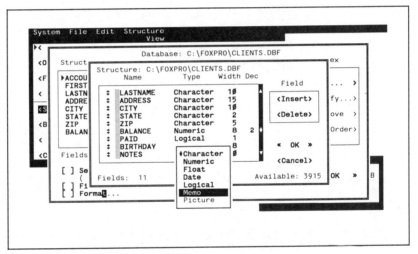

Figure 7.3: Adding a memo field

⑦ Select the OK button by pressing Ctrl-Enter or clicking on the OK button with the mouse.

⑧ When FoxPro asks if you want to make the structure changes permanent, answer Yes. FoxPro will occupy itself for a few moments and then take you back to the Setup dialog box. You can tab to the field list and use PgDn to move through it to verify that your changes have been made.

If you look at your directory, you will see that a new file, CLIENTS.BAK, has been added. This is a "backup" file, identified by its .BAK extension. When you change the structure of a file, FoxPro automatically takes the old version of the file and saves it as a backup file in case you change your mind.

If you want to insert a field somewhere in the middle of the field list, just move the highlight to the field above which you want to insert the new one and press the Insert key on your keyboard. A new line will open up in the list and you can type in a new field definition.

Deleting Fields

Deleting fields works in essentially the same way as adding fields. In this example, we will delete "PAID" and "BIRTHDAY." Start by getting back into the Setup dialog box. Then, to delete a field:

① Select the "Structure" Modify button to go to the Structure dialog box.

② Move the cursor to the field list (using the Tab key or the mouse). Then move it down to the PAID field, as shown in Figure 7.4, and press Enter to select that field. An up-arrow will appear in the shaded area to the left of the PAID field, indicating that it has been selected.

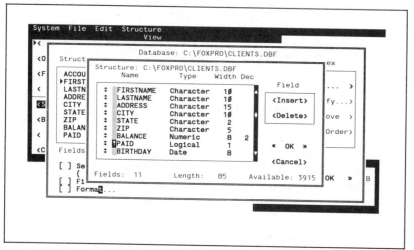

Figure 7.4: *Selecting a field to delete*

③ Press the Delete key on your keyboard or click on the on-screen Delete button with the mouse. The PAID field will disappear, and the next field (BIRTHDAY) will move up to take its place.

④ Now, suppose that we've changed our minds about sending birthday cards to clients every year. Let's go ahead and delete the BIRTHDAY field as well.

⑤ Press Ctrl-Enter or click on the OK button with the mouse. When FoxPro asks if you want to make the structure changes permanent, answer Yes. FoxPro will occupy itself for a few moments and then take you back to the Setup dialog box.

Changing a Field Definition

You change a field definition the same way you add or delete fields: by going through the Setup and Structure dialog boxes. For example, you might find that a size of 15 characters isn't wide enough for the ADDRESS field.

To make the change, you would go to the Structure dialog box, just as if you were going to add or delete a field. Then you would move the cursor to the ADDRESS field and tab over to the Width column. You would then type in your new field length—for example, 25—and press Ctrl-Enter to save the change. Everything works the same way.

If you want to bypass the View window and the Setup dialog box, you can go directly to the Structure dialog box by typing **modify structure** in the Command window and pressing Enter.

Lesson Summary

You must specify the type of data you will be using in FoxPro. FoxPro recognizes the following field types:

- *character* (for text and numbers treated as text)
- *numeric*

- *float* (for numbers used in scientific calculations)
- *date*
- *logical* (for true/false data)
- *memo* (for text of variable length)

To display your file's structure, select the Setup button in the View window or type **display structure** in the Command window.

To add a field, select the Modify button next to the word "Structure" in the Setup dialog box. Then move the cursor to the bottom of the field list in the Structure dialog box. Type in your new field name, data type, and width. Press Ctrl-Enter to exit and then answer Yes to confirm the changes.

To insert a field in the middle of the field list, highlight the field before which you want to insert the new field, then press the Insert key on your keyboard and type in the new field definition.

To delete a field, highlight it in the field list and press the Delete key on your keyboard.

To change a field definition, highlight the field in the field list and simply type in the new value(s).

To bypass View and Setup, and go directly to the Structure dialog box, type **modify structure** in the Command window.

Hot Tips

- If you're putting numbers into a character field, e.g., for customer number, be sure to pad them out to the left with zeros. Otherwise, FoxPro may handle them incorrectly. For example, in sorting your records, FoxPro (and most other database management systems) will list a character value of 10 before a character value of 1. If the field is a numeric field, you don't need to worry about this.

- If you make structure changes in a file and then use the View window's Browse button to display your data, it will look as if the structure wasn't changed at all. This happens because the Browse button tells FoxPro to execute the command **BROWSE LAST**—meaning that your data will be shown as it was the last time you closed the file. Of course, the last time you closed your file, the new fields weren't in it yet, so they aren't displayed. The only way around this is to go to the Command window (press Ctrl-F2 or use the mouse), type **browse,** and press Enter. This will clear the old Browse window settings and display all your new fields.

LESSON 8
Viewing Your Client Data

Featuring

- How to enter data into memo fields
- How to move columns in the Browse window
- How to resize columns in the Browse window
- How to display selected columns in the Browse window

NOW THAT WE'VE SEEN HOW TO MODIFY THE STRUCTURE of a database file, in this lesson we'll look at how you can modify the way your file is displayed in the Browse window.

First, however, let's tie up a loose end from Lesson 7, where we learned how to create memo fields but didn't find out how to put anything into them.

Entering Data Into Memo Fields

The technique for putting data into an ordinary field is obvious: you highlight the field on the screen and simply type the data into the appropriate blank. A memo field, however, is designed to hold a variable amount of data—from a few words to a long document. You can't just move the cursor to a memo field and start typing, as you can with other field types.

Let's enter some data into a memo field. First, open your Clients database file by using the View window. Then,

① Open the Record menu and select "Change." A window should pop open on the screen, displaying your records in form view.

② Use the down arrow or the mouse to go to the Notes memo field in the record for John Jones.

③ Press Ctrl-PgDn. The memo field window will pop open.

④ Type the information you want into the memo field. Notice that when you come to the right edge of the window, your text automatically wraps around to the next line just as it would in a word processor. You can see an example of this in Figure 8.1.

⑤ To save your memo data, press Ctrl-W or click the mouse on the frame's close button; your data will be saved automatically. If you change your mind about entering data into the memo field, press the Escape key and answer Yes when FoxPro asks if you want to discard changes. In either case, you end up with the cursor back on the Notes field in your record.

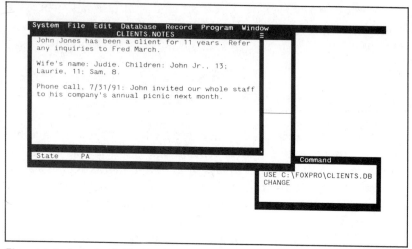

Figure 8.1: *A memo field, demonstrating word-wrap*

Rearranging the Browse Window

There may be times when you want to modify the Browse window's display to suit your particular needs. For example, you might decide to do any or all of the following:

- Rearrange the information in the Browse window so that it appears in a different order than usual.

- Make some of the columns narrower so that you can display more fields on-screen.

- Display only two or three of your database's fields in the Browse window.

FoxPro makes these operations easy. Moving and resizing columns is especially easy because it's similar to moving and resizing windows, which we learned about in Lesson 4.

How to Move a Column

Moving columns in the Browse window is the easiest of all. Let's move the Account column so that it's to the right of the Lastname column. First, display your client records in a multicolumn table. Then,

① Make sure that the cursor is positioned on the column you want to move—in this case, "Account."

② Open the Browse menu and press *M* on your keyboard to select the "Move Field" menu option.

③ Tap the right arrow key twice. Each time you tap the arrow key, the Account column will move over one slot to the right. When it's to the right of the Lastname column, press Enter to end the "Move Field" operation. Your screen should look like Figure 8.2.

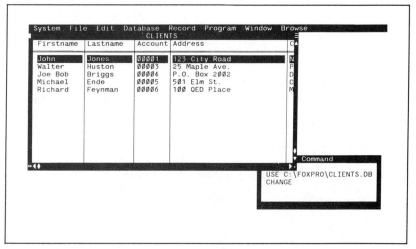

Figure 8.2: *The Account column in its new position in the Browse table*

④ Now, to see how it's done with a mouse, let's move the Account field back to where it started. (If you don't have a mouse, then simply repeat Steps 1 through 3 to move the Account column two slots back to the left, this time using the left arrow key, of course.) Move the mouse cursor onto the column title itself ("Account"). Then hold down the left mouse button and drag the column two slots back to the left so that it's back where it started. When it's in the correct position on the screen, release the mouse button.

Lesson 8

That's all there is to it! You can move any column anywhere you want.

By the way, don't worry about what this will do to the structure of your database file. Rearranging the columns in the Browse table has no effect on the file itself. Neither does resizing or selecting columns in the Browse table, which we'll talk about next.

How to Resize a Column

Resizing a column works in pretty much the same way as moving a column. Make sure that your database is still displayed as a multi-column table in the Browse window. Then, to resize a column,

① Position the cursor somewhere in the Lastname column in the table.

② Open the Browse menu and press *S* on your keyboard to choose the "Size Field" menu option.

③ Tap the right arrow key 15 times to expand the column to a width of 25 characters, then press Enter. Your screen should look like Figure 8.3.

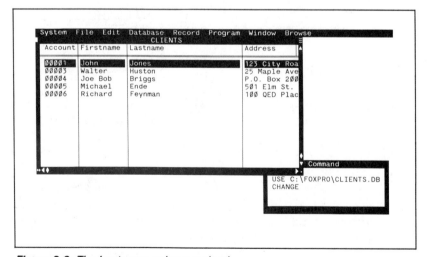

Figure 8.3: *The Lastname column resized*

Viewing Your Client Data   71

④ If you don't have a mouse, then reopen the Browse menu and choose "Size Field" again. Tap the left arrow key 15 times to restore the column to its original width. If you do have a mouse, move the mouse cursor onto the vertical line between the Lastname and Address columns. Then hold down the left mouse button and drag the line to the left until the Lastname column is back to its original size.

Selecting Columns to Display

You can also tell FoxPro to display only certain columns in the Browse window. First, exit from the Browse window by pressing the Escape key; this should take you back to the View window. Once you are there,

① Select the Setup button in the View window by pressing *S* on your keyboard or clicking the button with the mouse.

② Tab to the "Set Fields" checkbox at the lower left and press the space bar (or click between its brackets with the mouse) to display what FoxPro calls the "Field Picker" window.

③ Press the Tab key until you highlight the Account field in the "Database Fields" list box. Press the Enter key, and the Account field moves to the "Selected Fields" box. This indicates which fields will be displayed when you go back to the Browse window.

④ Press the down arrow to highlight "Lastname" and press Enter to select it for display.

⑤ Highlight "Balance" and press Enter to select it for display. Your screen should look like that shown in Figure 8.4.

⑥ Press Ctrl-Enter or click on OK to exit from the Field Picker window. Press Escape to exit from the Setup dialog box and return to the View window.

Now, let's take a look at how our changes affected the Browse window. Because only three fields are selected—Account, Lastname,

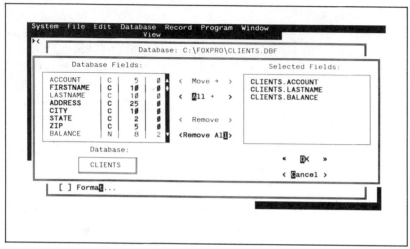

Figure 8.4: Fields to be displayed using the Field Picker window

and Balance—those three should be the only ones displayed in the Browse window.

Unfortunately, when you push the Browse button in the View window, FoxPro executes a **BROWSE LAST** command, as we mentioned at the end of Lesson Six. This command causes FoxPro to display the Browse window as if no changes had been made in the Field Picker window. This isn't a bug, since FoxPro is supposed to work this way, but it certainly seems like a design flaw.

To get around this problem, press Ctrl-F2 to get to the Command window, type **browse**, and press Enter. The Browse window will now display as we intended, as shown in Figure 8.5.

Returning Your Browse Window to Normal

To finish up, let's reverse the process so that all your fields are displayed again. Press Escape to exit from the Browse window. If you're in the Command window, press Ctrl-F1 or use the mouse to return to the View window. Then,

① Select the Setup button and click on the "Set Fields" checkbox again to open the Field Picker window.

Viewing Your Client Data   73

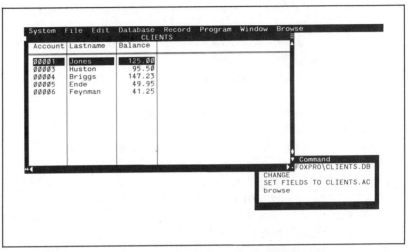

Figure 8.5: The Browse window displaying selected fields only

② Push the Remove All button in the middle of the window by tabbing to it and pressing Enter, or by clicking on it with the mouse.

③ Press Ctrl-Enter or click on the OK button. You'll return to the Setup dialog box. Notice that the "Set Fields" checkbox is now turned off (unchecked). Press Escape to exit from the Setup dialog box.

④ Remembering the problem with the Browse button, press Ctrl-F2 to go to the Command window.

⑤ Type **browse**, and press Enter. The Browse window will pop open, and all your columns should now be displayed.

Lesson Summary

To enter data into a memo field, position the cursor on the memo field and press Ctrl-PgDn, or double-click on it with the mouse. Type the information in the memo window. Then press Ctrl-W or click on the close button to exit. To discard what you've entered, press Escape.

To move a column in the Browse window, position the cursor on the column you want to move. Then pick "Move Field" from the Browse menu and use the arrow keys to move the field; press Enter when you're done. With a mouse, position the mouse cursor on the column title, hold down the left mouse button, and drag the column to its new position.

To resize a column in the Browse window, position the cursor on the column you want to resize. Then pick "Size Field" from the Browse menu and use the right or left arrow key to expand or shrink the field; press Enter when you're done. With a mouse, "grab" the vertical line on the right side of the column (position the mouse cursor on it and hold down the left mouse button) and drag it to the right or left.

To select columns to display in the Browse window, use the "Set Fields" checkbox in the Setup dialog box to go to the Field Picker window. For each field you want to display, highlight it and press Enter. Exit from the Field Picker window by pressing Ctrl-Enter and go to the Command window. Type the command **browse** and the Browse window will show only the fields you picked.

Hot Tips

- There was a bug in version 1.00 of FoxPro that made the cursor jump to the next record whenever you exited from a memo field. If you have this problem, the only thing to do is use the arrow keys or mouse to move back up to the appropriate record. This bug is fixed in versions 1.01, 1.02, and 2.00 of FoxPro.

- You might have noticed that the Field Picker window has three other middle buttons. "Move" moves a highlighted field into the Selected Fields list; "Remove" takes a highlighted field out of the Selected Fields list. Naturally, the "All" button moves all fields into the Selected Fields list. However, since all you need to move a field from one list to another is to highlight it and press Enter, the first two buttons are a less efficient way of selecting and deselecting fields. You might as well ignore them.

LESSON 9
Creating Simple Reports

Featuring

- Parts of a report
- How to create a table report
- How to use Page Preview
- How to create a form report
- How to print your report

UP TO NOW, WE'VE BEEN MAINLY CONCERNED WITH putting data into your computer. However, it doesn't do much good to put data into your computer if you can't get it out again. We've already learned how to display data on the screen with the Browse window. In this lesson, we'll see how to create and print reports using the information in your database.

FoxPro makes it easy for you to print any reports you need, from simple multicolumn reports to customized layouts with data grouping and automatic math calculations.

First, we'll create a simple report, just to impress you with how fast and easy it is. Then, like Hercule Poirot, Agatha Christie's fictional Belgian detective, we're going to explain how we did it.

Creating a Quick Report

First, make sure that your client database file is open. Then simply do the following:

① Select the "New" menu choice from the File menu.

② When the File Type dialog box appears, choose the "Report" file type.

③ The Layout window will open on the screen, and a new Report menu will appear on the menu bar. Open this menu, then press *Q* on your keyboard to select "Quick Report."

④ Select the OK button in the Quick Report dialog box (shown in Figure 9.1). Your Quick Report is automatically set up.

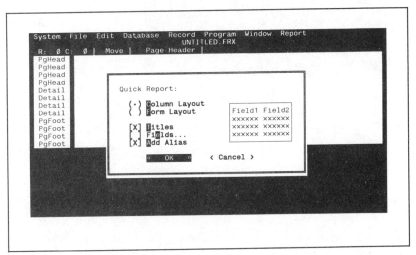

Figure 9.1: *The Quick Report dialog box*

⑤ To see how your report will look when it is printed, select "Page Preview" from the Report menu.

Creating your report took only four steps. The fifth step was just to see what you created. Now, let's go back and look at the details.

The Layout Window

Press Escape to get out of Page Preview and you'll find yourself back in the Layout window, which is a good place to begin (see Figure 9.2). There's now a Report menu in the menu bar above the Layout window, as we saw while creating the report. It has menu choices for layout operations, such as adding or moving fields, drawing boxes, or inserting and deleting lines—as well as the Page Preview feature, which you've already seen. The menu items not currently available (because of the type of report we're doing) are displayed in dimmer text.

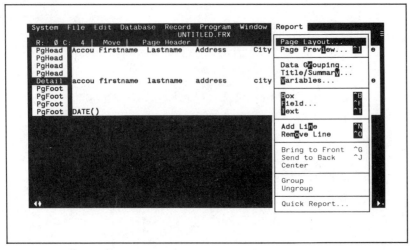

Figure 9.2: The Layout window

The first line of the Layout window shows the title of your current report layout. You can save this layout through the File menu (which we'll do in a minute) and reuse it again and again to print standard reports. Right now, the report layout is untitled, since we haven't given it a name yet.

The second line of the Layout window is the *status line*. This shows information about the cursor location and what FoxPro thinks you want it to do at the moment. At the left are two items—R: and C:—to show the row and column location of the cursor. Try moving the cursor around a little bit with the arrow keys to see how these numbers change. You can also move the cursor instantly to a new location by single-clicking the mouse on the place you want the cursor to be.

The operation that FoxPro is currently set to perform is indicated to the right of the row and column information; in this case, it is set to let you move fields and text around in the window. If you choose another operation from the Report menu, such as drawing a box, this part of the status line will display the new operation that you've picked.

Parts of the Report Layout

The last item on the status line indicates the part of the report layout in which the cursor is now located. (You should be able to see the cursor as a flashing underline beneath the *A* in *Account*.) This can be useful when you can't see all the layout "bands" in the window at one time.

The PgHead (page header) band is where you put column headings and other information that should be printed at the top of every page of the report. (In a Quick Report, FoxPro automatically takes your field names and makes them upper-and-lowercase column headings.)

The Detail band is where the actual data from your database will be printed. When you are laying out a report, the placement and width of each field is indicated by an all uppercase field name that occasionally appears chopped off, or truncated. Don't be alarmed by the apparently arbitrary chopping phenomenon. The chopping of the name serves to indicate the width that has been specified for that field. Thus, in Figure 9.2, you see only the first five letters of ACCOUNT because, as you might remember, the account field has been specified to be only five characters wide. Of course, the incomplete words themselves won't appear on the report once it has been created; they appear in the layout merely as placeholders for the data to be included in the report.

The PgFoot (page footer) band corresponds to the PgHead band. It is where you put information that should be printed at the bottom of each report page. FoxPro assumes that in a Quick Report, you want the current date printed in the bottom left corner of each page and the page number printed in the bottom right corner of each page. In Figure 9.2,

Lesson 9

you can see where the date will appear—the DATE ( ) in the footer band. The page number footer is off to the right of the screen display.

Modifying Your Quick Report

Even though your Quick Report was created automatically, you have considerable freedom to change it as needed. Let's start out by adding a title.

Adding a Title to Your Report

① Open the Report menu and select the "Title/Summary" option. The Title/Summary dialog box will pop open.

② Select "Title Band," as shown in Figure 9.3, by pressing *T* on your keyboard or clicking in the checkbox with the mouse. Then select the OK button.

③ A Title band will appear in your report layout. Type **Current Clients** and press Enter.

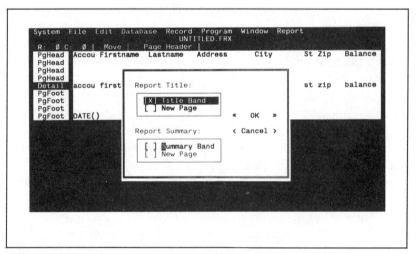

Figure 9.3: *The Title/Summary dialog box, with the "Title Band" checkbox selected*

Creating Simple Reports

④ Select the "Add Line" menu choice from the Report menu to add a line to the Title band. Do this two more times so that there are four lines in the Title band. (You can also press Ctrl-N, which is the speed key to add a line.)

⑤ Position the cursor on any letter in the words "Current Clients," then press the space bar or click the mouse. This turns "Current Clients" into a text "object" that you can move around the screen.

⑥ Press the up arrow on your keyboard two times. Your title moves up into the second line of the Title band.

⑦ Select "Center" from the Report menu and your report title will be centered on the page. It won't appear to be in the center of the screen, but that is because the screen cannot show you the full width of the page. Press Enter to confirm the new location.

Adding a Box to Your Report Title

Now, we're going to give your report a more professional appearance by drawing a box around your report title. However, before going ahead with this procedure, be sure to read the Hot Tip at the end of this lesson: it might affect whether you can continue.

① Move the cursor to the line above your title, two spaces to the left (R:0, C:30 on the status line). Then choose "Box" from the report menu.

② Use the arrow keys to move the cursor to the line below the title, two spaces to the right (R:2, C:48). Press Enter to tell FoxPro that this is where you want the opposite corner of the box. Figure 9.4 shows the on-screen result of this operation.

Adding a Finishing Touch

The way it's currently laid out, the report has three lines in the PgHead band between the column headings and the actual client names. Let's reduce that to one line and draw a solid bar between the column headings and the actual data:

① Position the cursor in the line underneath the column headings in the PgHead band (R:5).

Lesson 9

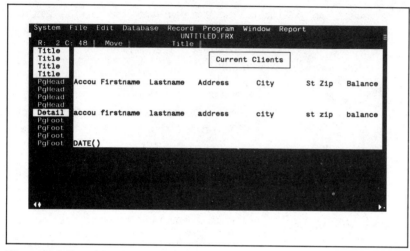

Figure 9.4: *Drawing a box around the title*

② Select "Remove Line" from the Report menu or press Ctrl-O, the speed key to remove a line. Do this one more time, so that there are now only two lines remaining in the PgHead band.

③ With the cursor in the second line of the PgHead band, choose the "Box" menu choice from the Report menu or press Ctrl-B (the speed key).

④ We're going to use FoxPro's box-drawing feature to draw a line: that is, this "box" is going to be completely flat. Press the up arrow once to turn the box into a horizontal line. Use the right arrow key to move the cursor to column 79, then press Enter to tell FoxPro that you're finished drawing. (You could draw your line with the mouse, but in this case, using the mouse is tricky and I don't recommend it.)

If you want to see what your report will look like when it's printed, select "Page Preview" from the Report menu or press Ctrl-I (the Page Preview speed key).

Saving and Printing Your Report

① Select "Save" from the File menu. The Save Report dialog box will pop open on the screen.

② Type **cli-rpt** into the space at the bottom left of the dialog box.

③ Select the OK button by pressing Ctrl-Enter or clicking the mouse on OK. When FoxPro asks if you want to save the environment information (open files, etc.) simply press Enter to answer yes.

④ Press the Escape key to close the Layout window.

To print your report, first make sure that your printer is turned on and is on-line. Then do the following:

① Select "Report" from the Database menu. The Report Generator dialog box will appear.

② Select the Form button by pressing *M* on your keyboard or clicking on "Form" with the mouse. A directory selection box will appear.

③ Scroll down the list of directories and select "CLI-RPT.FRX" by highlighting it and pressing Enter or by double-clicking on it with the mouse.

④ Press *P* on the keyboard to select the "To Print" checkbox at the bottom of the dialog box.

⑤ Press Ctrl-Enter or click on OK to tell FoxPro to go ahead and print your report. The report will appear on the screen as it prints.

⑥ In the Command window, type **eject** and press Enter to eject the page from the printer.

Creating a Form Report

FoxPro does not limit you to table reports, even if you're just doing a "quick report." You can also print out your data in form view, and move or delete fields as you need to.

Let's create a form-view quick report. First, make sure that your client database file is still open. Then,

① Select "New" from the File menu and "Report" from the File Type dialog box.

② When the Layout window appears, select "Quick Report" from the Report menu.

③ When the Report Type dialog box opens, press *F* to select a form-view report.

④ Let's include only account number, name, and current balance in this report. In the Report Type dialog box, press *E* to select the "Fields" checkbox. The Field Picker dialog box appears.

⑤ Highlight "Account" and press Enter to select it.

⑥ Then, in order, select "Firstname," "Lastname," and "Balance" by highlighting each and pressing Enter.

⑦ Press Ctrl-Enter or click on OK. When the Report Type dialog box reappears, press Ctrl-Enter again.

⑧ Add a Title band and delete three of the PgHead lines.

⑨ Enter **Client Account Balances** in the Title band and center it in the same way you centered the "Current Clients" title in the last report.

*M*odifying a Form Report

Let's do a couple of things to make the report easier to read.

① Position the cursor in the Balance field in the last line of the Detail band. Remember that the field itself is the one that appears in all lowercase letters (on the right), while the field label is in both capital and lowercase letters. Press the space bar to select the field (or click on it with the mouse).

② Using the arrow keys or the mouse, drag the field to the second line of the Detail band so that it's to the right of the Account field. The *B* in *BALANCE* should be in column 40. Press the Enter key to anchor the field in its new location.

③ Select the Balance field label in the same way, and drag it to the same line but to the left of the Balance field itself. The *B* in the "Balance" label should be in column 31. Press Enter.

④ On second thought, we really don't need to list the client's first name in this report. Move the cursor into the Firstname field label and select it by pressing the space bar. Then press the Delete key on your keyboard. Do the same thing with the Firstname field.

⑤ Press Ctrl-O to delete the empty line.

⑥ In the last line of the Detail band, draw a horizontal line by holding down the hyphen key so that it repeats, forming a line. The line should extend to column 47. When it's drawn, press Enter. Your screen should match the one in Figure 9.5.

⑦ Press Ctrl-I (the Page Preview speed key) to see what your report will look like when you print it.

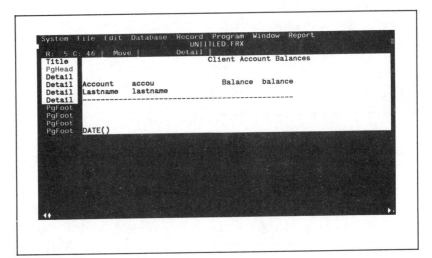

Figure 9.5: *A form report*

⑧ Save your report layout as **cli-rpt2**.

⑨ Press Escape to close the Layout window.

Lesson Summary

To create a Quick Report, select "New" from the File menu and "Report" from the File Type dialog box. Then select "Quick Report" from the Report menu and choose whether you want a table or a form report.

To perform any operation on a field or text object in a report, select it by moving the cursor into it and pressing the space bar, or by clicking on it with the mouse. Then you can move, center, or delete it.

To draw a box or a line in your report, move the cursor to where you want the top left corner and choose "Box" from the Report menu. Then move to where you want the lower right corner, and press Enter. (With the original version of FoxPro, use the hyphen and vertical bar characters to draw lines and boxes.)

To save your report, select "Save" from the File menu.

To print your report, close the Layout window and select "Report" from the Database menu. Then select the Form button to choose which report layout to print, and select the "To Print" checkbox. Press Ctrl-Enter to send your report to the printer. After printing, type **eject** and press Enter to eject the last page of your report from the printer.

Hot Tip

- If you're using some versions of FoxPro (1.00, 1.01, 1.02, or any 1.0*x* version), boxes and lines in your printed report will look strange. The reason for this is that each different brand of printer (IBM, Okidata, etc.) uses different codes to control special effects such as boxes and boldfaced type. These versions did not let you configure FoxPro to send the codes required to produce special printing effects. To create boxes with the original version of FoxPro, then, you need to draw your own—using the hyphen for horizontal lines and the vertical bar (¦) character for vertical lines. The vertical bar character is on the same key as the backslash; it's at the top right on some keyboards and the lower left on others.

PART III

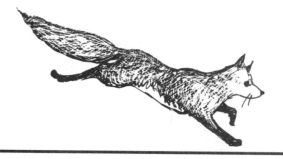

Intermediate-Level Skills

LESSON 10
Sorting a Database File

LESSON 11
Indexing Your Client File

LESSON 12
Finding Specific Records

LESSON 13
Creating Sophisticated Reports

LESSON 10
Sorting a Database File

Featuring

- What sorting does
- How to sort on more than one field
- Sorting on letters and numbers

CAN YOU IMAGINE WHAT IT WOULD BE LIKE TRYING TO find a person's telephone number in the Los Angeles phone directory if the entries weren't arranged (sorted) by name? It wouldn't just be difficult; it would be virtually impossible. Although this is an extreme case, it illustrates the fact that sorting helps us get things done more easily: compare looking for an invoice in an unsorted stack of papers with looking for the same invoice in a stack that is sorted by invoice number.

Sorting is a complicated process. All you have to do to prove this to yourself is to try to teach a computer how to do it. The task of making computers sort things efficiently has launched multimillion-dollar companies and scores of Ph.D. dissertations in computer science.

With FoxPro, however, the details have already been worked out. You just tell FoxPro to sort your database file and in what kind of order. It leaves your original file "as is" and creates a new, sorted file for you.

Getting Ready to Sort Your Client File

At this point, we have only five records in the client file. (Remember we deleted Archie Leach back in Lesson 5.) To get a really clear picture of how sorting works, we'll need to add a few more. Using the Append window (see Lesson 3 if you need a quick review), add the following records to your client database:

Account: 00007

Firstname: John

Lastname: Huston

Address: 353 Moravec Dr.

City: Pittsburgh

State: PA

Zip: 15230

Balance: 14.30

Account: 00008

Firstname: Carol

Lastname: Huston

Address: 10 Berliner St.

City: Pittsburgh

State: PA

Zip: 15230

Balance: 7.50

Account: 00009

Firstname: Andy

Lastname: Jones

Address: 10 Minsky St.

City: New York

State: NY

Zip: 10016

Balance: 10.50

Account: 00010

Firstname: Jennifer

Lastname: Jones

Address: 2899 Garden St.

City: Menlo Park

State: CA

Zip: 94025

Balance: 46.75

You may notice that some of the last names and zip codes are the same as records already in the database. This will come in handy when we're learning how to sort on more than one field.

Sorting on a Single Field

Currently, your client records are simply in the order they went into the database. With only nine records, it's no great problem to find a particular client. If you had a hundred or a thousand records, however, it would be imperative that you be able to see the records in order by name or account number; otherwise, you'd have a very difficult time finding anything.

As a first step, let's try sorting the records by last name. Do the following:

① Open your client database file through the View window.

② Select "Sort" from the Database menu. The Sorting dialog box will appear on the screen (Figure 10.1).

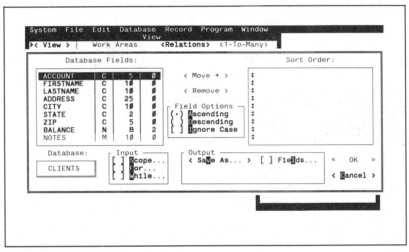

Figure 10.1: The Sorting dialog box

It's worth pausing for a moment to look at the features of this dialog box. You should recognize the Sorting dialog box as being a "field picker" type of dialog box. In addition to the familiar Move, Remove, OK, and Cancel buttons that we've seen before, there are several new buttons and checkboxes.

In the middle of the dialog box, the "Field Options" buttons let you specify if you want an ascending (A to Z, 1 to 10, etc.) or descending (Z to A, 10 to 1, etc.) sort order. Selecting the "Ignore Case" checkbox tells FoxPro that it should consider "Jones" and "jones" as the same word, even though one starts with a capital letter and the other does not. If you do not specify otherwise, FoxPro assumes you want a case-sensitive and ascending sort.

Along the bottom of the Sorting dialog box, the first item on the left shows the name of the database file that's being sorted. The checkboxes in the "Input" box help you to specify which records you want in the sorted file. If you don't specify anything here, FoxPro assumes you want to include all of the records.

The next name along the bottom, the "Output" box, is where you enter the name for your sorted database file. The "Fields" checkbox within the "Output" box lets you tell FoxPro to include only certain fields from your original file in the sorted file. This is important when your original file has many fields that you don't need in the sorted version.

Now, let's continue sorting your file:

③ Press the down arrow or use the mouse to highlight the LASTNAME field in the "Database Fields" box on the left. Then press Enter or double-click the mouse to move the LASTNAME field to the "Sort Order" box on the right. (As before, the Move → button works but is less efficient than highlighting a field and pressing Enter.)

④ Press *V* on your keyboard to select the "Save As" button. Type **clisort1** and press Ctrl-Enter. When the Sorting dialog box reappears, press Ctrl-Enter again to create the sorted file.

⑤ Using the View window, open your new CLISORT1 file. Then select the Browse button to to display your records.

The sort was a success, as far as it went: all our records are in order by last name. Unfortunately, the first names are still out of order: Walter Huston comes before John Huston and Carol Huston, and John Jones comes before Andy and Jennifer Jones. The first names still have the same positions—relative to each other—that they had in the original file. To correct the problem, we need to sort on both the Lastname and the Firstname fields.

*S*orting on Multiple Fields

For situations like the preceding, Foxpro lets you sort on more than one field at a time. The first field you pick in the Sorting dialog box will be the main field for the sort, while any other fields will be secondary sort fields.

Let's do it again, this time sorting by zip code, last name, and first name (a common sort order for bills and other mailings):

① Reopen your clients database file.

② Select "Sort" from the Database menu to call up the Sorting dialog box.

③ In the "Database Fields" box, highlight ZIP and press Enter to move it to the "Sort Order" box. Then do the same with LASTNAME and FIRSTNAME. Your screen should look like that shown in Figure 10.2.

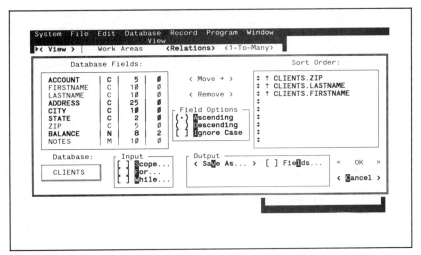

Figure 10.2: The Sorting dialog box, showing that the CLIENTS file will be sorted on three fields

④ For this particular sorted file, we're not going to include the ACCOUNT or BALANCE fields, so move the highlight to the "Fields" checkbox and select it. The original Field Picker dialog box appears; this will let you choose which fields to include in the sorted file.

⑤ In order, select FIRSTNAME, LASTNAME, ADDRESS, CITY, STATE, and ZIP. Then press Ctrl-Enter to confirm your choice. The Sorting dialog box will reappear.

⑥ Press Tab once to move to the "Save As" button in the "Output" box. Type **clisort2** and press Ctrl-Enter to create the sorted file.

⑦ Open and browse the CLISORT2 file, then zoom it to a full-screen by selecting "Zoom" from the Window menu. It should appear as in Figure 10.3.

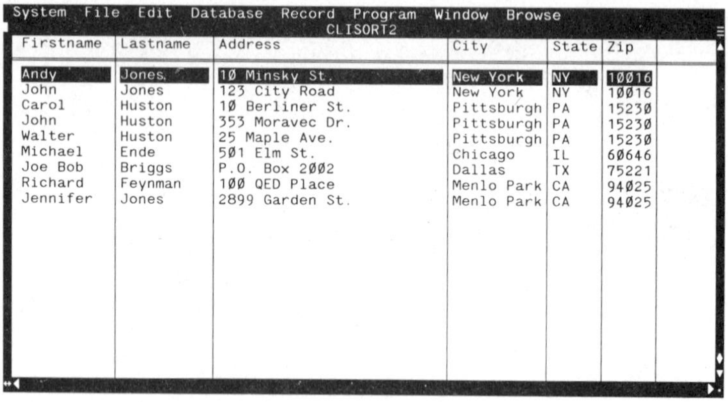

```
System  File  Edit  Database  Record  Program  Window  Browse
                              CLISORT2
Firstname  Lastname  Address         City         State  Zip
Andy       Jones     10 Minsky St.   New York     NY     10016
John       Jones     123 City Road   New York     NY     10016
Carol      Huston    10 Berliner St. Pittsburgh   PA     15230
John       Huston    353 Moravec Dr. Pittsburgh   PA     15230
Walter     Huston    25 Maple Ave.   Pittsburgh   PA     15230
Michael    Ende      501 Elm St.     Chicago      IL     60646
Joe Bob    Briggs    P.O. Box 2002   Dallas       TX     75221
Richard    Feynman   100 QED Place   Menlo Park   CA     94025
Jennifer   Jones     2899 Garden St. Menlo Park   CA     94025
```

Figure 10.3: *The CLISORT2 database file*

At first glance, it might seem as if something has gone wrong: the last names are out of order. But if you look at the zip codes column, you can see that the zip codes are in perfect order. That's because we specified ZIP as our first sort field.

Furthermore, within each zip code the last names are in order, because LASTNAME was our second sort field. And whenever two or more people in the same zip code share a last name, the first names are in order, because FIRSTNAME was our third sort field. Thus, in the 94025 zip code, Richard Feynman comes before Jennifer Jones. In the Hustons of Pittsburgh, Carol comes before John and Walter.

Finally, as advertised, the new file includes only the fields that we selected in the Field Picker dialog box.

Sorting on Letters and Numbers

There's one final point we should make about sorting—as well as about indexing, which we'll discuss in the next lesson.

When you have numbers in a character-type field, they are sorted as characters, not numbers. In case you've been wondering, that's why all of the account numbers in our client database are padded out to the left with zeros: because we specified ACCOUNT to be a character field. If we didn't pad the account numbers with zeros, then a sorting operation on the ACCOUNT field would put account 10, for example, before account 2.

With numeric fields, such as the BALANCE field, you don't have to worry about this problem. It only occurs with numbers in character fields.

Lesson Summary

To create a sorted version of a file, open the file and select "Sort" from the Database menu, Then, in the Sorting dialog box, select the options you want for ascending or descending order and whether or not to ignore case, and pick the sort fields in their order of priority.

The order of fields in the "Sort Order" box determines which field will be the primary sort field. If ZIP appears first, then the new file will be in order by zip code.

The "Input" area in the Sorting dialog box lets you select only certain records to be included in the sorted file.

The "Fields" checkbox in the "Output" area of the Sorting dialog box calls up the Field Picker dialog box to let you pick which fields from the original file to include in the sorted file.

When entering numbers into a character-type field, be sure to pad the numbers to the left with zeros. This will prevent them from being put in the wrong order if you ever sort on that field.

Hot Tips

- Even if you're sorting a file that's in a different directory, Fox-Pro will normally put the sorted version of your file into the FoxPro program directory. That's because the FoxPro directory is the "default" directory, and all newly created files go

- there. If you want to use a different directory for your database files (which is generally a good idea), you need to reset the default to the directory you want. Press Ctrl-F2 to go to the Command window. Then, if your data directory is C:\MYDATA, you should type **set default to c:\mydata** and press the Enter key.
- Once you learn how, it's faster to sort files from the Command window. For example, if you wanted to do the multiple-field sort we did to create CLISORT2, you would type the following all on one line in the Command window, pressing Enter only at the end:

    sort on zip, lastname, firstname to clisort2 fields firstname, lastname, address, city, state, zip
- If you want to sort a fairly large file, first make sure that you have enough disk space to store the sorted version of the file. Sorting is also time-consuming. Depending on what you need to accomplish, it might be better to *index* a large file instead of *sorting* it (see Lesson 11).

LESSON 11
Indexing Your Client File

Featuring

- Sorting vs. indexing
- How to index a database file
- How to index on multiple fields
- How to use more than one index file
- How to create a view file

AS USEFUL AS SORTING IS, IT'S NOT ALWAYS THE BEST way to go. First, it takes disk space: a sorted file can take up as much disk space as the original file. Second, it takes time: not only does it take time for FoxPro to carry out the sorting process itself, but it takes time for it to create each new, sorted file on disk.

Because of these factors, sorting is appropriate mainly for files that don't change very often—either in the sorting order itself or in the contents of the file. If you need to view a file in several different sort orders, or if you frequently add new records to the file, then indexing is a better method.

Indexing differs from sorting in that it doesn't create a new database or even rearrange the records in your old file. What it does is build a kind of "table of contents" that tells FoxPro what the order of the records would be if they *were* sorted—e.g., record #37 would come first, record #80 would come second, record #11 would come third, and so on.

By using this table of contents, called an *index file*, you can view your data in a variety of sorted orders without making any change in the database itself. And because it doesn't create a new database, indexing is both faster than sorting and uses less disk space.

How to Index a Database File

Let's create an index file for your client database. Like before, we'll use LASTNAME as our primary sort field and FIRSTNAME as our secondary field. Do the following:

① Using the View window, open your unsorted client database file, CLIENTS.DBF.

② Select the Setup button. When the Setup dialog box appears, select the Add button on the right, under "Index."

③ When the Open Index File dialog box appears, select the New button on the lower right to create a new index file (see Figure 11.1).

④ If we were indexing on last name only instead of last and first names, we could just select LASTNAME in the field list by highlighting it and pressing Enter (or double-clicking on it with the mouse). Since we need to include two fields in the index, however, select the Expr button to display FoxPro's Expression Builder dialog box. This will enable you to create

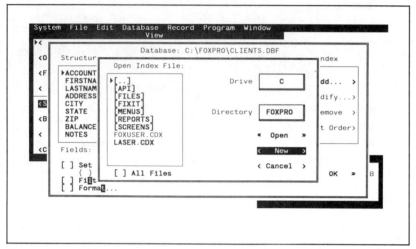

Figure 11.1: Adding an index file

what is called an "expression," which tells FoxPro what criteria to follow when performing such operations as indexing or searching.

⑤ LASTNAME is still the first field we want to index on, so tab to the field list, highlight LASTNAME, and select it by pressing Enter (or double-click on it with the mouse). The field name will appear in the expression box (labeled "Index On: <expr>").

⑥ The mouse and keyboard techniques differ quite a bit for this next step. If you're using a mouse, move the cursor to the rectangular button labeled "String" and hold down the left mouse button; a list of "string operators" should pop open on the screen. (The rectangular buttons you run into from time to time in FoxPro are called "popup buttons.") While still holding down the mouse button, move the highlight to the plus sign (+) and release the mouse button. If you're working from the keyboard, open the Expression menu by pressing Alt-X; then select "String Functions," use the arrow keys to highlight the plus sign, and press Enter.

⑦ Tab back to the field name list, highlight FIRSTNAME, and press Enter (or double-click on it with the mouse). The field name **firstname** will appear to the right of the plus sign in the expression box above, as shown in Figure 11.2.

⑧ To verify that your index expression is valid, click on the Verify button or select "Verify" from the Expression menu. FoxPro should display the message **Expression is valid**.

⑨ Press Ctrl-Enter to accept the index expression. You should now be in the Indexing dialog box (see Figure 11.3).

⑩ Move to the Output box at the bottom center of the screen and highlight "IDX." FoxPro 2.0 offers you the choice of several different index formats, but we're just going to create a standard *.IDX* index file. With the highlight on "IDX," press the space bar to select IDX format.

⑪ Press Tab twice to highlight the "Compact" checkbox, and press the space bar to deselect it.

⑫ Press Tab once to highlight the "Save As" button, then press Enter and type **name** as the name of the index file. Press Ctrl-Enter to return to the Indexing dialog box.

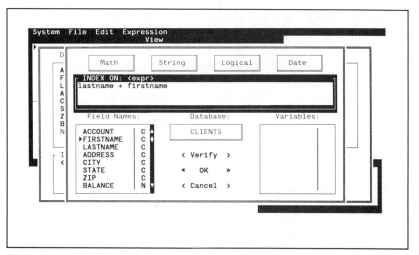

Figure 11.2: *The Expression Builder dialog box, showing the expression that determines on which fields to index*

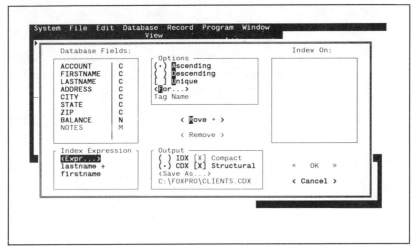

Figure 11.3: Indexing dialog box

⑬ Highlight the "Move" button in the center of the dialog box and press Enter. Your index expression will appear in the Index On box.

⑭ Press Ctrl-Enter to create the NAME.IDX index file. You will automatically return to the Setup dialog box, where "NAME" is shown in the "Indexes" box (see Figure 11.4).

Figure 11.4: The Setup dialog box with NAME index open

⑮ Press Escape to return to the View window. Browse your records to verify that both the last and first names are in ascending alphabetical order.

On your own, you should now go back and create a new index file called ZIPCODE by indexing your client file first on the ZIP field, then on LASTNAME and FIRSTNAME. Your index expression should read

zip + lastname + firstname

This will give you an indexed version of the zip-sorted file we created in the previous lesson.

Keeping Index Files Up-to-Date

When you sort a file, you must re-sort it when you add more records. Otherwise, the new records will simply be added to the end of the file, out of order.

Keeping your index files up to date is equally important. An outdated index file can cause all sorts of headaches. If you add new client records without updating your index, for example, FoxPro may not be able to find those records when you do a search or print out a report. As a result, you'll get inaccurate information.

Opening Your Index Files

To update your index files for a database, you simply need to make sure that the index files are open whenever you make any changes in the database:

① Using the View window, close your client file.

② Reopen your client file and select the Setup button in the View window.

③ Select the Add button in the Setup dialog box.

④ When the Open Index File dialog box appears, move the highlight to NAME.IDX, as shown in Figure 11.5, and press Enter.

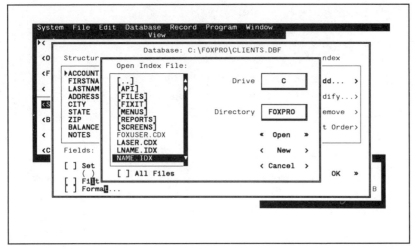

Figure 11.5: Opening an index file

⑤ Select the Add button again. In the dialog box, move the highlight to ZIPCODE.IDX and press Enter. The Setup dialog box will reappear.

If you look at the Indexes list in the Setup dialog box, you'll see that both the NAME and ZIPCODE index files are now open. The ZIPCODE index is marked because it is the primary index file, which determines the order in which your client records are displayed. The little up-arrow shows that the records are indexed in ascending order. Press Ctrl-Enter or click on OK to confirm your choices. When the View window reappears, you can see that CLIENTS is similarly marked; in this case it is to indicate that index files are open in this database. Because your index files are open, they will automatically be updated with any changes you make in your data.

Updating Index Files After Changes

If you forget to open your index files when you make changes in a database, don't worry; all is not lost. You can manually update an index file by using the REINDEX command.

Simply open your database file, open the index file you need to update, and select "Reindex" from the Database menu. If you prefer to use the Command window, you can type **reindex** and press Enter. Either way, your index file will be updated.

Closing Your Index Files

Any time you want to close one or more open index files, you can do so through the Setup dialog box: you may have noticed that below the Add button, there's a Remove button as well.

To close the ZIPCODE index file, for example, do the following:

① Make sure that your client database is open with the NAME and ZIPCODE index files open.

② Open the Setup dialog box and highlight the ZIPCODE index by tabbing to the index list and using the arrow keys or by clicking on ZIPCODE with the mouse. The three buttons below the Add button will light up.

③ Select the Remove button. The ZIPCODE index will disappear from the indexes list. It is now closed.

If you want to close all your index files at once, you can simply move to the Command window and type either **set index to** followed by nothing or **close index**; then press Enter. All your open index files will be closed.

Working with Multiple Index Files

FoxPro lets you have as many as 21 index files open for a database file. The fact that you can have that many, however, does not mean it's a good idea.

Apart from being confusing, having a lot of open index files tends to slow down FoxPro's operations. Each time you make a change in your data, FoxPro has to update each index file. The more index files you have open, the more time it takes. By all means, use as many index files as you need—but try not to use any more than that.

Setting the Index Order

Take a minute now to reopen the NAME and ZIPCODE indexes, as shown in Figure 11.6.

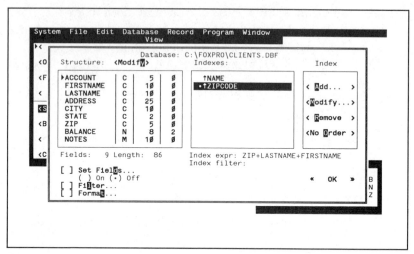

Figure 11.6: *Two index files open, with ZIPCODE as the primary index*

If you chose to display your records right now, they would be displayed in zip code order. However, let's say that, after going to the trouble of reopening ZIPCODE, you decide you want to see your records in order by client name. Do you have to close everything down and start over? No—you simply change the order of the index files so that NAME is the primary index. Let's try it:

① With your client database in the View window and indexed on ZIPCODE and NAME (with ZIPCODE as the primary index), open the Setup dialog box. The two indexes should be listed in the "Indexes" box, with a dot or a diamond next to ZIPCODE to show that it is the primary index file.

② Highlight NAME in the "Indexes" box, then press *O* on the keyboard to select the Set Order button. The mark will move to NAME, indicating that it is now the primary index file. Press Ctrl-Enter to exit from the Setup box.

③ Browse your client database to verify that it is now in order by client name.

An alternative to using the menus for this procedure is to use Fox-Pro's SET ORDER command in the Command window. If NAME is the first index you opened and ZIPCODE is the second, you can make NAME the primary index by entering **set order to name** in the Command window. To switch back to ZIPCODE as the primary index, you enter **set order to zipcode**.

Simplifying Your Work by Using View Files

Especially when you go through the menus, it takes a lot of steps to open your database file and then open all the associated index files. If you have several index files, there's even a chance that you'll forget to open one of them, resulting in an out-of-date index.

To avoid this problem—and make it easier on yourself—FoxPro lets you create *view files*. In essence, a view file is a "snapshot" of a particular database and index file setup. After you take the snapshot, you no longer have to open all the files separately: you can just open your view file, and FoxPro reconstructs your database setup so that it matches the snapshot.

Creating a view file is easy.

① Make sure that your client database is open with the ZIPCODE index primary and the NAME index secondary.

② Display your file in the View window.

③ Select "Save As" from the File menu.

④ When the dialog box to create a View file appears, type **clients** in the name blank at the bottom. Press Ctrl-Enter to exit, then close your client database file.

That's it! Your view file has been created. Now, instead of opening the clients file, opening the ZIPCODE index, and opening the NAME index every time you make changes to your client database file, you can simply open your client view file and let FoxPro do the work:

① From the File menu, select "Open."

② From the file-type selection box in the Open dialog box, select "View," as shown in Figure 11.7.

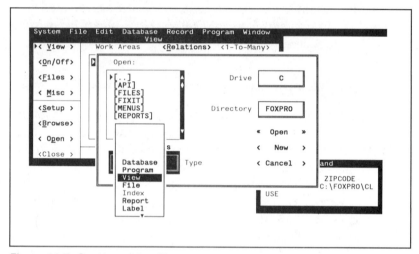

Figure 11.7: Opening a view file

③ Select CLIENTS.VUE from the file list in the dialog box.

If you want, open the Setup window to verify that the client file is open with ZIPCODE as the primary index and NAME as the secondary index.

Lesson Summary

Sorting versus indexing: Sorting is appropriate primarily for files that don't change too often or are fairly small. For other files, indexing is usually a better choice.

To index a database file, select the Add button in the Setup dialog box. Then, either pick a single field on which to index or construct an index expression in the Expression Builder. You can combine several different fields in an index expression by linking them with the plus (+) sign.

Before making changes in your data, be sure that all your index files for that database are open, so they can be updated automatically. If you forget, open all your index files for that database and select "Reindex" from the Database menu.

To save a particular database and index setup in a view file, select "Save As" from the File menu and name your view file. Then, whenever you want to retrieve that setup, select "Open" from the File menu, choose "View" from the file-type selection box, and open the view file you want.

*H*ot Tips

- The same problem with default directories occurs with indexing as with sorting. If you want your database and index files to go into a separate directory, you need to use the SET DEFAULT TO command to change the default to that directory.

- Unless you specify otherwise, FoxPro thinks that indexing should be case-sensitive: that is, "John," "JOHN," and "john" are considered different words. You can safeguard against potential problems by using the FoxPro UPPER function from the String functions list (accessed by selecting the String popup control in the Expression Builder). For example, by providing only uppercase versions of the words in the Lastname and Firstname fields, the expression

    upper(clients->lastname) + upper(clients->firstname)

    prevents FoxPro from listing JOHN JONES before Jeff Jones. (If you compare these two names *without* converting them to the same capitalization style, FoxPro will list them according to ASCII value—which would put any uppercase word before any word containing a lowercase letter.)

- Even if you haven't created a view file, you can skip the menus to open an indexed database by using the Command window. For example, to open your client file together with the name and zip code index files, you would go to the Command window and type

use clients index name, zipcode

and press Enter.

- Indexing a file from the Command window is similar to sorting, but it is not identical. To index your client file on lastname and firstname, for example, you would enter

index on lastname + firstname to cli_ndx

where CLI_NDX is the name of the index file you create. (To index on multiple numeric fields, you need to convert them to character fields; see your FoxPro reference manual for details.)

- You can use either the index name or its order number when specifying index order with the SET ORDER command. For example, if you opened the NAME index and then the ZIPCODE index, you can make NAME the primary index by typing either **set order to name** or **set order to 1** in the Command window.

LESSON 12
Finding Specific Records

Featuring

- How to set up search conditions
- How to use LIST, LOCATE, and SEEK
- How to show records with SET FILTER

IN THIS LESSON, YOU WILL LEARN HOW TO FIND ANY records you need—whether your database has nine records or nine million. It helps if your database has been put in order by sorting or indexing, but it's not absolutely necessary.

Search Conditions

The phrase "search conditions" may sound a little imposing, but there's really nothing difficult about it. If you've ever seen a TV detective show, you're familiar with the idea of search conditions: for example, that "the suspect is a white male, 25 to 30 years of age, with a slight limp and either black or brown hair."

If we were to tell FoxPro to search for someone fitting the preceding description, we'd need to phrase things a little more formally, but there wouldn't be any essential difference:

locate for (white male .and. (age > = 25) .and. (age < = 30) .and. slight limp .and. (hair = "brown" .or. hair = "black"))

In a database, search conditions let you narrow down a large number of records into a smaller group that is easier to handle. You might be looking for the record of a specific client. You might be looking for all the clients who live in a certain city or whose account balance is over $100.00. If you plan on a direct marketing campaign, you might need the records of all the clients who have shown an interest in certain types of services you offer. The possibilities are endless.

A Simple Search with LIST

The simplest kind of search, of course, is one in which you're looking for records that satisfy just one condition. Let's try a simple search right now—say, for all clients who live in Pittsburgh.

① Open your client database file from the Command window (not through the View window) by typing **use clients** and pressing Enter.

② Type

list firstname, lastname for city = "Pittsburgh"

In response, FoxPro lists the record number, first name, and last name for three records, as in Figure 12.1.

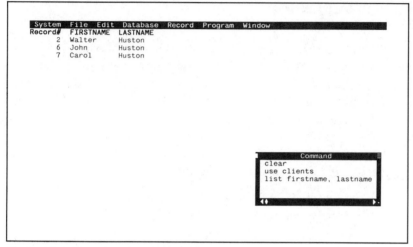

Figure 12.1: Searching for records with the LIST command

③ Now, let's try an experiment. In the Command window, type the same thing as in Step 2, but don't capitalize "Pittsburgh." Type

    list firstname, lastname for city = "pittsburgh"

and press Enter.

④ Nothing happened! That's because FoxPro is case-sensitive: as far as it's concerned, "Pittsburgh" and "pittsburgh" are different words, and it just didn't find any records where the city was pittsburgh with a lowercase *p*. You can see how this might cause problems if your data is not entered consistently. We'll see one solution to this problem in Lesson 14, when we see how to create data-entry screens.

⑤ For now, let's take a simpler approach. FoxPro has two functions—UPPER and LOWER—that convert letters to upper and lowercase, respectively. Let's try the same thing as in step 3, but using the LOWER function. Type

    list firstname, lastname for lower(city) = "pittsburgh"

and press Enter. The correct three records will be shown. You can use the UPPER function in a similar way.

Although in this case we've used LIST to search for multiple records that satisfy a search condition, it can also be used to display single records—e.g., **list for lastname = "Feynman"**. If you don't include field names with LIST, FoxPro assumes that you want all the fields listed—which can get a little messy on the screen.

Multiple Search Conditions

Sometimes, you need to narrow your search by entering more than one search condition. For example, there are three clients named Jones: two in New York and one in Menlo Park. This isn't much of a problem, but if there were three thousand clients named Jones, we'd have a very hard time finding the right one if all we had was the last name.

Logical Operators

To use multiple search conditions, we have to use *logical operators* to connect the conditions. There are four logical operators that you'll use very often:

- **.AND.** A condition with .AND. is true if the conditions on both sides of the .AND. are true. If, for example, we're looking for someone in our client database whose name is John *and* who lives in Pittsburgh, then only John Huston satisfies the search condition. John Jones is named John, but he doesn't live in Pittsburgh; Carol Huston lives in Pittsburgh, but her first name isn't John; and Michael Ende is neither named John nor lives in Pittsburgh.

- **.OR.** A condition with .OR. is considered true if either of the search conditions it connects is true. If we're searching for clients who either live in Dallas *or* are named Huston, then our search will find Joe Bob Briggs, who lives in Dallas, as well as Walter, John, and Carol Huston, who don't live in Dallas but whose last name is Huston.

- **EQUALS** is denoted by the equals sign, =. A condition with = is true if the part on the left of the = sign is equal to the part on the right. If we want to look for every client who lives in Pittsburgh, for example, we would enter **city = "Pittsburgh"** as a search condition.

- **NOT EQUAL** is denoted by <>. A condition with <> is true if the part on the left of the <> sign is not equal to the part on the right. If we want to find every client who *doesn't* live in Pittsburgh, we would enter the search condition **city <> "Pittsburgh"**.

There are many other search operators. Together, they let you create search expressions that do almost all of the work for you. (See your FoxPro reference manual for details.)

Doing a Multiple-Conditions Search

Let's try a multiple-conditions search. We want to find all the client records where (*a*) the client's last name is Huston and the account balance is over $50.00, or (*b*) the city is Menlo Park. Type the following all on one line in the Command window and then press Enter:

list for (lastname = "Huston" .and. balance > 50.00) .or. city = "Menlo Park"

The records for Walter Huston, Richard Feynmann, and Jennifer Jones should be displayed. Notice that, just as in our seventh-grade algebra class, we used parentheses to group the conditions that go together.

Printing Your Search Results

Until now, we've simply displayed the results of our search on the PC's screen. It's just as easy, however, to send the results to the printer: simply add the words **to print** at the end of your list command. Then, the records will be printed at the same time they are being displayed on the screen. If you have a printer hooked up, type **list firstname, lastname to print** in the Command window and press Enter.

Your records will be printed as they are displayed on the screen. To eject the page from the printer, type **eject** and press Enter.

Using LOCATE and SEEK

So far, we've found the records that match our search conditions and displayed them on the screen. But what if you need to edit each record that you find? Of course, you can use LIST, copy down the record numbers it displays, and choose "Change" from the Record menu for each record you want to edit.

Fortunately, there's an easier way. Searching for records with the LOCATE command (available from the Record menu, while LIST is not) lets you edit each matching record as you come to it, then move on to the next one. Another useful command, SEEK, is similar to LOCATE, except that it can be used only with indexed files.

LOCATE With Non-Indexed Databases

Here's an example using LOCATE to find the records of clients who live in Pittsburgh:

① From the Record menu, choose "Locate."

② When the Locate Records dialog box comes up, press *F* on your keyboard to select the "For" checkbox (see Figure 12.2).

③ In the Expression Builder dialog box, press Shift-Tab to back up to the field list, and use the down arrow key to highlight the City field. Then press Enter.

④ From the Logical functions selection box (which you can call either from the Expression menu or, if you're using a mouse, from the "Logical" popup control), select the equal sign (=) and press Enter.

⑤ From the String functions selection box, select "text" and press Enter. When the quote marks appear in the expression box, type **Pittsburgh** between the quote marks and press Ctrl-Enter (see Figure 12.3).

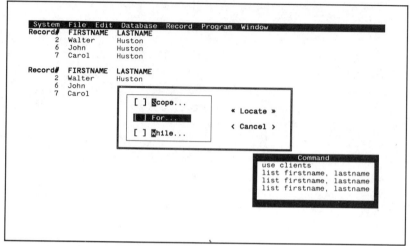

Figure 12.2: *The Locate records dialog box*

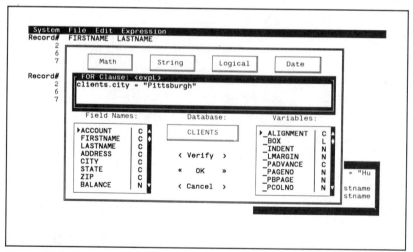

Figure 12.3: *Building a search expression*

- ⑥ Press Ctrl-Enter again to begin the search. FoxPro will display the message **Record = 2** to indicate that the first matching record has been found.

- ⑦ Let's say that Walter Huston has paid off his account balance. Type **edit** in the Command window and press Enter. Move down to the Balance field and type **00.00** as in Figure 12.4. Press Escape to close the Edit window.

⑧ Select "Continue" from the Record menu. (Alternatively, you can enter **continue** in the Command window or simply press Ctrl-K, which is the speed key.) The record pointer will move to the next matching record, even though you can't see it. Verify the pointer's position by opening the Browse window; the highlight should be positioned on the record for John Huston.

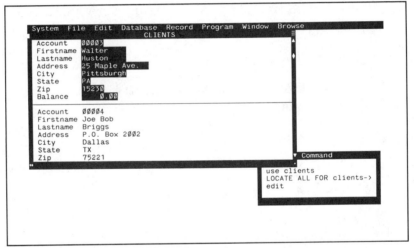

Figure 12.4: Editing a record found with LOCATE

⑨ Now close the Browse window (things will get confusing if you leave it open), and press Ctrl-K to continue locating matching records. The record pointer will move to record #7, Carol Huston.

⑩ Press Ctrl-K one more time. FoxPro displays the message **End of locate scope**, which means it can't find any more matching records.

SEEK with Indexed Databases

In a large, indexed database (and any large database file *should* be indexed), SEEK may find records much faster than LOCATE.

That's because SEEK looks only at the primary index field. Since the primary index file gives the order of the records based on that field, it's easy for SEEK to go right to the first matching record.

There's another difference between LOCATE and SEEK. Since SEEK looks at the primary indexed field only, you don't need to tell it which field to look at. With LOCATE, on the one hand, you might enter a search command like

locate for lastname = "Huston"

On the other hand, if you're using SEEK for the same search where the primary index field is LASTNAME, then you merely need to enter

seek "Huston"

Let's give it a quick run-through.

① Open the NAME index file by entering **set index to name** in the Command window.

② Select "Seek" from the Record menu.

③ Press Ctrl-S to pop up the String functions selection box, and select "text."

④ Between the quotation marks, type **Huston** and press Ctrl-Enter.

⑤ Open the Browse window to verify that the highlight is on the first record for which lastname = "Huston." Then close the Browse window.

Here's where we come to the drawback of using SEEK: you can't use "Continue" to find additional matching records. SEEK can only be used to find the first matching record, and "Continue" only works with LOCATE.

Now, that isn't all bad; it's just more complicated for beginners. If there's only one matching record in your database, you're home free. If there's more than one, then at least SEEK has moved the record pointer to the first of the matching records.

Since all the matching records are together (remember, the database is indexed on that field), you can then use LOCATE and CONTINUE to pursue the search from that point. With our database of nine records, it doesn't make a lot of difference; but if you had nine thousand records, using SEEK to go straight to the first matching record would be a real timesaver.

To continue the search, just enter

locate while lastname = "Huston" for firstname = "Walter"

in the Command window. Open the Browse window and you'll see that the highlight is on the record you want. (The "while" part of what you typed tells FoxPro to stop searching if it runs out of records with last name Huston.)

Using SET FILTER

Sometimes you don't want to do a lot of fancy searching. You want to open your Browse window and look at only those records that match your search conditions. You can do this easily with SET FILTER.

To see how SET FILTER works, do the following:

① Open the View window and select the Setup button to open the Setup dialog box.

② In the Setup dialog box, press *L* on your keyboard to check the "Set Filter" checkbox. The "Set Filter" Expression Builder dialog box will appear.

③ Enter **city = "Menlo Park"** in the expression box. Then press Ctrl-Enter to exit from the Expression Builder dialog box. Press Ctrl-Enter again to exit from the Setup dialog box.

If you now open the Browse window, you can see that only the clients who live in Menlo Park are displayed, as in Figure 12.5. To redisplay all of your records, you can simply move to the Command window and enter **set filter to** (followed by nothing) to turn off the filter.

Lesson 12

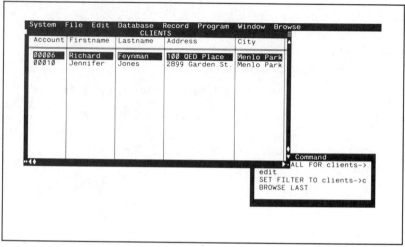

Figure 12.5: Displaying selected records with SET FILTER

Lesson Summary

To search for records and display them on your screen, open your database file and enter

   list *field1*, *field2*, . . . for *fieldn* = *something*

in the Command window. You should replace *field1* and *field2* (etc.) with the names of the fields you want to display, and *fieldn* with the field on which you're searching.

To print the records you've retrieved using LIST, as they're displayed on the screen, simply add the words **to print** at the end of your LIST command.

To use multiple search conditions, connect the individual search conditions with logical operators such as .AND., .OR., = (equal), and < > (not equal).

To make your search ignore whether letters in a word are upper or lowercase, you can use the UPPER and LOWER functions.

The commands LOCATE and SEEK both let you edit a searched-for record once you've found it. The main differences are that

- SEEK can search only the primary index field of an indexed database file.

- SEEK is faster than LOCATE for large files.
- SEEK will find only the first matching record: it has no option to CONTINUE.
- SEEK does not require a "for" clause like LOCATE. (In fact, it cannot use a "for" clause.)

The command SET FILTER allows you to display in your Browse window only those records that meet your search conditions. You can use SET FILTER either from the Setup dialog box or from the Command window.

Hot Tips

- Sometimes you may not be sure about the exact contents of the record you're trying to find. For example, you may not be sure if Richard Feynman's last name ends with one or two *n*'s. Instead of doing two searches (one for each spelling) you can use Fox-Pro's $ function to look for part of the name. Type

    list for "Feyn" $ lastname

    and FoxPro will find Feynman's record.

- The $ function is particularly powerful in searching for text in memo fields. With dBASE III Plus, you had to pull off some fairly complex programming maneuvers to find records based on what was in their memo fields. With FoxPro, you simply think of a word or phrase that is in the memo field you want, but isn't likely to be in the memo fields of other records. If the word is "quark" and the memo field is "notes," then you would simply enter

    list for "quark" $ notes

    in the Command window.

LESSON 13
Creating Sophisticated Reports

Featuring

- How to customize your report layout
- Grouping your data
- Formatting report fields
- Using report functions

IN LESSON 9, WE SAW HOW TO CREATE SIMPLE REPORTS by using FoxPro's "Quick Report" feature. In this lesson, we're going to learn some more sophisticated tricks to use in creating reports.

*L*aying Out Your Report

When you create a report, FoxPro assumes that you are using standard-size paper and that you want to use the whole page—no top, bottom, or side margins. This will undoubtedly get the most data on each page, but your report won't look as nice as it could.

*U*sing the Page Layout Dialog Box

We want our customized report to look good, so we'll change FoxPro's default settings. Do the following:

① Open your client database file. Index it on "city" to a new index file, which you should now name **by-city**.

② Select "New" from the File menu and choose the "Report" file type. Press Ctrl-Enter to confirm your choice. The Report window will appear.

③ From the Report menu, choose "Page Layout." The Page Layout dialog box will appear as in Figure 13.1, showing the standard page size of 66 rows (lines) and 80 columns.

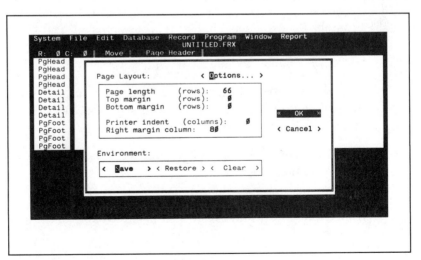

Figure 13.1: *The Page Layout dialog box*

④ Tab to the "Page Length" item. We're going to leave the page length at 66 lines, so simply press Enter.

⑤ Type **3** for the "Top Margin" item and press Enter. Do the same with "Bottom Margin."

⑥ Enter a "Printer Indent" of **5** (for a left margin that is five columns—spaces—from the edge of the page) and a "Right Margin Column" of **75** (for a right margin that is five spaces from column 80—the edge of the page).

⑦ Press Ctrl-Enter to confirm your choices.

⑧ Choose "Save As" from the File menu and type **cli-rpt3** in the blank for the file name. Press Ctrl-Enter to save this report form.

Entering Title Information

You'll recall from Lesson 9 that page header information (anything in the PgHead band) is printed at the top of every page. Page footer information (in the PgFoot band) is printed at the bottom of every page. In addition to header information, let's give this report a title that will appear only on page 1.

① From the Report menu, choose "Title/Summary." The Title/Summary dialog box will open as in Figure 13.2. Press *T* to select "Title Band" and press Ctrl-Enter to accept your choice.

② One line won't be enough for our title, so add a second line to the Title band by pressing Ctrl-N. (Make sure that the cursor is in the Title band when you do it.)

③ In the first line of the Title band, type **My Computer Company** and press Enter.

④ Press the space bar to select the text, then choose "Center" from the Report menu. Press Enter again to confirm the new position.

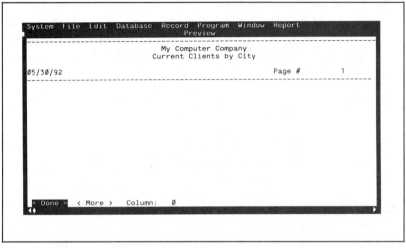

Figure 13.2: *The Title/Summary dialog box*

⑤ On the second line of the Title band, type **Current Clients by City** and press Enter. Center the text just as you did before.

Date Stamping and Page Numbering

Now, let's do something a little different. We want each page of our custom report to show the current date and the page number. These were included automatically in our Quick report. To put these in our new report, we'll use several of FoxPro's built-in functions:

① Move the cursor down to the second line of the PgHead band (you should see R:3 C:0 at the top left on the status line).

② Call up the Field dialog box by pressing Ctrl-F, and select the "Expr" button by pressing Enter. This opens the Expression Builder.

③ Select DATE( ) from the list of Date functions available through the Expression menu or, with the mouse, from the list you pop up by clicking on the Date popup button. Press Ctrl-Enter twice to return to the Layout window.

④ You'll see the DATE() function positioned at the left of the PgHead band. Each time you use this report format to print a report, the DATE() function will check your PC's system clock to find out the current date, which will then be displayed on each printed page in the header part of the report.

⑤ Now, let's add page numbering. Move the cursor to column 55 of row 3 (R:3 C:55). Type **Page #** and press Enter.

⑥ Now move the cursor one column to the right of the number symbol to position the page number. Press Ctrl-F to open the Field box, and press Enter to open the Expression Builder.

⑦ Move to the "Variables" box at the lower right. (If you're using the keyboard, press Tab five times to get there. With a mouse, just click in the box.) Move the highlight down to _PAGENO and press Enter or double-click to select it.

⑧ Press Ctrl-Enter twice to return to the Layout window.

⑨ Using hyphens, draw a line across the full width of the page in the third line of the PgHead band, and press Enter. Then press Ctrl-I to activate Page Preview (see Figure 13.3).

Modifying the Date Format

This looks all right, but we can make it look better. The numeric date, 05/30/92, would be easier to read as "Saturday, May 30, 1992." It will take a little extra work to set this up, but it demonstrates how much power FoxPro has under the hood.

First, however, we need to understand what a function is. In essence, a function simply takes one value and turns it into another. Often, you end up with the same kind of value you started with; that is, one number turns into another number. In this case, however, we're going to use some FoxPro functions to take the current numeric date (05/30/92) and transform it into a character day (Saturday) and month (May), and a slightly different numeric form of the day of

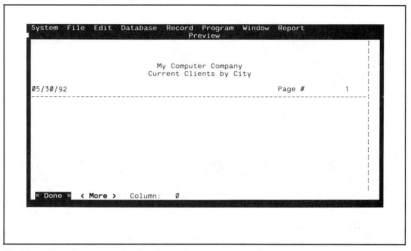

Figure 13.3: *Preview of date and page number information*

the month and year. Press Escape to get out of Page Preview and back into the Layout window, then do the following:

① Move the cursor to the *D* in DATE( ) and press the Delete key. This deletes the entire DATE( ) function.

② Press Ctrl-F to call up the Field box; then press Enter to open the Expression Builder.

③ Press Ctrl-D to pop up the list of Date functions. Highlight CDOW( ) and press Enter to select it. CDOW( ) stands for "character day of the week"; it takes the current numeric date and transforms it into Monday, Tuesday, etc. Notice that in the expression box, the cursor is between the parentheses in the CDOW( ).

④ Pop up the Date functions list again and select DATE( ). This function will appear where the cursor was: between the parentheses of CDOW( ). As shown in Figure 13.4, the expression should read CDOW(DATE( )). Press Ctrl-Enter twice to return to the Layout window.

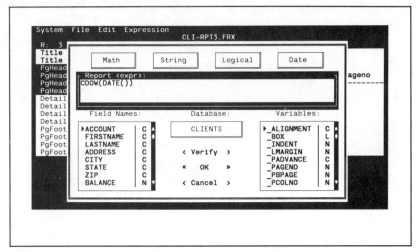

Figure 13.4: A nested function in the expression box

⑤ Using the right arrow key (not the space bar), move the cursor so that it is just to the right of the function we just entered. You will notice that only the first few letters of the function are displayed; thus, you will be moving the cursor to R:3 C:6. Type a comma and press Enter.

⑥ Using the arrow key again, move the cursor to column 8 (R:3 C:8). Press Ctrl-F to call up the Field box and Enter to open the Expression Builder.

⑦ From the Date functions list, select CMONTH( )—the function for "character month," e.g., May, June, July. With the cursor between the parentheses, pop up the Date functions again and select DATE( ). Press Ctrl-Enter twice to return to the Layout window.

⑧ Using the arrow key, move the cursor to the very next space after the end of "CMONT" (the part of the function name that is shown in the Layout screen). The cursor should be at R:3 C:13.

⑨ Open the Expression Builder again and select DAY( ) from the Date list. With the cursor inside the parentheses of DAY( ),

Creating Sophisticated Reports **133**

pop up the Date list again and select DATE( ). Press Ctrl-Enter twice to go back to the Layout window.

⑩ At R:3 C:16, type a comma and press Enter. Use the arrow key to move the cursor to the very next column (R:3 C:17).

⑪ Open the Expression Builder. From the list of Date functions, select YEAR( ). Then, with the cursor between the parentheses in YEAR( ), select DATE( ) from the Date functions list. Press Ctrl-Enter twice to return to the Layout window.

⑫ Now, we can see the results of our work! Open "Page Preview" by pressing Ctrl-I. Your screen should look like Figure 13.5.

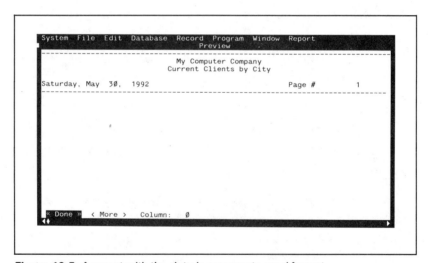

Figure 13.5: *A report with the date in an easy-to-read format*

Let's add one more header feature before we move on. Position the cursor on the last line of the PgHead band and press Ctrl-N to add another line. Then, in the same line (R:5), add column headings to start at the following positions: Account (C:0), Last name (C:10), City (C:30), State (C:42), and Current Balance (C:50). In the last line of the PgHead band, draw another horizontal line across the width of the page by using the hyphen key.

Grouping Records

FoxPro makes it easy for you to group your report records any way you want. You can group records based on city, account balance, income level, buying habits, or almost anything else in a database. You can also combine different groupings: for example, one group might contain records of people in Pittsburgh who subscribe to computer magazines and have at least two cars; another group might be the same except that the people would live in Miami.

Your database file should be indexed on the grouping fields. In our client report, which is currently indexed by city, we're going to group the records on city so that all client records for a given city will print together. To get started, do the following:

① Select "Data Grouping" from the Report menu.

② When the Group dialog box comes up, select the Add button.

③ When the Group Info dialog box comes up, press Enter to select the Group button (see Figure 13.6).

④ When the Expression Builder window opens, highlight and select CITY from the field list on the left. Press Ctrl-Enter three times to get back to the Layout window. You'll notice

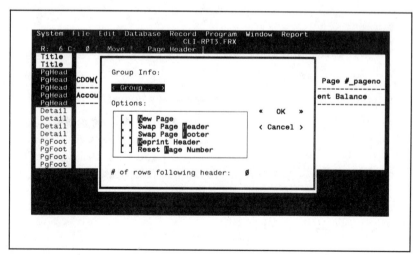

Figure 13.6: The Group Info dialog box

that a line labeled "1-city" now wraps around to the lines above and below the Detail band. The "1" indicates that it's the first level of grouping, while the "city" indicates the field used for grouping.

5. Now it's time to place the fields for our report. In the first line of the Detail band, position the cursor at C:0 and press Ctrl-F to call up the Report Expression dialog box. Press Enter to open the Expression Builder dialog box, and select ACCOUNT from the field list on the left. Press Ctrl-Enter twice to get back to the Layout window. You should see the first five letters of the word "account"—that is, "accou"—in the Detail band.

6. Repeat the process in step 5 to position the LASTNAME (C:10), CITY (C:30), STATE (C:42), and BALANCE (C:50) fields on the same line as the account field.

7. In the Layout window, move to the line below the fields and press Ctrl-O three times to remove the other lines in the Detail band.

8. On the line underneath the Detail band (the bottom half of the "1-city" wrap-around line), draw a horizontal line with the hyphen key. Your layout screen should look like Figure 13.7.

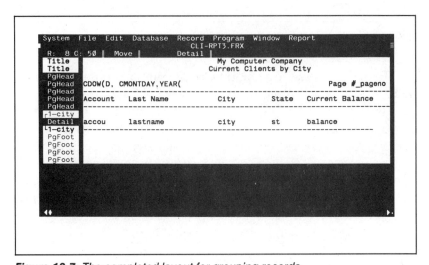

Figure 13.7: *The completed layout for grouping records*

⑨ Press Ctrl-I to call Page Preview. Your records are grouped by city, with a horizontal line separating each group (see Figure 13.8).

*F*ormatting Report Fields

There's one other thing you ought to know about, even though we're not going to do it in our report. FoxPro allows you to use predefined formats for your report fields.

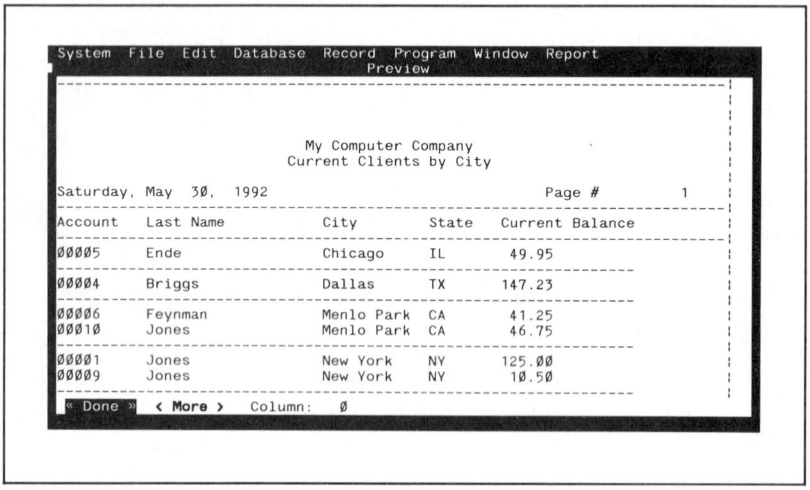

Figure 13.8: Report records grouped by city

To apply a format to a report field, you simply choose the field in the Expression Builder and then, when you back out to the Report Expression box, choose "Format." A Field Format dialog box opens and you can choose the format(s) you want. There are several. For example, you can tell FoxPro to put a dollar sign and commas into currency fields; you can have character fields (such as last name) in all capital letters; you can justify left or right; and many other possibilities. The formats are different for each of the four field types that you can apply them to: character, numeric, date, and logical. A dialog box for numeric field formats is shown in Figure 13.9.

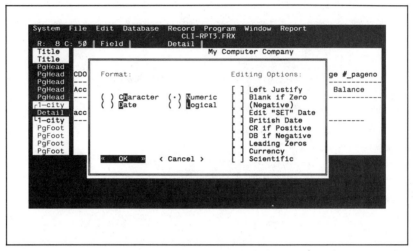

Figure 13.9: Format options for numeric report fields

*F*iltering Records in Your Report

Sometimes, of course, you won't want to include all your records in a report. Instead of including many different cities, you might want to look only at records for Menlo Park, or where the account balance is over $100.00.

You handle this not by doing anything to the report format itself, but by using a dialog box (shown in Figure 13.10) when you print the report. We first encountered it in Lesson 9, when we used it simply to print a Quick Report. To open this dialog box, you must first exit from your Report Layout screen, and then select "Report" from the Database menu.

To limit your report to certain records, highlight and select the "For" checkbox on the right. An Expression Builder box will appear where you can build the condition that records must satisfy to be included in the report. This works exactly the same as all the other uses of the Expression Builder. To limit your report to clients whose balance is over $100.00, for example, you would enter **balance > 100.00** in the expression box.

The "Scope" and "While" checkboxes provide alternate ways of limiting the records included in your report; see your FoxPro user's manual or Charles Siegel's *Mastering FoxPro 2* (SYBEX, 1991) for details.

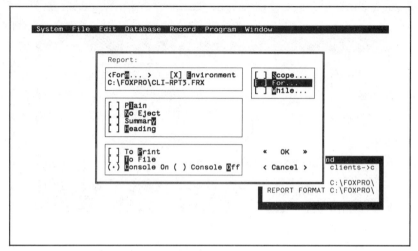

Figure 13.10: Report printing dialog box

Two other features of the Report printing dialog box are worth noting. At the bottom left are checkboxes to send the report to the printer or to a text file on disk. As you already know, your report will be printed if you select the "To Print" box. If you select "To File," you'll be prompted to enter a file name under which your report will be saved on disk. The "Preview" checkbox simply displays the report in the same manner as Page Preview on The Report Layout screen.

The "Console On" button displays your report on the screen as it is created (regardless of whether it's also being printed). "Console Off" turns off the report screen display.

Lesson Summary

The Page Layout dialog box, available from the Report menu, lets you set paper size as well as top, bottom, left, and right margins for your report.

The DATE( ) function causes the current date (when the report is printed) to appear on your report. You can also combine different functions to display the information in different formats, such as CDOW(DATE( )), which prints the character day of the week when the report is printed. Date functions are available from the Date functions list, which can be called either from the Expression menu or with Ctrl-D, the Date functions speed key.

The _PAGENO function, available from the "Variables" box at the bottom right of the Expression Builder, causes the current page number to print on each page of your report.

You can group records on any field or combination of fields. Your database file must be indexed on the fields you use for your grouping. You call up the Grouping dialog box from the Report menu.

When you place a field on your report layout, you have the option of using a field format. To use one of FoxPro's predefined formats in a report field, pick "Format" in the Report Expression box; then, in the Field Format dialog box, just select the formats you want for that field.

To print only selected records in your report, choose "For" in the Report Printing dialog box that appears when you choose "Report" from the Database menu.

Hot Tips

- One function that is often used in FoxPro reports is TRIM. This function takes a character field and filters out any trailing spaces on the right. In a form letter, for example (which is just a special type of report), the first line might contain both the first and last name of the recipient. If the person's first name is Joe and the firstname field is ten characters wide, then there will be seven spaces between the person's first and last names in the letter. To eliminate this problem, you would simply type in

    trim(firstname) + " " + lastname

    Notice the single space between the quotes: because TRIM filters out all of the spaces after the first name, it is necessary to insert this one space to separate the first and last names.

- As noted in Lesson 9, some versions of FoxPro do not support special printer effects such as boldfaced type and box drawing. While these effects would display on the screen, they could not be printed. If special printer effects are absolutely essential, and your version of FoxPro does not support them, you can print the report (with "Report" from the Database menu) to a text file on disk and then import the text file into your word processor for final formatting and printing.

PART IV

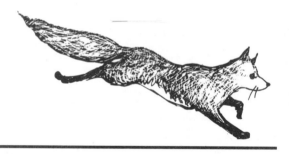

Advanced-Level Skills

LESSON 14
Creating Your Own
Data-Entry Screens

LESSON 15
Linking Files

LESSON 16
Creating Multifile Reports

LESSON 17
Creating Your
Own Menu System

LESSON 14
Creating Your Own Data-Entry Screens

Featuring

- How to start FoxView
- How to create a customized data-entry screen
- How to include formats and data validation

WE'VE ALREADY SEEN THAT FOXPRO LETS YOU ENTER new database records by choosing "Append" from the Record menu. However, new records may sometimes be entered by people who are unfamiliar with your database, and they may need a little more explanation of what they are doing and how it should be done.

That's when FoxPro comes to your rescue. It makes it easy for you to create customized data-entry screens with on-screen help messages, as well as screens that only display your data without letting the user change it—a capability that can be tremendously valuable in safeguarding your data against accidental loss or change.

Customized data entry screens have other advantages. You may recall from the earlier lessons on sorting, searching, and indexing that inconsistent capitalization can be a real problem. When you're searching for a city name, for example, your search will find only those records that exactly match your search condition: if you have several people entering data, the city name might be "Pittsburgh" in some records, "pittsburgh" in others, and "PITTSBURGH" in others.

The data checking capability that you can build into customized data-entry screens will solve this problem—and many others—for you.

Using FoxPro's Screen Painter

If you used the previous version of FoxPro, you'll be surprised to learn that FoxPro 2 no longer includes "FoxView," a program which made it easy to create custom screens and menus. In version 2, these functions are more tightly integrated into FoxPro itself. Instead of running FoxView to create a screen or a menu, you simply choose the New option from the File menu and select "Screen" or "Menu" in the File Type dialog box (see Figure 14.1).

Unfortunately, there is a slight complication. For reasons that are a little obscure, Fox Software decided to remove the screen painter's ability to create screen formats that you could simply "plug in and use." Until now, both FoxPro and dBASE let you create "format files" that you could invoke any time you wanted them. Thus, once you had created such a format file, such as, "clients.fmt," you could type **set format to clients** in the Command window and that format would be used to put new records in the data file.

That isn't true any longer. The screen files that you create by choosing New/Screen from the File menu are not screen formats, but full-blooded FoxPro programs. In order to use these screen programs effectively, however, you must know a good deal about FoxPro

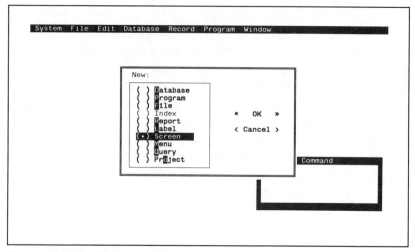

Figure 14.1: The File Type dialog box

programming—which means that the FoxPro screen painter has become far less helpful to the average PC user (and even to programmers).

Fortunately, though, you can paint screens with the screen painter and then, with a simple procedure, convert them into screen format files that you can easily use. That is the method we will use here. In order to understand what you're doing, you'll need to know a little bit more about FoxPro programming than you did with earlier versions, but it still won't be too difficult.

Starting the Screen Painter

Start FoxPro if you haven't already, and open the clients data file by typing **use clients** in the Command window and pressing Enter. Then do the following:

① Choose "New" from the File menu and, in the File Type dialog box, select "Screen," as shown in Figure 14.1.

② Press Ctrl-Enter to open the Screen Painter. Notice that a new Screen menu has been added to the menu bar.

③ Open the Screen menu with the mouse or by pressing Alt-C. Because it is the easiest way to create a screen, select "Quick Screen." The Quick Screen dialog box will open, as shown in

Creating Your Own Data-Entry Screens   147

Figure 14.2. Simply press Ctrl-Enter to accept the default choices.

④ All of the fields in your client file will appear on-screen, as shown in Figure 14.3. (If we had wanted to include only certain fields, we could have done so by positioning the cursor on the screen and pressing Ctrl-F to insert a field at that point.)

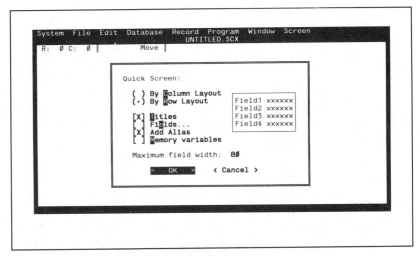

Figure 14.2: The Quick Screen dialog box

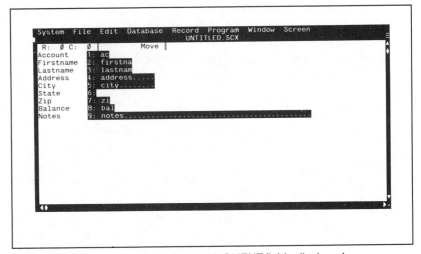

Figure 14.3: FoxPro Screen Painter with CLIENT fields displayed

Notice that the field labels appear in normal text, while the fields themselves are highlighted. Press Ctrl-A to select all fields and field labels.

⑤ Using the arrow keys, move the fields and field labels until the row/column indicator at the top left of the screen reads "R:5 C:2." Notice that the word "Move" appears to the right of the row and column numbers. This indicates that the Screen Painter is in "Move" mode.

⑥ Press Enter to exit the Move mode and to confirm the new location for the fields.

Now we want to move the fields around the screen a bit. There's nothing special about the locations where we're placing the fields; you can arrange them in a different manner if you prefer. We're also going to put a title on the screen.

⑦ First, let's create the title. To do this, you need to realize that each item on the screen is a particular kind of "screen object" that can be moved and manipulated. Using the arrow keys—not the space bar—move the cursor to row 2, column 27 and type **My Computer Company**. Then press Enter to confirm the title's location on the screen.

⑧ Using the arrow keys, move the cursor to the field *label* "Firstname" (not the field itself). Press the space bar to select it, then use the arrow keys to move it to row 5, column 25. If you're using a mouse, simply click on the field label and, while holding down the mouse button, drag it to the new location.

⑨ In the same way, move the firstname field to row 5, column 36.

⑩ Move the other items as follows: Lastname label to 5,49; lastname field to 5,59; Notes label to 14,2; notes field to 14,8; Balance label to 12,30; balance field to 12,38; Zip label to 12,2; zip field to 12,6; State label to 10,61; state field to 10,67; City label to 10,39; city field to 10,44; and Address label to 10,2; address field to 10,10.

We've now accomplished a fair amount, so it's a good time to save our work. Open the File menu and select "Save." When you're prompted for a file name, type in **clients** and press Ctrl-Enter. A dialog box will appear, asking if you want to save the environment information. Simply press Enter to answer "Yes." Your screen should now look like Figure 14.4.

Now, let's change the field names a little on the screen.

① Move the cursor back to the account field. We're going to expand the field label, so we need to move the field to R:5 C:17.

② Move the cursor one space to the right of the "Account" label (R:5 C:10), and type **Number**. Then press Enter.

③ What we've just done has one problem. Use the space bar or the mouse to highlight "Number" and you'll discover that it's a separate screen object from the word "Account." This doesn't make any real difference here, but with the other labels, we'll do things another way.

④ Move the cursor to "Firstname" and press the Delete key. The field label disappears. In its place, type **First Name** and press Enter. This creates a new "First Name" screen object.

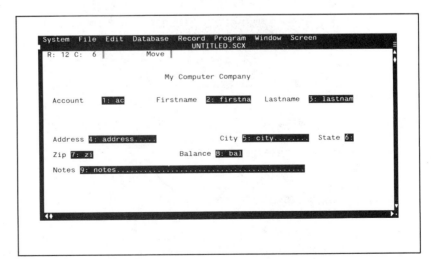

Figure 14.4: *Fields rearranged on the layout screen*

⑤ Do the same with the Lastname field label. Move the cursor to "Lastname" and press the Delete key. Then, in its place, type in **Last Name** and press Enter.

⑥ Let's make one more change—"Address" will become "Street Address." First, move the address field to R:10 C:17. Then move the cursor to "Address" and press the Delete key. In its place, type **Street Address** and press Enter.

⑦ Once again, open the File menu and save your work.

Adding Boxes to Your Screen

We're going to add one more cosmetic touch to the data-entry screen: a box that will enclose the client's name and account number. You'll be surprised at how easy this is:

① Move the cursor to R:4 C:1. Then open the Screen menu.

② Highlight and select the "Box" menu option, as shown in Figure 14.5. (Note that you could also use the Box speed key, Ctrl-B.) A small box appears above and to the left of the Account field label.

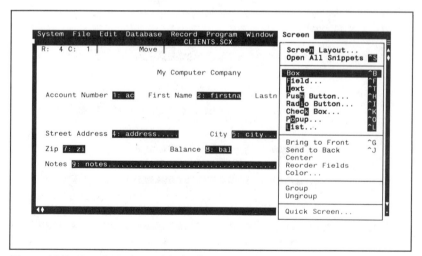

Figure 14.5: Drawing a box with the Screen menu

③ Tap the down arrow key once. The box stretches downward to row number six, just below the fields we want to place in the box.

④ Hold down the right arrow key until the box stretches to R:6 C:70. Your screen should now look like Figure 14.6. Open the File menu and save your work.

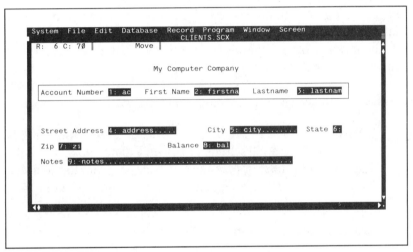

Figure 14.6: The data-entry screen with a box added

Adding Formats and Data Validation

If your data is entered incorrectly, it doesn't matter how nice your data-entry screens look. In addition to the cosmetic changes that we've already seen, the FoxPro Screen Painter lets you build some basic data validation measures into your screen. This can help protect your database from some common data-entry mistakes. You can catch incorrect data and prevent it from being entered. You can also reformat data to match a standard format; then, no matter how it's typed, it will be stored and displayed correctly. This eliminates problems caused by inconsistent capitalization, and a hundred other database headaches.

Adding Field Attributes

It's beyond the scope of this book to discuss every field attribute that you can use, though we will look at a few of them in Lesson 18, "Advanced Field Techniques." Here, we'll only discuss two of the most important.

The first thing we will do is make sure that our "firstname," "lastname," "city," and "state" entries are stored in all uppercase letters, no matter how they are typed. This is one way to avoid problems that could result from inconsistent capitalization. (Another way, as we saw in the lesson on searches, is to use the UPPER( ) and LOWER( ) functions in search expressions.)

After that, we'll put a format into the balance field so that it displays entries in currency (dollars and cents) format. Let's get started:

① Move the cursor to "firstname." This time, we won't simply select the field: we'll select it and open a dialog box by double-clicking the mouse or pressing the space bar twice in rapid succession. The Field dialog box opens, as shown in Figure 14.7.

② In the Field dialog box, select "Format." This opens the Format dialog box, as shown in Figure 14.8.

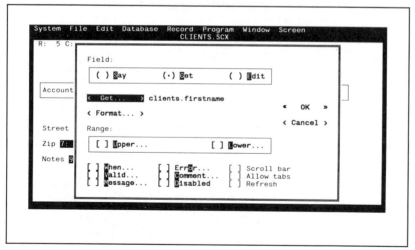

Figure 14.7: The Field dialog box

Creating Your Own Data-Entry Screens

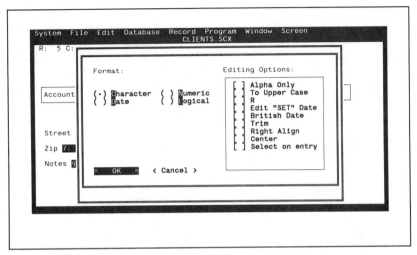

Figure 14.8: The Format dialog box

③ Highlight the "To Upper Case" checkbox and select it by pressing the space bar or clicking between the square brackets with the mouse. Then press Ctrl-Enter to return to the Field dialog box.

④ In the Field dialog box, notice that "@!" now appears next to the Format button. This is actually a piece of FoxPro programming code that converts all the letters in a field to uppercase. Your format for the firstname field is now complete, so press Ctrl-Enter one more time to return to the Screen Painter.

⑤ Using the same method, insert an uppercase-only format into the lastname, city, and state fields.

⑥ Finally, move the cursor to the balance field and open the Format dialog box. Because "balance" is a numeric field, you automatically open a numeric-format dialog box, as shown in Figure 14.9. Select "Currency" and press Ctrl-Enter twice to return to the Screen Painter. Then save your work.

There's one more step we need to take in the Screen Painter. So far we've created a special kind of database file that contains data about the screen objects and layout. We now need to have FoxPro generate a code for our screen, which we will then modify slightly to create a screen format file.

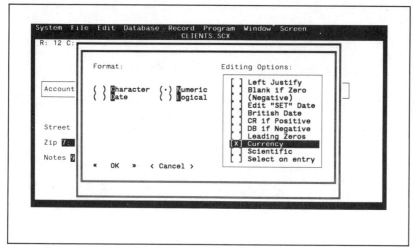

Figure 14.9: Format dialog box with numeric formats

⑦ After saving your work, open the Program menu and select "Generate." The Generate dialog box will open, as shown in Figure 14.10. Deselect all the checkboxes under "Code Options" so that none of them has an "X" between the square brackets. Then press Ctrl-Enter to accept the default file name of CLIENTS.SPR and FoxPro will generate the code for you.

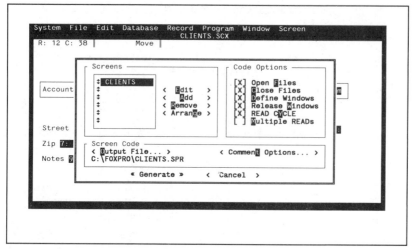

Figure 14.10: The Generate dialog box

Creating Your Own Data-Entry Screens **155**

⑧ After FoxPro has finished generating the code, press Escape to exit from the Screen Painter and return to the Command window.

Now, we're going to alter the CLIENTS.SPR file so that it is usable as a screen format. Although it is unorthodox, this is the easiest method for a non-programmer to create a screen format file. In the Command window, type **modify command clients.spr** and press Enter. A text-editing window will open, as shown in Figure 14.11.

Press Ctrl-F10 or click on the window's zoom button to zoom the editing window to full-screen so that it's easier to work with. What you see is FoxPro programming code, some of which is unnecessary for a screen format. Therefore, we'll delete that which we don't need.

① First, open the File menu and select "Save As." Save the file under the new name **clients.fmt**.

② Then, move the cursor to the very beginning of the file, to the left of the box that says "CLIENTS.SPR." Hold down the shift and down arrow keys to highlight everything down to and including the line that says **#REGION 1** under the box that says "CLIENTS Screen Layout," as shown in Figure 14.12.

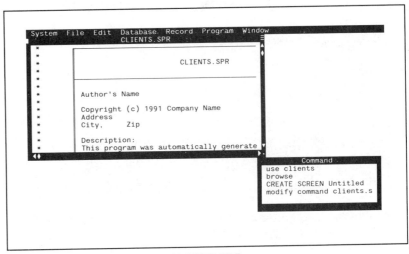

Figure 14.11: *Preparing to edit CLIENTS.SPR*

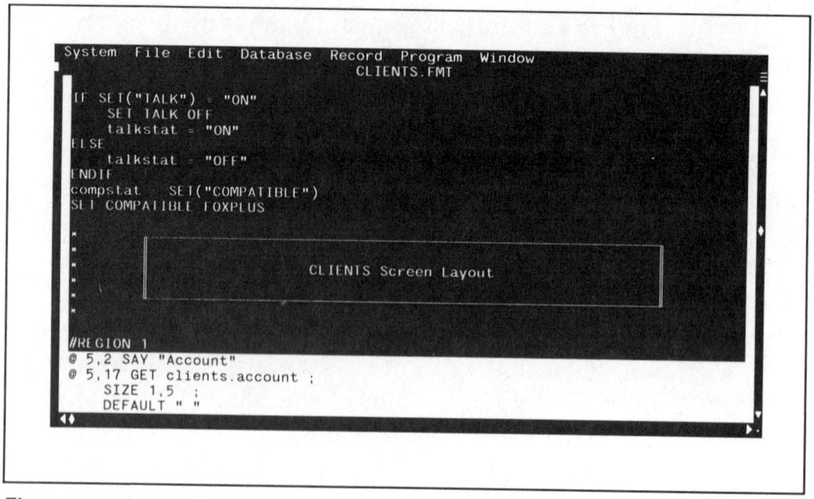

Figure 14.12: Highlighting material for deletion

③ Press the Delete key to delete the highlighted code.

④ Now go down to the bottom of the file, to the line under the READ statement that says **#REGION 0**. Highlight and delete everything from that line to the end of the file, as shown in Figure 14.13.

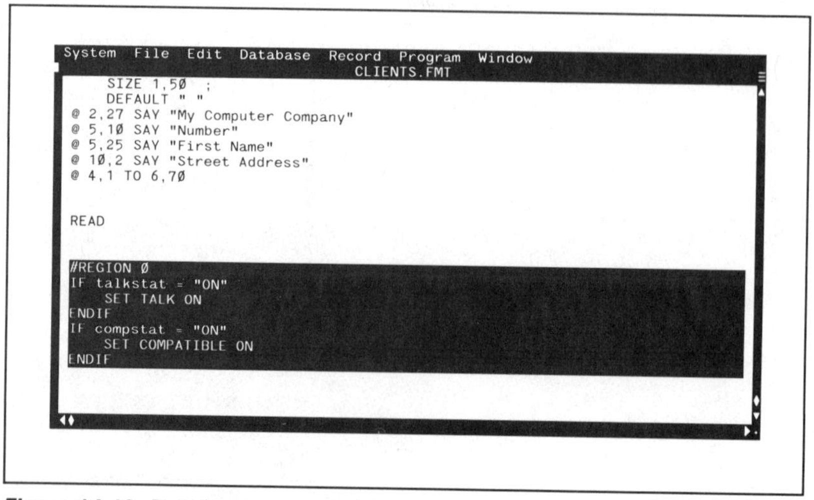

Figure 14.13: Deleting more material

The screen format should now match Figure 14.14. If it does, then it is now ready to use, so save your work and press Escape to return to the Command window.

```
@ 5,2 SAY "Account"
@ 5,17 GET clients.account ;
       SIZE 1,5 ;
       DEFAULT " "
@ 5,36 GET clients.firstname ;
       SIZE 1,10 ;
       DEFAULT " " ;
       PICTURE "@!"
@ 5,49 SAY "Lastname"
@ 5,59 GET clients.lastname ;
       SIZE 1,10 ;
       DEFAULT " " ;
       PICTURE "@!"
@ 10,17 GET clients.address ;
       SIZE 1,15 ;
       DEFAULT " "
@ 10,39 SAY "City"
@ 10,44 GET clients.city ;
       SIZE 1,15 ;
       DEFAULT " " ;
       PICTURE "@!"
@ 10,61 SAY "State"
@ 10,67 GET clients.state ;
       SIZE 1,2 ;
       DEFAULT " " ;
       PICTURE "@!"
@ 12,2 SAY "Zip"
@ 12,6 GET clients.zip ;
       SIZE 1,5 ;
       DEFAULT " "
@ 12,30 SAY "Balance"
@ 12,38 GET clients.balance ;
       SIZE 1,6 ;
       DEFAULT 0 ;
       PICTURE "@$"
@ 14,2 SAY "Notes"
@ 14,8 GET clients.notes
@ 2,27 SAY "My Computer Company"
@ 5,10 SAY "Number"
@ 5,25 SAY "First Name"
@ 10,2 SAY "Street Address"
@ 4,1 TO 6,70

READ
```

Figure 14.14: The CLIENTS.FMT screen format file

Using the Screen Format

Now it's time to try our new screen format. In the Command window, do the following:

① Type **use clients** and press Enter to re-open your client data file, just in case it was accidentally closed.

② Type **set format to clients** in the Command window and press Enter.

③ Type **append** in the Command window and press Enter. Your data-entry screen should appear.

④ Type **00011** into the account field. Because you completely filled the field, FoxPro beeps and then automatically moves to the next field.

⑤ Type **max** and press Enter. Notice that the letters are automatically converted to uppercase.

⑥ In the lastname field, type **zorn** and press Enter. Again, the letters are converted to uppercase.

⑦ Press Ctrl-W to save the new record and exit from the data entry screen.

Pushing Ahead with the Screen Painter

From what we've done in this chapter, it must seem as if FoxPro's Screen Painter is a useful but flawed tool. In fact, the Screen Painter is a very powerful tool—but using it requires the use of some programming techniques that are beyond the scope of this book.

However, let's take a brief look at the power of the Screen Painter, just so that you know what it can really do when you let it loose. Make sure that your client file is open and then re-open your screen file by typing **modify screen clients** in the Command window. Then do the following:

① Open the File menu and select "Save As." Save the file as CLIENTS2.SCX.

② Move the cursor down to R:17 C:4 and select "Push Button" from the Screen menu, as shown in Figure 14.15.

③ The Push Button dialog box will open. Under "Push Button Prompts," enter **Append** and **Browse**, as shown in Figure 14.16.

Creating Your Own Data-Entry Screens **159**

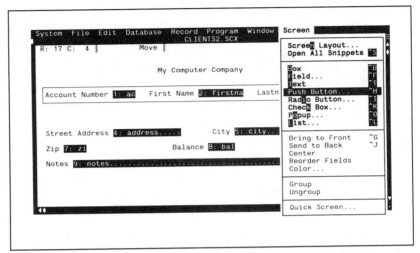

Figure 14.15: Preparing to add push buttons with the Screen menu

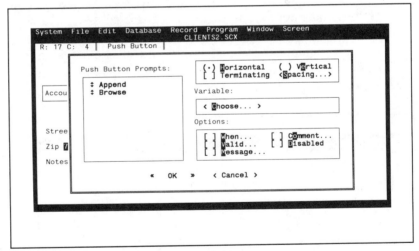

Figure 14.16: Entering prompts for push buttons

④ Tab to the Options box and press **V** to select the "Valid" checkbox. When the Valid dialog box opens, make sure that the Edit button is highlighted; then just press Enter to return to the Push Button dialog box.

⑤ Press **C** to select the "Choose" push button. The Expression Builder box will appear. Enter **actnum** in the box and press Ctrl-Enter to exit.

⑥ When you are back in the Push Button dialog box, press Ctrl-Enter. An editing window will open in the upper left corner of the screen. Type the following code into it, as shown in Figure 14.17, and then press Ctrl-W to exit.

```
do case
   case actnum = 1
      append
   case actnum = 2
      browse
endcase
```

When you return to your screen, you'll see that it now has two push buttons that can be selected with the Tab key or the mouse, as shown in Figure 14.18. FoxPro's Screen Painter makes it easy to add push buttons, radio buttons, and many other sophisticated features to your screens—but you do need to know a little about programming. If you want to create sophisticated screens like the one shown in Figure 14.18, you should refer to your FoxPro user's manual or Charles Siegel's *Mastering FoxPro 2* (SYBEX, 1991).

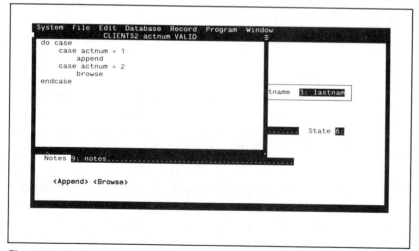

Figure 14.17: Entering the programming code for a push button

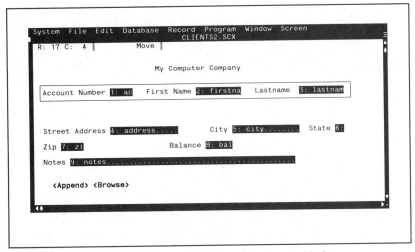

Figure 14.18: *The data entry screen with push buttons added*

Lesson Summary

The easiest way to create a customized data entry screen in Fox-Pro is to select New/Screen from the File menu and use the built-in Screen Painter. You can then delete unnecessary code from the screen file and save it as a standard screen format file that is compatible with dBASE and FoxPro 1.0.

The easiest way to paint a screen that includes all of the fields in a data file is to choose "Quick Screen" from the Screen menu. Individual fields can be included in a screen by positioning the cursor and pressing Ctrl-F.

To create a box, position the cursor at the location for the upper left corner of the box and press Ctrl-B to start the box. Stretch the box down and to the right, and press Enter to complete the box.

To put a standard format into a field, select the field by double-clicking with the mouse or double-pressing the space bar. A dialog box will open up in which you can specify formats and formulas for data validation.

To use a screen format, open the data file with which it is associated. In the Command window, enter **set format to** <file>, where <file> is the name of your format file. Then, type **append** in the Command window and press Enter.

LESSON 15
Linking Files

Featuring

- How (and why) to design a multifile database
- How to link files
- How to view data from multiple files

BEFORE WE TALK ABOUT HOW TO LINK DATABASE FILES, let's spend a little time on why anybody would want to. It's extra work, extra complication—so why bother?

Setting Up a Transaction File

Consider the client records of "My Computer Company," the mythical firm for which we've created a database file. Each client record contains account number, name, address, current balance, and a notes field for miscellaneous information.

What our client records don't contain is information about specific sales and services for each client. We'd like to be able to track what we've sold to each client, when we sold it, and how much the client was billed for it.

The Non-Linking Approach

The common-sense approach to this problem is simply to include fields in the client database file to hold transaction information. This is, in fact, the way almost everyone does it the first time he or she sets up a database. For each transaction, we'll need one field for the date, one for the product or service sold, and one for the amount billed to the client. If we displayed a Browse table, our database would look something like CLIENTS2.DBF, shown in Figure 15.1. (You don't need to create this database yourself.)

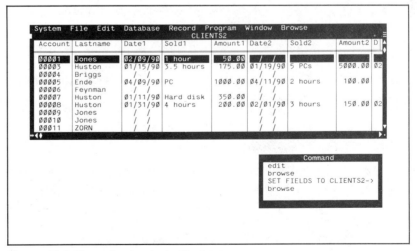

Figure 15.1: Example of a single-file database

For reasons that are a little obscure, this way of setting up a database is called the "flatfile" approach: you try to put all the data you need into one database file. In many database packages other than FoxPro, the flatfile approach is the only one available to you.

But there are serious problems with this approach. As sensible as it may seem to keep all your client data in a single database file, it's tremendously wasteful of disk space because you're mixing two radically different kinds of data in the same file.

Let's think about that for a second. In your client file as it now stands, exactly the same type of information goes into each record: account number, name, address, city, state, zip, balance, and notes. If you try to add fields for each transaction, you face two problems.

First, you must add enough fields to cover the maximum number of transactions that you expect in any record. Suppose that John Huston is your most active client, and that you expect 10 transactions from him in the foreseeable future. Allowing enough fields (30) for 10 transactions in John Huston's record means that you have to allow the same number of fields in the record of Max Zorn, who hardly ever buys anything. The same applies to all of your clients who are less active than John Huston: there are going to be a lot of empty fields in their records, as you can see in Figure 15.1.

Your second problem is that, sooner or later, you're going to run out of transaction fields for some clients. When that happens, you'll have to add still *more* fields to the database file, even if most of your client records are a long way from being filled up.

The bottom line is that in this type of situation, the flatfile approach is a tremendously inefficient way to handle your data. FoxPro's ability to create links between database files is a far superior way of handling such problems.

*T*he Linked-File Approach

Let's take another look at how we might solve our problem. We know that we need certain information about each client, and that this information doesn't vary from one client record to another. Likewise, we know that we need certain information about each transaction, and that this information doesn't vary from one transaction to another.

Because we have two distinct types of information, a two-file solution is the best approach: one file for client information and one file for transaction information. All we need now is a way to link the client information in one file with the transaction information in the other. That way, we can draw information from both files to find out who bought what, when they bought it, and how much they were billed.

Separating Different Types of Information

If the records in a file vary too widely in the amount of information they contain—if some have data in every field while others have many empty fields—then you probably haven't set up your database correctly.

File linking lets you treat multiple linked files as if the information they contain were all in a single file. You should take advantage of this capability when you need it.

A Note on "Relational"

If you've had much exposure to computer jargon, then you were probably expecting to see one word which we *haven't* used: "relational." People commonly refer to multifile database operations as "relational," but this is incorrect. A relational database package is one that follows a particular theory (the relational data model) about how databases should be handled. A database package can link files without being relational.

Nonetheless, you need to know that when people call a database package "relational," they often mean that

- it can create links between different files;
- it can generate reports based on information from multiple linked files; and
- it can support data-entry into multiple files from a single data-entry screen.

FoxPro can do all these things, even though it isn't a relational database package in the strict sense. Because of its multifile abilities, you will often hear FoxPro referred to as "relational" and links between files called "relations."

What You Need to Link Files

For two files to be linkable, one field in each must duplicate the information in one field of the other. That is, there must be a field, such as account number, that appears in both files. Having this field in common enables records in the *primary* or *master file* (e.g., "clients") to be matched up with the correct records in the *secondary file* (e.g., the transaction or sales file we're going to create in a moment).

Take account number 00001 as an example. Because the sales file also has an account number field, FoxPro can scan through the sales file and find all the transactions with that account number. Then, it can produce a report showing what client 00001 has purchased.

There are two requirements for the common field. First, it must be *unique for each record* in the master file. If there were two clients with account number 00001, for instance, FoxPro would have no way of telling which account 00001 transactions went with which client 00001.

Second, the secondary file must be *indexed on the common field*, and you must make sure that the index files are kept up to date. This is so that when FoxPro scans for matching records, it knows where to find them in the transaction file.

Creating a Linked-File Database

Our first step in creating our linked-file database is to set up a transaction file called SALES.DBF. Then, we'll index the transaction file on the Account field and link it up with our clients file.

Creating the Transaction File

As we discussed above, we need four pieces of information for each transaction: the date of the transaction, the account number for the client making the purchase, what was purchased, and how much the client was billed. Do the following:

① From the File menu, select "New." Press Enter to choose the Database file type.

② On the first line of the dialog box, type **SALEDATE** for the field name. Then choose "Date" for the field type; FoxPro will automatically assign a width of 8.

③ On the next line of the dialog box, type **ACCOUNT** for the field name. Then choose "Character" for the field type and type in **5** for the field width. (It's not essential that the field *name* be the same as in our clients file, but field *type* and *width* have to match.)

④ For field number 2, type **ITEM**. Choose the Character field type and a width of 10.

⑤ For field number 3, type **AMOUNT**. Choose the Numeric field type and enter a width of **7** with **2** decimal places. Your database definition should match Figure 15.2.

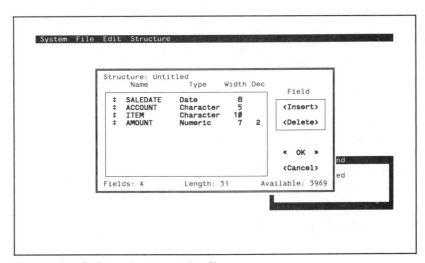

Figure 15.2: Defining the transaction file

⑥ Press Ctrl-Enter to accept the definition, and name the file **SALES**. When prompted

> **Input data records now?**

answer Yes.

Now, simply enter the following records:

Sale Date: 07/15/91
Account: 00001
Item: 1.5 hours
Amount: 75.00

Sale Date: 07/15/91
Account: 00009
Item: PC
Amount: 750.00

Sale Date: 07/15/91
Account: 00003
Item: Hard disk
Amount: 350.00

Sale Date: 07/16/91
Account: 00001
Item: 5 PCs
Amount: 3750.00

Sale Date: 07/17/91
Account: 00001
Item: 2 Printers
Amount: 600.00

Sale Date: 07/17/91

Account: 00010

Item: 4 hours

Amount: 200.00

Sale Date: 07/17/91

Account: 00005

Item: 3 hours

Amount: 150.00

Sale Date: 07/18/91

Account: 00011

Item: LAN instal

Amount: 2250.00

Sale Date: 07/18/91

Account: 00010

Item: 2.5 hours

Amount: 125.00

Sale Date: 07/18/91

Account: 00001

Item: Software

Amount: 350.00

Sale Date: 07/19/91

Account: 00004

Item: Hard disk

Amount: 350.00

After entering the records, move to the Command window and type **index on account to sales** and press Enter.

How to Link the Client and Sales Files

Now we come to the easy part. Open the View window and you'll see that the sales file you just created is in Work Area A. Because the file is indexed, there should be a small diamond on its left.

Now, in order to link the sales file to another file, we need to open another file. But you can only have one file open in each work area at a time, so change to Work Area B—by moving the highlight to "B" in the "Work Areas" box and pressing Enter (with a mouse, just double-click on the "B")—and FoxPro will prompt you to open a file. (If it doesn't, just select the "Open" button in the View window.) Open your client database file in Work Area B, making sure that it's indexed on the Account field. If you haven't already indexed the clients database on the account field, do it now. Then change back to Work Area A and do the following:

① With the SALES file highlighted, select the Relations button at the top right of the View window by pressing *R* on your keyboard or clicking on it with the mouse. The name of the sales file will appear, with an arrow coming out of it, in the "Relations" box.

② Move the highlight in the "Work Areas" box down to CLIENTS and press Enter. The Expression Builder dialog box will appear.

③ Select ACCOUNT from the field list on the left (see Figure 15.3).

④ Press Ctrl-Enter to exit. The View window will now show both the sales and client files in the "Relations" box, as in Figure 15.4. The arrow going from the sales file to the client file shows that SALES is the master file in this case.

Your sales and client database files are now linked. If we wanted to, we could now draw information from both files to include in a report. (We'll cover that in the next lesson.)

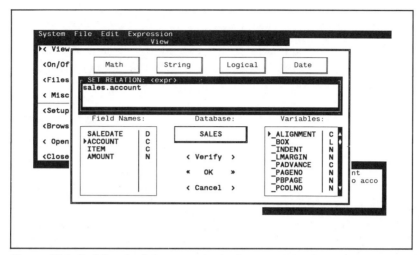

Figure 15.3: Building the link expression in the expression box

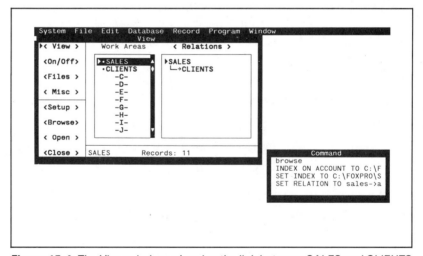

Figure 15.4: The View window, showing the link between SALES and CLIENTS

Unlinking the Files

You may at some point want to unlink two files that you've previously linked. This is just as easy as linking them in the first place.

For example, if you want to unlink the client file from the sales file, simply highlight the clients file in the "Relations" box and press

Enter. Then when the Expression Builder opens, just press the Delete key, and the link expression disappears. Press Ctrl-Enter to exit from the Expression Builder. The View window will reappear, and the "Relations" box will be empty, showing that the link is gone. (If you try this out, be sure to relink the two files before proceeding. We're going to use that link in the next section.)

We should note that links between files are not permanent unless you save them as a view file (see below). If you close both the sales and client files and then reopen them, they will no longer be linked.

Saving Your Link Setup as a View File

You'll recall from an earlier lesson that view files let us save indexes along with database files so that when we open the view file, our database and index files are automatically opened in the correct order.

This also works with links between database files. Once we have a link established, we can save the setup as a view file. Then, when we reopen the view file, each database will be indexed on the link field and the link will be set up. To save your setup as a view file:

① Select "Save As" from the File menu.

② Type **csales** as the name for the view file. Press Ctrl-Enter to save the file.

And we're done! The benefits of file linking will become apparent in the next lesson, when we create a multifile report.

Lesson Summary

To be linked, a file must contain a field that duplicates the information in a field in another file. The field must have the same type and width in each file, though it need not have the same name. The secondary file must be indexed on that field.

The values in the common field must be unique in the master file. In other words, no two master file records can have the same value: there can be only one account number 00014, for example.

To link two files, first open each in a different work area. Select the master file and select the Relations button in the View window. Then select the secondary file and press Enter; choose the link field and put it into the expression box of the Expression Builder. Press Ctrl-Enter to exit, and the files will be linked.

To unlink two files, highlight the secondary file in the "Relations" box of the View window and press Enter. Delete the link expression from the expression box and press Ctrl-Enter.

To save a linked-file setup, select "Save As" from the File menu and save the setup as a view file.

*H*ot Tip

- When you use the View window to switch to a different work area, FoxPro will open a Browse window if there's already an open file in that work area; if there isn't an open file, FoxPro will prompt you to open one. Don't let this little glitch bother you. Just close the Browse window (unless you wanted to open a Browse window anyway) or open a file in response to the prompt.

LESSON 16
Creating Multifile Reports

Featuring

- How to include fields from linked files
- Creating a simple linked report with LIST
- How to create linked Quick Reports
- How to create linked custom reports
- How to use advanced report functions

IN THE LAST LESSON, WE SAW HOW TO SET UP LINKS between different database files so that information can be drawn from both files at the same time. In this lesson, we'll complete the sequence by showing how to put information from multiple files into reports—both Quick Reports and custom reports.

Creating Linked-File Reports

To create a linked-file report, whether it's a Quick Report or a custom report, all of the linked database files must be open—each in a different work area. (In speaking of linked files, I will often distinguish between the "current file"—whichever linked file is in the current work area—and its links in other work areas.) Each file must be indexed on the common field that links it to the next file, and the indexes must be up to date.

FoxPro provides menu-driven support for "many-to-one" reports. This means that you can, in the example we've created, print a report that lists each transaction (many) and its associated client (one). In this sort of report, you'd have something like Table 16.1.

Table 16.1: A "many-to-one" report

TRANSACTION	CLIENT
1.5 hours	John Jones
5 PCs	John Jones
2 printers	John Jones
Software	John Jones
Hard disk	John Huston
Hard disk	Joe Bob Briggs

This differs from a "one-to-many" report, which in the case of our client and sales files, would look something like Table 16.2.

Obviously, this second kind of report is a little more useful. And even though you technically can't create one-to-many reports in FoxPro, you can create reports that look just like them, so the theoretical nuances aren't that much of a handicap.

Table 16.2: A "one-to-many" report

CLIENT	TRANSACTION
John Jones	1.5 hours
	5 PCs
	2 printers
	Software
John Huston	Hard disk
Joe Bob Briggs	Hard disk

Creating a Simple Linked Report with LIST

You can use FoxPro's LIST command to create a simple linked report just as we used it in Lesson 9 to create a single-file report. The only difference is that, because we're using more than one database file, you have to tell FoxPro where to find any fields that aren't in the current work area's database file.

To create a simple linked report with LIST, do the following:

① Select "Open" from the File menu.

② In the dialog box, open the CSALES view file. Open the View window to verify that the sales file in Work Area A and the client file in Work Area B are open, with the relation SALES –> CLIENTS shown in the "Relations" box. In the "Work Area" list, each file should have a diamond on the left, indicating that it is indexed. The highlight should be on the sales file.

③ Press the Escape key to close the View window. In the Command window, type

list account, item, clients->lastname

and press Enter. (You make the arrow with the hyphen key and the angle bracket key that's over the period on your keyboard.)

The data from each field will be listed as shown in Figure 16.1. The account and item fields come from the sales file, and the lastname field comes from the clients file.

Note that because you were in Work Area A and SALES was the currently selected file, you simply entered the names of the fields that you wanted. CLIENTS, however, was in a different work area, so you had to preface the field name with "clients −>" to tell FoxPro where to find the field you wanted.

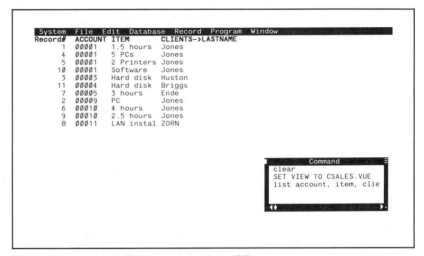

Figure 16.1: *A simple linked report using LIST*

No matter what you're doing in FoxPro (using LIST, creating a Quick Report, etc.), this is how you always refer to fields in linked database files: with the name of the linked file, an arrow (a hyphen and an angle bracket), and the name of the field.

If you wanted to print this list report, you would merely add the words **to print** at the end of the command, so that the new command would read

list account, item, clients −>lastname to print

How to Create a Linked Quick Report

It's not all that much harder to create a linked Quick Report than it is to use the LIST command. To create a linked Quick Report, do the following:

① Choose "New" from the File menu and the "Report" file type in the dialog box. Press Ctrl-Enter to select the OK button, and the Report Layout window will appear.

② Select "Quick Report" from the Report menu. When the dialog box appears, select the "Fields" checkbox by pressing *E* or clicking in the box with the mouse.

③ Notice that the Database popup button at the lower left of the Field Picker dialog box shows that SALES is the currently selected database. However, we want our first column to be from our client file, which is linked to SALES. To use a field from CLIENTS, highlight the Database button and press Enter, then select CLIENTS from the file-selection list that appears, as shown in Figure 16.2. (Using a mouse, click on the Database button, drag to highlight CLIENTS, and release.)

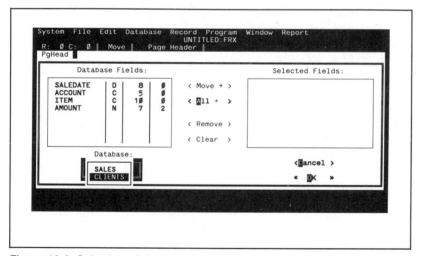

Figure 16.2: *Selecting a linked database file from the Database popup*

④ The Database popup button should now show the file name CLIENTS. Move to the "Database Fields" list on the left and, in order, highlight and select ACCOUNT, FIRSTNAME, and LASTNAME so that they are moved into the "Selected Fields" list on the right.

⑤ Once again, highlight and select the Database popup button. This time, select SALES from the popup list. We'll take our next report field from the transaction file.

⑥ In order, highlight and select ITEM and AMOUNT from the "Database Fields" list so that they move into the "Selected Fields" list.

⑦ Press Ctrl-Enter or click on OK to exit; then do the same in the Quick Report dialog box. You should end up back in the Layout window.

⑧ Select "Page Layout" from the Report menu. In the dialog box, enter the following: top margin **3**, bottom margin **3**, printer indent **5**, right margin column **80**. Highlight the "Save Environment" button and press Ctrl-Enter to exit.

⑨ Save your work so far by selecting "Save" from the File menu and entering **cli-rpt4** in the file name dialog box.

Now, take a quick look at our Quick Report by pressing Ctrl-I for Page Preview. You can see that the fields have been included from both of the linked files as in Figure 16.3.

Enhancing Our Quick Report

The fact that this is a Quick Report doesn't mean that we can't pretty it up a bit. Let's add a title and a few other changes that will make the report easier to read:

① Add a Title band by choosing "Title/Summary" from the Report menu; then choose "Title" in the dialog box and return to the Layout window. Add an extra line to the Title band by pressing Ctrl-N.

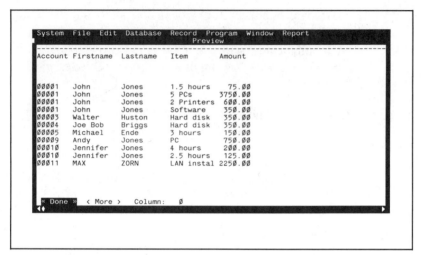

Figure 16.3: A linked Quick Report

② On the top line of the Title band, type **My Computer Company**, press Enter, and press the space bar to select this title as a text object. Center it by selecting "Center" from the Report menu and pressing Enter.

③ Delete the bottom two lines from the PgHead band by positioning the cursor at R:3 C:0 and pressing Ctrl-O twice. On the remaining PgHead line under the column labels, draw a double horizontal line by holding down the key for the equal sign.

④ The columns are just a little too close together for easy reading, so let's space them out a bit. Select the AMOUNT field (in the Detail band, not the PgHead band) by pressing the space bar. Then move it to R:4 C:50 and press Enter. Then, in the same way, move the "Amount" column label in the PgHead band to R:1 C:50.

⑤ Move the ITEM field to R:4 C:35 and the "Item" column label to R:2 C:35.

⑥ We're done, so press Ctrl-I to see the result. Don't forget to save your work at this point. Exit from the Layout window by pressing Escape.

Creating a Linked Custom Report

Our linked Quick Report is fine as it stands. However, we could enhance it even more by adding page numbers and by grouping. Further, it is not as flexible as we might like; in particular, it repeats the client name on each line, even if it's the same name as on the previous line.

To design more flexible reports, we can use the Layout window for a linked custom report. It's a little more work, but in return we get a more useful format. To get started, do the following:

① In the Command window, type **create report cli-rpt5** and press Enter. The Layout window will appear. Open the Page Layout box from the Report menu and set up our usual dimensions: top and bottom margins of 3, printer indent 5, right margin 80, and save environment.

② Add two more title lines as we did before, then type and center **My Computer Company** on the top line.

③ Delete two lines of the PgHead band. On the top remaining line, type **Account No.** at R:2 C:0 and then press Enter. In the same way, enter **Name** at R:2 C:16, **Item** at R:2 C:35, and **Amount** at R:2 C:50. Use the equal sign to draw a horizontal line on R:3 under the column headings.

④ In the first line of the Detail band, at R:4 C:0, press Ctrl-F to place a field. In the Expression Builder, switch to the CLIENTS database file and enter **Account** in the expression box. Press Ctrl-Enter once to return to the Report Expression dialog box.

⑤ In the Report Expression dialog box, press *R* to check the "Suppress" checkbox shown in Figure 16.4. In the Supress Repeated Values dialog box, select "On." Then press Ctrl-Enter twice to return to the Layout window.

⑥ Move to R:4 C:16 and press Ctrl-F again. In the expression box, type the following:

trim(clients->firstname) + " " + clients->lastname

Lesson 16

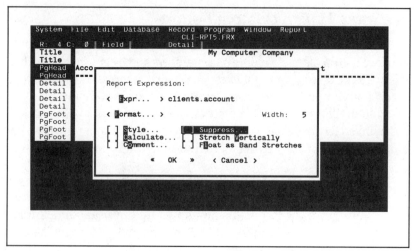

Figure 16.4: The Report Expression dialog box

(You can also build this expression by using the menus if you prefer.) Press Ctrl-Enter once to move to the Report Expression box, and once again check "Suppress Repeated Values." Press Ctrl-Enter to return to the Layout window.

⑦ At R:4 C:35, add the Item field from the SALES file. Then, at R:4 C:50, add the Amount field.

⑧ Let's group this report according to account number. Select "Data Grouping" from the Report menu. When the Group dialog box opens, select the Add button. At the Group Info box, just press Enter.

⑨ When you enter the Expression Builder, select "Account" from the CLIENTS database file. (We could just as easily use the Account field from the SALES file, but this is a little neater.) Press Ctrl-Enter three times to return to the Layout window.

At this point you should notice that the appearance of the Layout window has changed, reflecting our decision to group our records according to account number. Specifically, it now shows a "group header" and a "group footer" band directly above and below the Detail band. A number attached to the field name within each group band identifies the level of grouping. In our case, the bands show "1-accou," because the account field is our first (and only) level of grouping.

The group header band is similar to the PgHead band, only it's where you put information that you want to print at the start of each group rather than at the top of each page. Similarly, the group footer band is where you put things you want to print at the end of each group. Let's try it out by putting some space and a horizontal line below each group:

⑩ Delete the three extra lines from the Detail band by positioning the cursor on R:6 C:0 and pressing Ctrl-O three times. Add two lines to the group footer band by moving the cursor to R:7 C:0 and pressing Ctrl-N twice.

⑪ Draw a single horizontal line in the bottom group footer line (R:8) by holding down the hyphen key on your keyboard. Stop and press Enter when the cursor is at R:8 C:61. Your Layout screen should match the one shown in Figure 16.5.

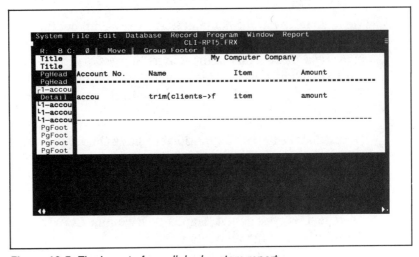

Figure 16.5: *The layout of your linked custom report*

And that's our linked custom report! Press Ctrl-I to take a look at how the report will look when printed.

Using Advanced Report Functions

As nice as our linked custom report is, we could still make it better. For instance, we have each client's purchases grouped together, but we don't have a total amount paid by each client.

FoxPro has a large number of summary functions that let us include this type of information in a report: everything from totals and subtotals to record counts, averages, and highest and lowest values.

Let's use just one of these functions to add subtotals to our report. What we want is a total dollar amount billed to each group—that is, to each client.

To add subtotals to our report, do the following:

① Move the cursor to the middle group footer line and, at R:7 C:28, type **Total amount billed:** and press Enter.

② Move the cursor to R:7 C:50, so that it's right under the Amount field. Press Ctrl-F to put a field in that position.

③ We're going to put the Amount field there again, but this time with an important difference: we're going to make it a summary field. Press Enter at the Report Expression box to open the Expression Builder. Then enter the Amount field from SALES and press Ctrl-Enter to return to the Report Expression box.

④ Notice that the Report Expression box has a checkbox marked "Calculate." Press C to check that box, and the Calculate dialog box will appear, as in Figure 16.6.

⑤ There are seven options (besides "Nothing"): Count, Sum, Average, Lowest, Highest, Standard Deviation, and Variance. We want to add the amounts billed for each transaction, so select "Sum" by pressing S.

⑥ Press Ctrl-Enter.

Creating Multifile Reports 185

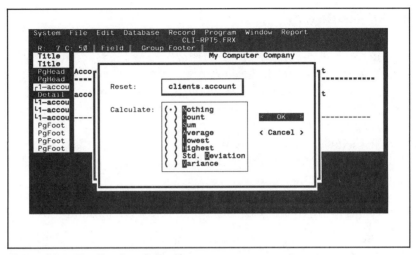

Figure 16.6: The Totaling dialog box

⑦ Move the cursor to the top line of the group footer band and use the hyphen key to draw a line from R:6 C:28 to R:6 C:56.

⑧ Press Ctrl-I to activate Page Preview. Your report should look like Figure 16.7.

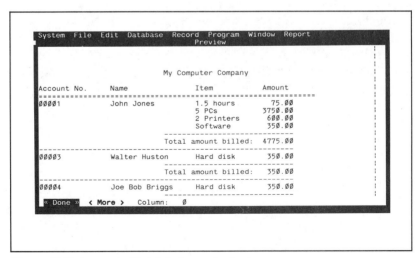

Figure 16.7: A report with totals for each client

Lesson Summary

Before you can create a linked report of any kind, you must have your linked files open, indexed (up to date) on the link field, and linked together. The best way to handle this is by creating and using a view file that will take care of the details for you—and will never forget any of them.

To include a field from a linked file, you must preface the field name with the name of the linked file and an arrow, for example, "clients->lastname".

To create a simple linked report with LIST, type list in the Command window followed by the field names from the primary and the linked files: for example,

list account, item, clients->lastname

To create a linked Quick Report, select the "Quick Report" option from the Report menu and check the "Fields" checkbox. Then select the fields you want in the Field Picker box; you can change from the primary to the linked database file by selecting the Database popup button at the lower left.

To create a linked custom report, you place the fields just as in a single-file custom report. However, you can suppress repeated values (account number, name, etc.) so that the report is easier to read.

You can put various items of summary information in your report through the "Totaling" checkbox of the Report Expression box. This provides options for record counts, totals, averages, and high or low values.

LESSON 17
Creating Your Own Menu System

Featuring

- How to create a customized menu system
- Using your menu system

BECAUSE YOU CREATED A FOXPRO DATABASE, YOU naturally know how it works. You know how to add records by using "Append," how to mark records for deletion, and how to print the reports you've created. You also know the names of your database files and your index files, and you know whether or not your files are linked.

But other people in your office may not know any of these things. A secretary can't be expected to learn to use FoxPro just to enter some records. Even if your secretary does learn to use FoxPro, what happens when he or she is sick and you get a "temp" for the day? What happens when you're in another city and your boss needs to get a report from your FoxPro database?

Creating a Menu System

You learned how to solve part of the problem in Lesson 14, when you set up a customized data-entry screen. The complete solution is to set up a menu system that will take users by the hand and lead them through your database. It will provide menu choices that make it easy for them to select the database file they need, to add records, to print reports, and to accomplish other standard database tasks that you learned the hard way.

Even these days, you can still expect most people to be absolutely terrified of working with a computer. The easier you can make things for them, the more certain you can be that they'll be able to do what they need to do with a minimum of hassle.

There's one other important reason for creating a menu system: to protect your data. If you allow people who don't know anything about FoxPro to go rummaging around in your databases without guidance or supervision, you run the risk that they will accidentally delete records or somehow scramble your database. By providing a simple menu system, you limit their actions to tasks that are safe and easy to understand.

With many other database packages, you must be a programmer to create a menu system like the first one presented in this lesson. But with FoxPro, creating such a system is as easy as making menu choices and typing in a few file names. FoxApp, a program included with FoxPro, does all of the programming for you. After that, you have a complete menu-driven application which you can use "as is."

However, if you want to create more sophisticated menu systems, FoxPro 2 does require you to do a little programming. FoxPro's programming language is amazingly simple, however, and we'll see later in this lesson how *you* can create a menu system—even if you've never written a program before! (FoxPro 1.0 included a utility called "FoxView" that could create sophisticated menu systems, but FoxView is not included in FoxPro 2.)

Starting FoxApp

Both your client database files and FoxApp must be in the same directory. If you've created a separate disk directory from your FoxPro program directory for your client files, be sure to copy the file FOXAPP.APP to that directory. Then start FoxPro. You're going to be amazed by how easy it is to set up a simple menu system for your sales file. (We'll set up a menu system that includes your client file later.)

In FoxPro's Command window, type **do foxapp** and press Enter. The FoxApp dialog box should appear, as shown in Figure 17.1; if there is a problem, it's most likely that FoxApp is not in the current default directory.

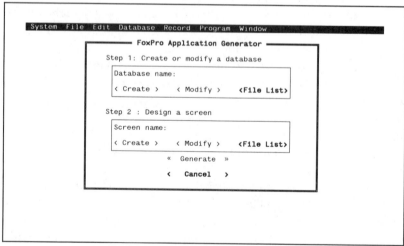

Figure 17.1: The FoxApp dialog box

Select "File List" in the dialog box and, when the file list pops up on the screen, highlight and select the SALES data file, as shown in Figure 17.2. The FoxApp dialog box will reappear, showing the name

Figure 17.2: Selecting the SALES data file

of the SALES data file as well as the name of the screen file that Fox-App will create; your screen should look the same as that in Figure 17.3. To command FoxApp to generate your application, just press Ctrl-Enter to select the "Generate" button.

After working for a few moments, FoxApp will prompt you to name your application. For our purposes, simply press Ctrl-Enter

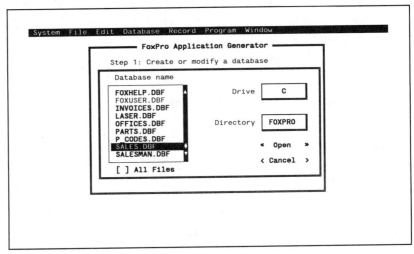

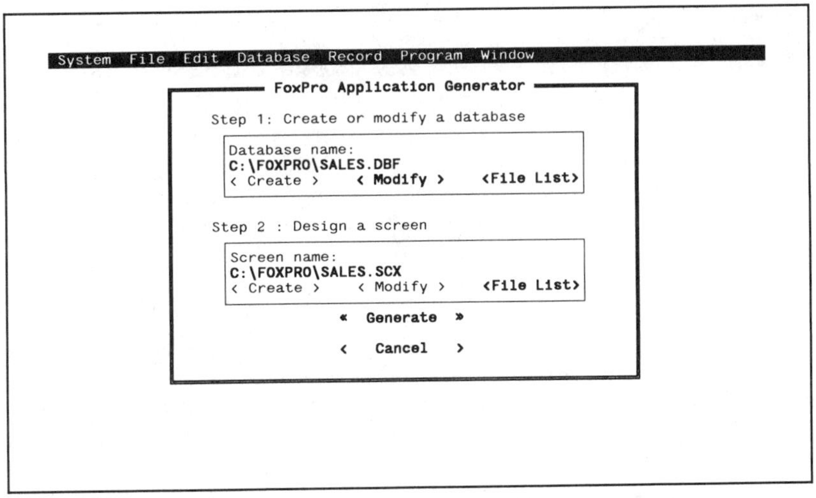

Figure 17.3: The FoxApp dialog box with the SALES file selected

to accept the default name of SALES.APP. After you select the name, FoxApp will continue to work for a few more moments. When it has finished building your application, it will display the message "Press any key to start your application." Press the space bar to continue.

Running Your FoxApp Menu System

As you can see in Figure 17.4, FoxApp has created a menu system for your SALES file that includes drop-down menus across the top of the screen and push buttons across the bottom, with the current SALES record displayed in the middle. Let's look at each part of this screen and how it works.

We'll start with the simplest part: the push buttons. These buttons allow you to move around in your data file:

- "Top" takes you to the first record in the file.
- "Prior" takes you to the previous record in the file.
- "Next" takes you to the next record in the file.
- "Bottom" takes you to the last record in the file.
- "Search" allows you to search your data file for a particular string or value, such as "LAN" or 15.25.

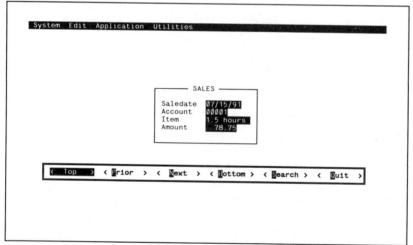

Figure 17.4: *The SALES application created by FoxApp*

We are already at the first record in the file, so let's try out some of these push buttons. First, press *B* for Bottom or select that button with the mouse. The last record in the file is displayed immediately on the screen. Pressing *T* or selecting the "Top" button moves you at once back to the first record in the file. The "Next" and "Prior" buttons work the same way.

The only button whose operation is at all complicated is the "Search" button. Try using the Search button now by pressing the *S* key or selecting that button with the mouse. The Search dialog box will open, as shown in Figure 17.5.

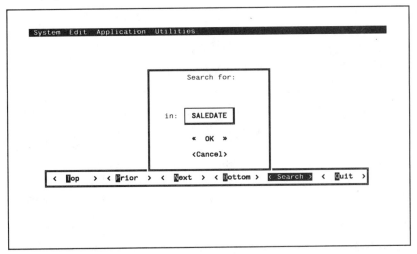

Figure 17.5: *The Search dialog box*

The initial field selected for the search is SALEDATE, but we're not interested in searching for a particular date. Instead, highlight the box containing SALEDATE and press Enter; a field list pops open, as shown in Figure 17.6. Select the ITEM field and press Enter.

In the "Search For" blank, type **LAN** and then press Ctrl-Enter to start the search. After a few moments, the application announces "Found It!" and displays the located record on the screen.

Now, let's look at the drop-down menus. The System menu does several of the things that the "real" FoxPro System menu does: it gives you access to on-screen help (for FoxPro, not your menu system), macros, and utilities. The Edit menu, likewise, allows you to copy, cut and paste, and select fields in your data file.

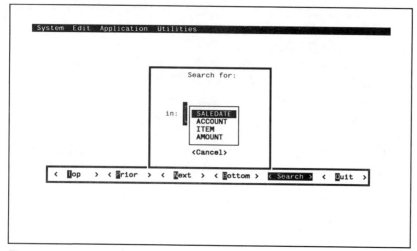

Figure 17.6: Changing the field to be searched

The real heart of your application, however, is the Application menu, shown in Figure 17.7. This menu allows you to browse through the data in your file; to add, copy, or delete records; to search for particular values; to sort your data file; and to generate reports. These operations work in the same manner as in FoxPro itself.

Finally, the Utility menu allows you to create new index files, although this is not necessary because FoxApp creates a comprehensive

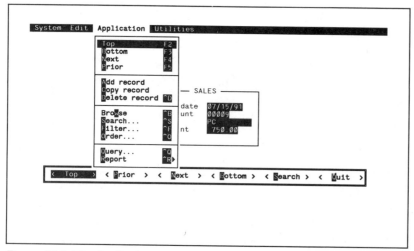

Figure 17.7: The Application menu of your SALES application

index for your data file when it generates the application. You can also "pack" your data file to permanently remove records marked for deletion, and you can set a few options for your application environment, such as whether or not a status bar will be shown on-screen.

After you've played around with your application a bit, exit by selecting the "Quit" button. A dialog box will ask if you want to run another application: to return to FoxPro, just select "Cancel."

A More Sophisticated Menu System

As attractive and easy as the FoxApp-generated system is, it suffers from a few limitations. The most important of these limitations is that FoxApp will only create a single-file application system. Thus, it cannot create a menu system that will handle our linked-file database, which includes both the client and sales files. Creating a more sophisticated menu system, however, requires us to do a little FoxPro programming.

Basic Programming Concepts

If you've had some exposure to programming and found it impossibly hard, don't worry: FoxPro's programming language is designed to be easy. If you have no idea of what programming is all about, here are the fundamentals:

- A program is a very precise list of instructions that tells the computer what to do and in what order.

- Because English and other spoken languages are often not very precise, a computer program must be written in an artificial language. Each word of the language has a precise meaning and must be used according to very strict rules.

- Once a program is written, it must be translated into the computer's own machine language. This is done either by an "interpreter" or a "compiler." FoxPro includes an interpreter for its built-in programming language.

Now you know all the essential concepts of writing computer programs! Everything else is just a matter of detail.

IF and CASE Statements

The most important detail is understanding how to use IF and CASE statements. The idea is a familiar one:

IF it rains, shut the car windows;
OTHERWISE, leave them open.
IF you're hungry, have something to eat;
OTHERWISE, go jogging.

The situation is a little more complex when there are several alternatives from which you must choose:

IF there's a sale on cottage cheese, buy 2 pints;
OTHERWISE,
IF there's a sale on carrots, buy 2 pounds;
OTHERWISE,
IF there's a sale on chocolate bars, buy 50 boxes.

FoxPro handles both simple and complex IF situations with ease. When you have only one alternative, you use an IF...ENDIF statement. Of course, FoxPro can't shut your car windows for you, but if it could, you'd tell it:

IF it rains
    SHUT car windows
ELSE
    LEAVE them open
ENDIF

The word "otherwise" isn't part of FoxPro's vocabulary; instead, FoxPro uses "ELSE" (which itself is optional.) The ENDIF is needed in case there's more than one thing that needs to be done; that way, FoxPro can be sure where the IF statement actually ends. (Although some words are in uppercase and indented, that's done only to make the statement easier for you to read. FoxPro usually doesn't care about case or indentation.)

More complex IF situations, such as on-screen menus, are handled with CASE statements. Our grocery store example above would translate to the following in FoxPro's language:

DO CASE
  CASE saleitem = "cottage cheese"
    BUY two pints

```
        CASE saleitem = "carrots"
          BUY two pounds
        CASE saleitem = "chocolate bars"
          BUY 50 boxes
          * but feel guilty about it
    ENDCASE
```

The CASE statement works pretty much the same way as the IF statement. It starts with the words **DO CASE** and ends with the word **ENDCASE**. In between, it lists the various cases that you want to handle and what to do in each case.

The only other new thing in the CASE statement is the second to last line, *** but feel guilty about it**. This is a program "comment," and is used to explain parts of a program to anyone who is reading the program code. FoxPro ignores any line that begins with an asterisk, so the comment is not actually part of the program itself. You can put comments anywhere in a program in order to make processes clearer, and the liberal use of comments is good programming practice.

Creating a "dBASE-Compatible" Menu

The basic idea of a menu system is simple. You create a main "menu program" that does nothing but display a menu on the screen and get the user's choice. Based on the user's choice, the menu program calls *another* program that does what the user wants. This is the simplest (although not the most sophisticated) way to set up a menu system in FoxPro. The structure of our menu system is shown in Figure 17.8.

The first of the two menu programs we will create is a "dBASE-compatible" menu of the kind that people have been writing for years. It will run under FoxPro, dBASE III or IV, Clipper, or any other dBASE-language package. (FoxPro uses a version of the dBASE language that has been specially enhanced by the people at Fox Software.)

In the FoxPro Command window, type **modify command menu1** and press Enter. Then:

① When the FoxPro text editor opens up a window, press Control-F10 to zoom the window to full-screen size. (If you'd like more information on the use of FoxPro's text editor, see Lesson 20.)

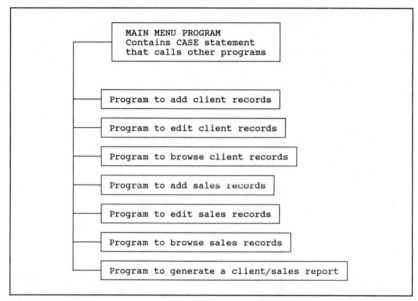

Figure 17.8: The structure of a simple menu program in FoxPro

② Type in the program shown in Figure 17.9. Be sure to enter it exactly as it appears in the figure.

③ After you have made sure that it's typed correctly, save the program by pressing Ctrl-W. (You can save the program without exiting from the text editor by selecting "Save" from the File menu.)

You can't do much with the MENU1 program yet, because you haven't created the supporting programs to add records, edit records, and so forth. However, you can run the program and then pick menu choice *8* to exit. To start the menu, type **do menu1** in the Command window and press Enter.

Reading User Input with @...SAY...GET...READ

You can simply type in the code for the MENU1 program without worrying about what it means. However, there are a few important things you should understand. (If you want to learn more about FoxPro programming, you should see Charles Siegel's *Mastering FoxPro 2*, published by SYBEX.)

```
* MENU1: "dBASE-compatible" menus for client/sales database
* author: Scott D. Palmer
* date: 23 May 1991

SET TALK OFF
SET ESCAPE OFF
SET STATUS OFF
SET SCOREBOARD OFF


* ---- set up a simple menu
CLEAR
menuchoice = 1
DO WHILE .T.
    @4,19 to 15,56 DOUBLE
    @5,23 SAY "CLIENT DATABASE MAIN MENU"
    @6,23 TO 6,47
    @7,23 SAY  "1. Add client records"
    @8,23 SAY  "2. Edit client records"
    @9,23 SAY  "3. Browse client records"
    @10,23 SAY "4. Add sales records"
    @11,23 SAY "5. Edit sales records"
    @12,23 SAY "6. Browse sales records"
    @13,23 SAY "7. Generate client/sales report"
    @14,23 SAY "8. Quit this program"
    @17,23 SAY "Enter your choice (1-8): " GET menuchoice;
                                            PICTURE "9"
    READ

    DO CASE
        CASE menuchoice = 1
            DO add_cli
        CASE menuchoice = 2
            DO edit_cli
        CASE menuchoice = 3
            DO brws_cli
        CASE menuchoice = 4
            DO add_sal
        CASE menuchoice = 5
            DO edit_sal
        CASE menuchoice = 6
            DO brws_sal
        CASE menuchoice = 7
            DO cs_rpt
        CASE menuchoice = 8
            CLEAR
            RETURN
    ENDCASE
ENDDO
CLEAR
RETURN
```

Figure 17.9: A simple "dBASE-compatible" menu program

The first bit of programming language you should understand is how to use the @...**SAY** and @...**SAY**...**GET**...**READ** commands. The @ character means simply "at," and you use an @...**SAY** command to display something at a specific location on the PC's screen. For example, **@5,10 SAY** "*FoxPro*" displays the word **FoxPro** at line 5, column 10 of your screen. **@...SAY** can also be used to draw single and double lines, as illustrated by the **@4, 19 to 15, 56 DOUBLE** command in Figure 17.9.

The **@...SAY...GET...READ** command not only displays text on the screen, but also receives input from the user—in this case, a menu choice. In Figure 17.10, it catches the user's keypress in a little "box" (a "variable") called *menuchoice* and then, based on the contents of the box, tells the CASE statement to start one of the sub-programs. You normally include a **READ** statement after one or more **GET** statements.

The menu screen that results from running the program in Figure 17.9 is shown in Figure 17.10.

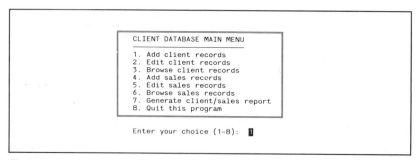

Figure 17.10: A simple dBASE-compatible menu screen

Repeating Actions with DO WHILE... ENDDO

The only other major feature of the MENU1 program is a **DO WHILE** "loop." This segment tells FoxPro to continue performing the statements between **DO WHILE** and **ENDDO** as long as the condition in the original **DO WHILE** statement remains true. Normally, the loop condition would become false at some point, but here, we want the menu to keep running until the user picks menu choice number 8, at which point the program terminates and you are returned to FoxPro.

Creating the Other Programs

The menu program includes calls to seven other programs that do specific jobs in our client/sales database. These programs are shown in Figures 17.11 through 17.17. For the most part, they do familiar things: opening data files and index files, browsing, editing,

```
* ADD_CLI: add client records

CLOSE DATABASES
USE clients INDEX clients
APPEND
USE
RETURN
```

Figure 17.11: A program to add client records

```
* EDIT_CLI: called from MENU1.PRG

CLEAR
CLOSE DATABASES
SET TALK OFF
USE clients INDEX clients
doanother = "Y"
DO WHILE UPPER(doanother) = "Y"
      acct_num = SPACE(5)
      @5,10 say "Enter account number of the record to edit: ";
            GET acct_num
            READ
      SEEK acct_num
      IF FOUND ()
            EDIT
      ELSE
            @6,10 SAY "Error: account number not in data file."
            WAIT
      ENDIF
      CLEAR
      @5,10 SAY "Do you want to edit another record (Y/N)? ";
            GET doanother
            READ
ENDDO
CLOSE DATABASES
CLEAR
RETURN
```

Figure 17.12: A Program to edit client records

```
* BRWS_CLI: called from MENU1.PRG

CLEAR
CLOSE DATABASES
USE clients INDEX clients
BROWSE
USE
CLEAR
RETURN
```

Figure 17.13: A program to browse client records

```
* ADD_SAL: add sales records

CLOSE DATABASES
USE sales INDEX sales
APPEND
USE
RETURN
```

Figure 17.14: A program to add sales records

```
* EDIT_SAL: called from MENU1.PRG

CLEAR
CLOSE DATABASES
SET TALK OFF
USE sales INDEX sales
DOANOTHER = "Y"
DO WHILE UPPER(doanother) = "Y"
    acct_num = SPACE(5)
    rightrec = "N"
    @5,10 say "Enter account number of record to edit: ";
        GET acct_num
        READ
    SEEK acct_num
    IF FOUND ()
        * ---- is the found record the correct one?
        DO WHILE UPPER(rightrec) <> "Y"
            CLEAR
            @4,5 SAY "Account Number: " + account
            @4,27 SAY "Date: " + DTOC(saledate)
            @4,50 SAY "Amount: $" + LTRIM(STR(amount))
            @6,10 SAY "Is this the record to edit (Y/N)? ";
                GET rightrec
                READ
            IF UPPER(rightrec) = "Y"
                EDIT
            ELSE
                SKIP
                IF account <> acct_num
                    EXIT
                ENDIF
            ENDIF            && of if upper(rightrec) = "Y"
        ENDDO                && of do while upper(rightrec) <> "Y"
    ELSE
        @6,10 SAY "Error: account number not in data file."
        WAIT
    ENDIF                    && of if found()
    CLEAR
    @5,10 SAY "Edit another record (Y/N)? ";
        GET doanother
        READ
ENDDO
* ---- end of loop to "do while upper(doanother) = "Y""

CLOSE DATABASES
CLEAR
RETURN
```

Figure 17.15: A program to edit sales records

```
* BRWS_SAL: called from MENU1.PRG

CLEAR
CLOSE DATABASES
USE sales INDEX sales
BROWSE
USE
CLEAR
RETURN
```

Figure 17.16: A program to browse sales records

```
* CS_RPT: called from MENU1.PRG

SET TALK OFF
CLEAR
CLOSE DATABASES
USE sales IN 1 INDEX sales
USE clients IN 2 INDEX clients
SELECT 1
SET RELATION TO account INTO clients

toprint = "N"
@5,10 SAY "Send report to the printer (Y/N)? " GET toprint
     PICTURE "!"
READ
IF toprint = "Y"
     REPORT FORMAT cli-rpt5 TO PRINT
     EJECT
ELSE
     REPORT FORMAT cli-rpt5
     WAIT
ENDIF
CLOSE DATABASES
CLEAR
RETURN
```

Figure 17.17: A program to generate a client/sales report

appending records, and so on. The only really new wrinkle comes in Figure 17.17, where we use the FoxPro **SET RELATION** command to link the sales and client files. We've already done this by using the View window, but we need to use a more direct method when we're writing a program.

Use FoxPro's text editor to create each of these programs. Be sure to assign each program the correct file name after you type **modify command** in the Command window. For example, to enter the program in Figure 17.11, you would type **modify command add_cli** in the FoxPro Command window. The correct program file names are:

Figure 17.11: ADD_CLI.PRG

Figure 17.12: EDIT_CLI.PRG

Figure 17.13: BRWS_CLI.PRG

Figure 17.14: ADD_SAL.PRG

Figure 17.15: EDIT_SAL.PRG

Figure 17.16: BRWS_SAL.PRG

Figure 17.17: CS_RPT.PRG

Once you have entered the sub-programs, you can run the MENU1 program and try each of the menu choices.

Creating FoxPro Drop-Down Menus

The menu program in Figure 17.9 might have been hot stuff in 1985, but today's users expect a little more sophistication. FoxPro provides a relatively easy way to write programs with drop-down menus just like those in FoxPro itself. Figure 17.18 shows how to set up drop-down menus, and while the program is not as simple as the one for the menu system in Figure 17.9, it's much simpler than drop-down menu programs in other programming languages.

```
* MENU2: FoxPro drop-down menus for client/sales database

SET TALK OFF
SET ESCAPE OFF
SET STATUS OFF
SET SCOREBOARD OFF

CLEAR

DEFINE MENU main
DEFINE PAD cli of main at 1,1 PROMPT "\<Clients"
DEFINE PAD sal of main at 1,9 PROMPT "\<Sales"
DEFINE PAD rpt of main at 1,16 PROMPT "\<Reports"
DEFINE PAD qt of main at 1,25 PROMPT "\<Quit"

ON PAD cli of main ACTIVATE POPUP cli_menu
ON PAD sal of main ACTIVATE POPUP sal_menu
ON PAD rpt of main ACTIVATE POPUP rpt_menu
ON PAD qt of main ACTIVATE POPUP quit_menu

DEFINE POPUP cli_menu from 2,0
DEFINE BAR 1 of cli_menu PROMPT "\<Add Record"
DEFINE BAR 2 of cli_menu PROMPT "\<Edit Record"
DEFINE BAR 3 of cli_menu PROMPT "\<Browse Records"
ON SELECTION POPUP cli_menu DO DO_MENU WITH POPUP(), PROMPT()
```

Figure 17.18: A menu program with FoxPro drop-down menus

```
DEFINE POPUP sal_menu FROM 2,9
DEFINE BAR 1 of sal_menu PROMPT "\<Add Record"
DEFINE BAR 2 of sal_menu PROMPT "\<Edit Record"
DEFINE BAR 3 of sal_menu PROMPT "\<Browse Records"
ON SELECTION POPUP sal_menu DO DO_MENU WITH POPUP(), PROMPT()

DEFINE POPUP rpt_menu from 2,16
DEFINE BAR 1 of rpt_menu PROMPT "\<Client/Sales Report"
ON SELECTION POPUP rpt_menu DO DO_MENU WITH POPUP(), PROMPT()

DEFINE POPUP quit_menu FROM 2,25
DEFINE BAR 1 of quit_menu PROMPT "\<Quit "
ON SELECTION POPUP quit_menu DO getout


ACTIVATE MENU main

PROCEDURE do_menu
  PARAMETER vpopup, vprompt
  HIDE POPUP ALL
  HIDE POPUP &vpopup
  HIDE MENU MAIN

  * ---- big CASE statement for entire menu bar
  DO CASE
    CASE vpopup = "CLI_MENU"
      * Nested CASE statement for Clients menu
      DO CASE
        CASE vprompt = "Add Record"
          DO add_cli
        CASE vprompt = "Edit Record"
          DO edit_cli
        CASE vprompt = "Browse Records"
          DO brws_cli
      ENDCASE

    CASE vpopup = "SAL_MENU"
      * nested CASE statement for Sales menu
      DO CASE
        CASE vprompt = "Add Record"
          DO add_sal
        CASE vprompt = "Edit Record"
          DO edit_sal
        CASE vprompt = "Browse Records"
          DO brws_sal
      ENDCASE

    CASE vpopup = "RPT_MENU"
      * nested CASE statement for Report menu
      DO CASE
        CASE vprompt = "Client/Sales Report"
          DO cs_rpt
      ENDCASE

  ENDCASE
  * ---- end of big CASE statement for menu bar choices

  CLEAR
  RETURN

PROCEDURE getout
  CLEAR
  DEAC MENU main
  RETURN
```

Figure 17.18: A menu program with FoxPro drop-down menus (continued)

The menu screen produced by the program in Figure 17.18 is shown in Figure 17.19. Note that we have only changed the menu program: all the other programs (Figures 17.11 - 17.17) can remain as we wrote them earlier. This is an example of compartmentalization, which is an important programming concept.

Enter the program shown in Figure 17.18 and save it as MENU2.PRG. To run it, simply type **run menu2** in the FoxPro Command window and press Enter.

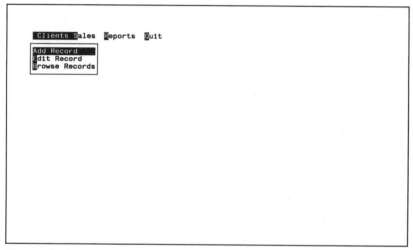

Figure 17.19: A drop-down menu system

Lesson Summary

- **The easiest way to create a menu system** is to type **do foxapp** in the FoxPro Command window, then select a data file and press Ctrl-Enter to generate the application. However, this approach can only produce simple, single data-file menu systems.

- **Writing a menu system program in FoxPro is relatively easy** in comparison to other programming languages. You create a main menu program that, based on the user's menu choice, calls one of several other programs; each sub-program does a specific database task.

- **A simple main menu program** displays a menu by using @...SAY statements and reads the user's choice with a GET...READ statement. The user's choice is then passed to a CASE statement, which calls the appropriate sub-program.

- **A drop-down menu program,** although it is much more complex, works in essentially the same way as a simple menu program: first it reads the user's choice and then passes it to a CASE statement, which calls the appropriate sub-program.

PART V

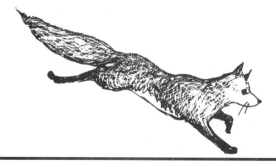

Specific Skills

LESSON 18
Advanced Field Techniques

LESSON 19
Using FoxPro's Command Window

LESSON 20
Using FoxPro's Text Editor

LESSON 21
Creating Form Letters

LESSON 22
Creating Mailing Labels

LESSON 23
Using Macros to
Speed Up Your Work

LESSON 24
Using FoxPro's Desk Accessories

LESSON 25
Introducing
FoxPro 2's Advanced Features

APPENDIX
Installing FoxPro

LESSON 18
Advanced Field Techniques

Featuring

- Field formatting
- How to set up field data-entry validation
- Using functions to change field types

WE'VE USED A LOT OF FOXPRO'S FEATURES IN THE course of developing our clients/sales database. One of the drawbacks of using an example, however, is that we can't include all of FoxPro's important features without making the example impossibly complicated. With the profusion of features, the most significant points might get lost in the shuffle.

In this chapter, we'll look at some features that, though important, didn't quite fit into our example. As in Lesson 17, this will involve a certain amount of typing, but the rewards will be well worth the effort.

First, we'll discuss how field options format and validate data. Then, we'll look at the nature and use of field functions in everything from printing reports to sorting database records, and examine some of the most important functions. Keep in mind that even this chapter will barely scratch the surface of what FoxPro can do.

Using Field Options

You've already seen a few field options. In Figure 14.14, the data-entry screen format file, we saw how to use the PICTURE and DEFAULT field options. Here, we'll look at these field options in more detail. We'll also examine how you can use VALID and RANGE clauses to limit the types of data that can be entered in certain fields—thereby catching most data-entry errors before they get into the database.

① Select "New" from the File menu and choose the "Database" file type.

② Enter the following fields in the new database file:

Name	Type	Width	Dec
FIRSTNAME	Character	10	
LASTNAME	Character	10	
HEIGHT	Numeric	2	0
WEIGHT	Numeric	2	0
PHONE	Character	13	

③ Once you've entered the fields, press Ctrl-Enter to confirm the file structure, and name the file **testfile**. It won't be necessary to input any records for this example, though you can do so later if you wish.

As we saw in Lesson 14, the FoxPro Screen Builder tends to produce fairly complicated programming code. What we're going to do here is very simple, so in the Command window, type **do foxapp** and press Enter. Then:

④ In the FoxApp dialog box, type **testfile** and press Enter. The name TESTFILE.SCX will be displayed as the default name for the screen format, as shown in Figure 18.1. Press Ctrl-Enter to accept the name and generate the application.

⑤ When the "Name your application" dialog box pops up, simply press Ctrl-Enter to name the application TESTFILE.APP.

⑥ As before, FoxApp will work for a few moments to build your application. Then it will display the message "Press any key to begin your application." Press the space bar to start your application.

The data-entry screen created by FoxApp is shown in Figure 18.2. It's a nice-looking screen, but it lacks data and formatting validation. Now we're going to see how to put some formatting and error-checking into those fields.

⑦ Exit from your application by selecting the "Quit" button.

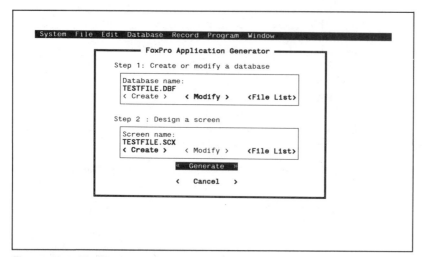

Figure 18.1: The FoxApp dialog box

Advanced Field Techniques 213

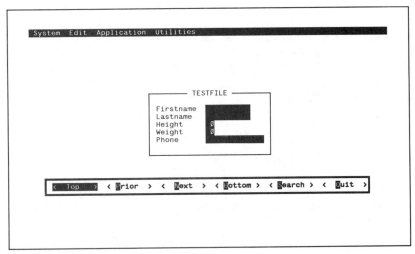

Figure 18.2: The TESTFILE.APP data entry screen

② In the "Application to run" dialog box, select "Cancel" to return to the Command window.

③ Once again, enter **do foxapp** in the Command window.

④ When the FoxApp dialog box reappears, type **testfile** as the file name and press Enter.

⑤ This time, however, we're going to do something different. In the Screen Name part of the dialog box, highlight the "Modify" button. Then press Enter (NOT Ctrl-Enter) to modify the data-entry screen. The Modify Screen window will appear as shown in Figure 18.3.

Before we proceed, let's talk briefly about the field options we're going to use. A PICTURE clause lets us restrict field entries to letters or numbers, and allows us to put "permanent" characters in a field—such as the parentheses surrounding the area code of a telephone number. A RANGE clause lets us set upper and lower bounds on the data entered in numeric fields; any numbers outside the limits we set will not be accepted by FoxPro.

A VALID clause allows us to limit entries to a specific value or list of values, such as "John," "Kymberly," and "Michael," or 1, 5,

Lesson 18

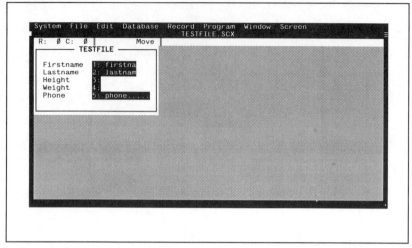

Figure 18.3: The Modify Screen window

10, and 15. Anything not in our list of acceptable values won't be allowed in the field.

*F*ormatting with PICTURE

① First, position the cursor in the Firstname field on the screen. This is the reverse-video highlighted space following the word "Firstname." Press Ctrl-F to enter a new field at that location.

② When the Field dialog box opens, press Enter to select the "Get" button, and in the "Choose a Field" box, select the Firstname field.

③ The Field dialog box will reappear. Select the "Format" button to open the Field Format dialog box, as shown in Figure 18.4.

④ Although it may not be visible on your screen, there is a blank at the top left under the word "Format." While the checkboxes on the right side of the dialog box allow you to perform most simple formatting tasks, this blank gives you a little more flexibility when you need it. Move the cursor to the blank and type **!AAAAAAAAA** (an exclamation mark followed by nine A's). Then press Ctrl-Enter to accept the field format. When you

Advanced Field Techniques   **215**

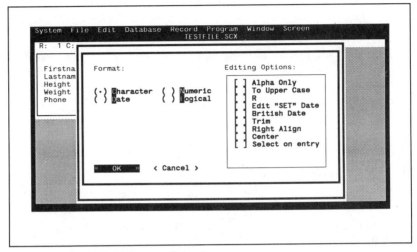

Figure 18.4: *The Field Format dialog box*

enter data in this field, only letters will be accepted, and the first letter will be converted to upper case.

⑤ When the Field dialog box reappears, press Ctrl-Enter to return to the Modify Screen window.

⑥ Now move the cursor down to the Lastname field and, once again, press Ctrl-F to enter a new field definition.

⑦ In the Field dialog box, select "Get" and choose the Lastname field in the "Choose a Field" box. On returning to the Field dialog box, once again select the "Format" button.

⑧ There's a hard way and an easy way to do this next step. We want this field to accept only letters (not numbers, punctuation, or other special characters), and we want all the letters to be uppercase. We could use the Format blank to do this by typing @**A**@!, but let's take the easy way. In the Editing Options box on the right, select the "Alpha Only" and "To Upper Case" checkboxes. Then press Ctrl-Enter twice to return to the Modify Screen window.

⑨ Move the cursor down to the Phone field and, in the same way as with the Firstname and Lastname fields, work your way to the Field Format dialog box.

⑩ In the Format blank at the top left, type **(999)999-9999**. Each 9 means that the field will only accept a number in that space, even though it's a character field. The parentheses and the dash will appear in the field as "permanent" characters when the field is displayed on-screen.

⑪ Press Ctrl-Enter twice to return to the Modify Screen window.

Data Validation with RANGE and VALID

For the purposes of this example, we're going to impose two rather odd restrictions on our data. First, we don't want anyone in the database who isn't 84 inches (seven feet) tall. And second, we don't want anyone in the database who weighs more than 80 pounds or less than 70 pounds.

① In the Modify Screen window, move the cursor to the Height field and press Ctrl-F to enter a new field definition. In the Field dialog box, select the Height field as a "Get" field.

② Highlight and select the "Valid" checkbox.

③ In the dialog box that opens up, press *E* to select the Expression radio button, and then highlight and select the "Edit" button.

④ In the Expression Builder, type or construct the expression **height = 84**, as shown in Figure 18.5. Select "Verify" to make sure that the expression you've constructed is valid, then press Ctrl-Enter three times to return to the Modify Screen window.

⑤ Now move the cursor down to the Weight field and press Ctrl-F again to enter a new field definition. In the Field dialog box, select "Get" and choose the Weight field.

⑥ In the Field dialog box, highlight and select the "Upper" checkbox. In the Upper dialog box that opens, press *E* for Expression and then select "Edit."

⑦ In the Expression Builder, enter the expression **weight <= 80** and select "Verify" to make sure that your expression is valid.

Advanced Field Techniques   **217**

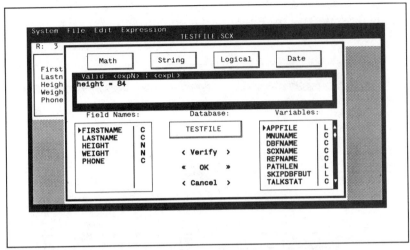

Figure 18.5: *Constructing a VALID expression for the Height field*

⑧ Press Ctrl-Enter twice to return to the Field dialog box. Then select the "Lower" checkbox.

⑨ Choose "Expression/Edit" to open the Expression Builder as before.

⑩ In the Expression Builder, enter the expression **weight > = 70** and select "Verify" to make sure that the expression is valid.

⑪ Press Ctrl-Enter three times to return to the Modify Screen window.

⑫ Select "Save" from the File menu.

Now, simply press Escape to exit from the Modify Screen Window and you're back at the FoxApp dialog box. (Remember that?) Press Ctrl-Enter twice to generate a new application with your modified screen format.

*A*ppending Records with Formats and Data Validation

When FoxApp has finished generating your modified application, it will display the message "Press any key to begin your application."

Press the space bar and the application screen will be displayed, as in Figure 18.6. Notice that the Phone field is pre-formatted with the parentheses and the dash.

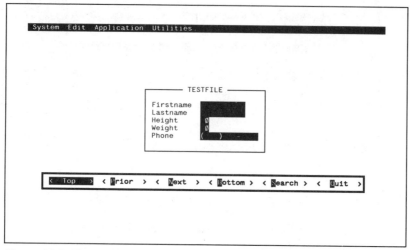

Figure 18.6: The application screen with formatting and data validation

Now let's try entering a record with invalid data. Move the cursor to the Firstname field and enter the following:

FIRSTNAME: joe
LASTNAME: jones
HEIGHT: 75
WEIGHT: 90
PHONE: 1234567890

FoxPro will initially accept the invalid data, but notice what happens then. The first and last names are automatically re-formatted as "Joe JONES." The cursor then moves to the Height field and the message "Invalid Input" is displayed. Once you correct the height (by changing it to 84), the same thing happens with the Weight field. You have now built simple formatting and data validation into your data entry screen with FoxApp.

Using Field Functions in FoxPro

Let's move on to a different sort of field formatting technique. In FoxPro, we can use functions to change a field from one type to another, to change its size, and to format it in various ways. Some of these functions are useful in making our reports look nicer; others are almost essential when we are sorting or indexing on numeric or date fields.

Report Formatting with Functions

Let's see if we can't improve on CLI-RPT5 (from Lesson 16) by adding the current date and page number in the header band at the top of each page. From the last time we did this (in CLI-RPT3, Lesson 13), you may recall that setting up the date was complicated and that the page number printed far to the right of our "Page #" text object. We're going to use advanced field techniques to make things simpler and neater.

① Open the CSALES view file, if it's not already open, by moving to the Command window and typing **set view to csales**, and pressing Enter. (It would also be a good safety measure to reindex your client file at this point, since we made changes during Lesson 17 and it's possible that the index file wasn't updated.) Then do the following:

② At the Command window, type **set century on** and press Enter. This will ensure that the year in any date will print out with four digits instead of two, as in November 3, 1992 instead of November 3, 92.

③ Select "Open" from the File menu. At the file type popup, choose "Report" and open CLI-RPT5.

④ Move the cursor to R:2 C:0 in the Layout window, so that it's on the *A* in *Account*. Press Ctrl-N twice to add two new PgHead lines.

⑤ Let's add the page numbers first. Move the cursor to R:2 C:60 and type **Page #**. Then press Enter.

⑥ Using the right arrow key (not the space bar), move the cursor to R:2 C:67. Press Ctrl-F to call up the Report Expression box; press Enter to open the Expression Builder.

⑦ In the Expression Builder, press Ctrl-S (or click on the String popup button) to open the String functions popup. Select LTRIM( ) and press Enter. We will use this function to trim blanks from the left side of the page number. **LTRIM( )** should appear in the expression box, with the cursor between the two parentheses.

⑧ Again from the String functions popup, select STR(, ,) and press Enter. Delete the two commas between the parentheses, but be careful not to delete anything else.

⑨ In the "Variables" box at the lower right, select _PAGENO and press Enter. Your screen should now look like Figure 18.7. If you want to be extra safe, select the Verify button to check the expression you've built.

⑩ Press Ctrl-Enter to return to the Report Expression box. Notice that the field width (at the right of the box) is set to 1, which won't be nearly enough. Change the width to **5** and press Ctrl-Enter to return to the Layout window.

What we just did was a two-step process. Because _PAGENO returns a numeric value, it has a default field width of 10. Since you

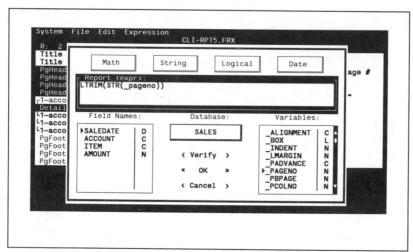

Figure 18.7: Trimming the spaces from _PAGENO

will seldom have need for page numbers in the billions, a lot of those 10 spaces will be unused. Of course, this can be a problem, because unused spaces still take up space. With numeric fields, the unused spaces appear to the left of the number, because the data in numeric fields is right-aligned.

The inner function, STR( ), takes the numeric value returned by _PAGENO and converts it to a string value—the same type of value as "John," which is not right-aligned. The outer function, LTRIM( ), takes the string version of _PAGENO that STR( ) creates and removes all the leading spaces (those on the left).

There are several versions of the TRIM( ) function: TRIM( ) by itself trims off spaces on the right, while ALLTRIM( ) trims off spaces on both the right and left sides of an expression. However, all of the TRIM( ) functions apply only to string (character) type fields; if you want to use them on another type of field, you must first convert it to a string with STR( ) for numeric fields or DTOS( ) for date fields.

Easier Date Formatting

Another thing we noticed in setting up CLI-RPT3 to print a live date was that it was fairly complex. First, we entered a function to convert the current date to the day of the week; then another function to convert it to the month, another for the day of the month, and still another for the year.

There's an easier way to do it using another of FoxPro's advanced functions.

① Move the cursor to R:2 C:0 and press Ctrl-F to call up the Report Expression box and the Expression Builder.

② As before, choose CDOW( ) (character day of the week) from the Date functions popup. Then, with the cursor between the parentheses in CDOW( ), choose DATE( ) from the Date functions popup. Select the Verify button to check the validity of the expression, then press Ctrl-Enter twice to return to the Layout window.

③ In row 2, just after the end of the field, enter a comma and press Enter. Move the cursor two spaces to the right and press Ctrl-F.

④ In the Expression Builder, select MDY( ) from the Date functions popup. Then, with the cursor between the parentheses in MDY( ), select DATE( ) from the Date functions popup. Press Ctrl-Enter twice to return to the Layout window. Your screen should look like Figure 18.8. Select "Save" from the File menu to save your report format.

If you press Ctrl-I to call up Page Preview, you'll see that the page number is one space to the right of your "Page #" text object, just as it was in CLI-RPT3, but with one useful difference: the space will be maintained automatically when your page numbers go into double or triple digits. Likewise, the date (day of the week and month/day/year) prints out as before—but in this case, it was easier to set up.

Before you proceed with any more exercises, be sure to enter **close databases** in the Command window.

Sorting and Indexing with Field Functions

Another important use of field functions is for sorting and indexing. If you are sorting or indexing on numeric and date fields, or on fields of different types, then field functions are an invaluable tool.

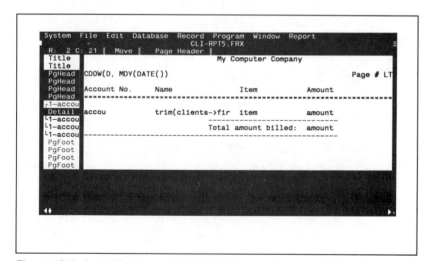

Figure 18.8: A modified layout for CLI-RPT5

It's no problem if you are sorting or indexing on just one field. However, if you want to sort on multiple numeric fields, or on a character plus a date field, you must convert some of the field types in order for things to work properly.

Multiple Numeric Fields

Sorting or indexing on a single numeric field is simple. You just set up the index in the Setup window. If we were to sort on the Height field in the testfile that we set up earlier, then the records would be in order by height. But remember how we sort and index on multiple fields? To sort on the Lastname and Firstname fields, we would enter

sort on lastname + firstname to testsort

With the Firstname and Lastname fields, this is no problem. But look how it applies to multiple numeric fields—e.g., if we wanted to sort on Height and Weight:

sort on height + weight to testsort

Instead of sorting (or indexing) the way we want it to, with multiple numeric fields, FoxPro will add the numbers together and sort on the sum of the two fields—hardly what we had in mind. What we need to do here is convert the numeric fields into character fields so that they won't be added together; and for that, we use the STR( ) function:

sort on str(height) + str(weight) to testsort

will give the correct result. The same method can be used for indexing on multiple numeric fields.

Multiple Fields of Different Types

Another problem is encountered when you want to sort or index on multiple fields that are of different types. FoxPro will only let you sort on multiple fields of the same type, so you must use functions to convert some fields from one type to another.

For example, we might want to sort or index a revised version of our client database and put the records in order by city and date of last purchase. FoxPro would refuse to accept a sort command such as

sort on city + saledate to client2

because CITY is a character field and SALEDATE is a date field. To make the sort (or index) operation work, we should instead use the command

sort on city + DTOS(saledate) to client2

which will give the correct result. By the way, when you're converting a date to a string (character) type for a sort or an index operation, it's important to use the DTOS( ) function and not one of the other date-to-character functions that FoxPro offers.

The DTOC( ) ("date to character") function, for example, normally converts your date to a string in the same format, such as 07/30/91. What you want for sorting or indexing, however, is something like 19910730. Otherwise, your records will be sorted by city, month, day, and year; all the records from July 1989, July 1990, and July 1991 will be grouped together—which isn't what you want.

*U*sing FoxPro's On/Off Panel

One final field technique can be of considerable help in data entry. If you open FoxPro's View window and select the On/Off button, you'll see the On/Off panel as shown in Figure 18.9. The On/Off

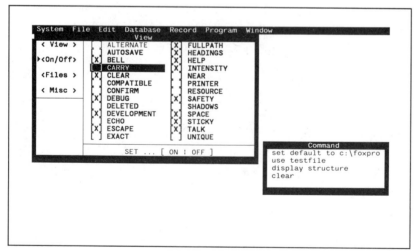

Figure 18.9: FoxPro's On/Off Panel

panel is used to set features of FoxPro that will be used by all database files, reports, and the like.

One important on/off box to know about is "Carry": checking this box is equivalent to entering **set carry on** in the Command window. When Carry is set to on and you are adding records to a database, the fields in a new record will already be filled in with the data from the previous record. If you are entering a lot of records that have most field data in common, then this can save you considerable time. You merely change the fields that are different in each record and leave the other fields untouched.

Lesson Summary

To add field formatting and data validation with FoxApp, first create your application. Then re-enter FoxApp and modify the screen it created by re-entering the field definitions with the formatting and data validation you want.

You can use field functions to help format your reports. One example is LTRIM(STR(_PAGENO)), which takes the page number, converts it to a string (character) value, and then trims off the leading spaces on the left. Sometimes, you must use a SET command, such as SET CENTURY ON, to make this work properly.

To sort or index on multiple numeric fields, you must first convert them to string (character) type fields so that their values won't be added together. To sort or index on fields of different types, you must first convert all fields to the same type—usually the character type.

FoxPro's On/Off box, accessible from the View window, lets you set toggles such as "Carry," which makes data from the previous record carry forward to a new record that you are adding.

LESSON 19
Using FoxPro's Command Window

Featuring

- The most important FoxPro commands
- Command window shortcuts
- Getting quick information about your data

FOXPRO'S MENUS AND DIALOG BOXES MAKE IT AN exceptionally easy program to learn and use. However, once you've used it for a while and become something of a FoxPro "expert," the menus may seem a little slow. First you open this menu and make a selection, then comes a dialog box, then another dialog box, an Expression Builder—and even then you're not finished, because you have to back out the same way, step by step.

That's fine for beginners, and even for experts on many tasks. But if you know what you're doing, you can use FoxPro's Command window both as a shortcut and to put even more power and flexibility at your fingertips. You can do anything in the Command window that you can do from the menus; you can also do quite a bit more that you can't do from the menus.

In this lesson, we'll look at the most important things you can do in the Command window. Unlike the FoxPro reference manual, which lists commands and functions in alphabetical order, this lesson will present commands in order of their significance: the commands you'll use most often come first, together with other commands that are normally used with them. This will provide a more direct route to learning FoxPro's Command window features than the alphabetical-reference approach. We've already covered some of these commands here and there in previous lessons, but this lesson draws them all together so that you can see where everything fits in. As we have done earlier in this book, we will present generic names in places where you should type the name of your own file or index or whatever is called for. In keeping with programming practice, we'll use angle brackets, as in <filename>, to indicate these general names when illustrating the commands. For instance, in the discussion of the USE command, you will be told to use the form **use** <**filename**>. To use an actual file, you would replace <filename> with the name of the file, as in **use clients**. Don't type the angle brackets!

Creating and Using Database Files

Before you can do anything with a database, you have to create it and put some data into it. This section will show how to perform these tasks from the Command window. Before doing anything else, you may want to type **clear** in the Command window and press Enter. This makes the screen easier to read by wiping it blank, though it won't close any onscreen windows.

Creating a Database

The first step in creating a database is to create the database's file (or files). In the Command window, type **create <filename>**. (Remember to replace <filename> with the name of the database file you're creating.) The actual process of setting up the file works the same as it does with the menus: you enter field names, types, and widths in a dialog box, and select the OK button when you're done.

CREATE, by the way, doesn't just apply to database files: you can also use it to set up report, label, and view files. If you don't specify a file type, FoxPro assumes that you want to create a database file, but you can create the other file types by entering **create report <filename>**, **create label <filename>**, or **create view <filename>**, as appropriate.

"Create report" opens the report layout screen, "create label" opens the label layout screen, and "create view" saves the current file, index, and file-link setup as a view file.

Opening Your Database and Adding Records

Opening your database and adding new records is as easy as creating it. To open your database file, enter **use <filename>** in the Command window. With the file open, enter **append**, and an append screen opens up. If you're using a screen format to append records (like the one we created in Lesson 14), you would enter **set format to <formatname>**. The command sequence would then go as follows:

> **use <filename>**
> **set format to <formatname>**
> **append**

The Append screen will open using your data-entry format. If your file is indexed, of course, you'll also want to make sure that all of its index files are open (see below).

Using the USE Command

It's worth pausing for a moment to look at what else you can do with the USE command. From previous lessons, you know about opening index files and FoxPro's ability to keep multiple database files open in different work areas. USE gives you a way to bypass the tedious process of going through the Setup dialog box to open index files and the View window to switch work areas.

To open a database file and its index file(s) in a single step, you simply enter

use <filename> index <indexname1>, <indexname2>, . . .

Of course, the " . . . " indicates that you can include more index file names—don't type three periods in the Command window!

There's one other important trick you can use with USE. If you want to open multiple database files in different work areas, there are two ways to do it from the Command window. The first is the long way:

use <filename> index <indexname>
select b
use <filename2> index <indexname2>
select c
use <filename3> index <indexname3>
. . .

SELECT, as you can guess from the example, is the way you switch from one work area to another. By the way, you can use either letters or numbers to refer to work areas; FoxPro doesn't care. "Select b" and "select 2" will both switch you to Work Area B.

But back to USE. If you're working with multiple files, there's a shorter way to open them in the appropriate work areas. Just enter:

use <filename> in 1 index <indexname>
use <filename2> in 2 index <indexname2>
use <filename3> in 3 index <indexname3>

and so on. The "in" clause tells FoxPro which work area to open the file in. As before, it makes no difference whether you use letters or numbers to denote work areas. If you want to try this out, you can open the View window to see what you've opened and which work area each file is in (see Figure 19.1).

Tip: How to Undo a Command Words that normally come after a command are called "parameters." In the command "use clients," for instance, the word "clients" is a parameter of the command "use." When a command normally comes with parameters, you can usually reverse the

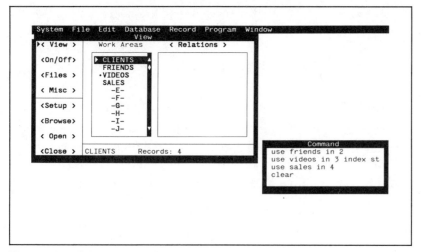

Figure 19.1: Opening multiple files with USE . . . IN

command by entering it without any parameters, as in the following examples:

- **use** <filename> opens a database in the current work area; **use** by itself closes the database in the current work area. (There *is* a command, incidentally—"close databases"—that closes all database files in all work areas.)

- **set index to** <indexname> opens an index file; **set index to** by itself closes all index files in the current work area.

Displaying a File Directory

You can display an on-screen list of your database files with the DIR command. Entering dir by itself makes FoxPro list all the database files in your current directory. If you want to look at another type of file, you must specify it by using "wildcards." A wildcard is a character that "stands in" for other characters. The most commonly used wildcard character is the asterisk (*). Examples of using the DIR command are

- **dir** displays a list of database files
- **dir *.*** displays a list of all files

- **dir *.idx** displays a list of index files
- **dir *.frx** displays a list of report format files
- **dir *.prg** displays a list of standard FoxPro program files

Viewing and Changing Your Database Structure

If you can't quite remember something about your database structure, it's easy to find out. Just enter **display structure** in the Command window, and the structure of the current database will be shown on the screen. (When you have other windows besides the Command window open on the screen, they may be "in front of" the structure listing. If this is the case, you should simply close them.)

Changing the structure is also easy. Enter **modify structure** in the Command window and the file structure dialog box will pop up, just as it did in Lesson 7 when you performed the same task from the menus.

The MODIFY command, by the way, doesn't just apply to database files. You can also use it to open the report or label layout screens to change existing format files, as follows:

modify report <formatname>
modify label <formatname2>

Operations within Your Database Files

Now that you know how to open your database files, it's time to learn how to get around in them and what to do when you get there.

GO TOP, GO BOTTOM, and SKIP: When You Know Where to Go

If you already know where you want to go—that is, if you know the record number or you want to go to the top or bottom of the database—then the following commands will take you there:

- **GO TOP** takes you to the first record that is displayed in the current database file. You should realize that this is not necessarily the same thing as the first record in the database file. If your database is indexed, it is displayed in a different order from that in which the records were entered; therefore, the "top" of the database file is unlikely to record #1. If your database is not indexed, then GO TOP will move the record pointer to record #1.

- **GO BOTTOM** takes you to the last record displayed in the current database file, subject to the same caveat noted for GO TOP.
- **GO <recordnumber>** takes you to whatever record you specify, e.g., **go 200**.
- **SKIP** moves you to the next record after the current one. You can also use SKIP with numbers to make bigger jumps: **skip 10** moves you ten records forward, while **skip −5** moves you five records back.

LIST and BROWSE: When You're Already There

If you just want to take a quick look at some of your data, then LIST and BROWSE are good ways to do it. With two or more linked database files, these commands can get information from all the linked files. (Remember that the link relationship must be many-to-one, as in the link between our sales and clients files: there can be many sales for each client record, but only one client record corresponds to each sale.)

Let's try out a couple of examples. First, type **set view to csales** and press Enter. This should open your sales file in Work Area A and your client file in B, with each indexed and linked on the account field. Then:

1. Just to be safe, reindex your sales file by typing **reindex** and press Enter. Then, reindex your client file by entering **select b** and **reindex**. Switch back to A with **select a**.

2. Type

    list account, item, clients −>firstname, clients −>lastname

    (all on one line) and press Enter. FoxPro displays data from both files, as shown in Figure 19.2.

Using FoxPro's Command Window   233

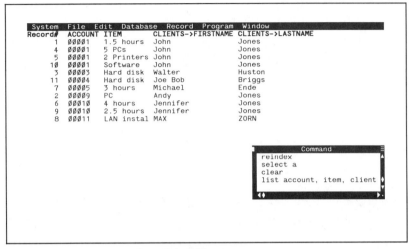

Figure 19.2: Listing data from linked files

③ To see something a little fancier, type

browse fields account, item, clients – >firstname, clients – >lastname

(again, all on one line) and press Enter. A Browse table will open that contains the selected fields from the two linked database files, as in Figure 19.3.

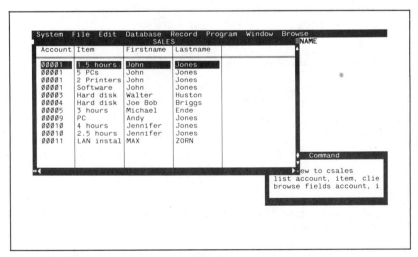

Figure 19.3: Browsing data from linked files

A Warning about File Links Once again, I should enter a warning note about how your file link is set up. It must be many-to-one. If you set up a link that has the client file (one) as the primary file with a link into the sales file (many) as the secondary file, you won't be able to get correct data.

A Browse table opened with the same sort of command as in the preceding Step 3—but for a one-to-many link—would look like Figure 19.4, which fails to provide a complete listing of items purchased by individual clients.

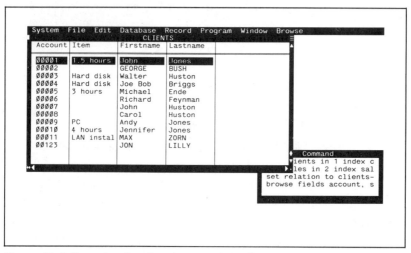

Figure 19.4: Browsing data from incorrectly linked files

Using "For" Clauses in a Command

You can do some very useful things by including a "for" clause in a command. For instance, if you do both consulting and sales work, you might want to list only those records where you have done consulting work. Since you bill your consulting work by the hour, you know that each transaction will have the word "hour" or "hours" in it. Thus, you can list all your consulting transactions by entering the command

list account, item, amount, clients – >lastname for "hour" $ item

(once again, all on one line). The result is shown in Figure 19.5.

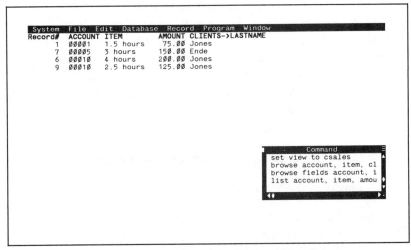

Figure 19.5: *Listing all records that include the word "hour"*

The dollar sign ($) in this command is referred to as the "included in" operator—it looks for whatever combination of characters you have placed between the quotation marks. In this case, the command that we entered tells FoxPro to list all the records that have the word "hour" in the item field. (Because the word "hours" itself contains the word "hour," we did not have to make a separate search for the singular and plural forms of the word.)

We might also want to know how much income we derived from selling PCs. In this case, we would enter the command **sum amount for "PC" $ item**. FoxPro scans through the records and returns the message

2 records summed. AMOUNT 4500.00

Similar in operation to SUM are the COUNT and AVERAGE commands. If we wanted to know how many sales have involved PCs or what the average bill for consulting work has been, then we would enter commands such as **count for "PC" $ item** or **average for "hour" $ item**.

We can even get fancier than that. Suppose that, when we first entered the amounts for our consulting transactions, we forgot that our state has a 5 percent tax on services. We can add the tax by using the REPLACE command with a "for" clause, as in

replace amount with amount * 1.05 for "hour" $ item

This tells FoxPro (*a*) to find all the records with "hour" in the item field and (*b*) to replace the number in the amount field by the same number times 1.05 (the number plus 5 percent). If you then list the account, item, amount, and clients->lastname fields again, you can see that the replacements have been made, as in Figure 19.6. Only the records with "hour" in the item field have been altered; the amounts for the other records are the same as before.

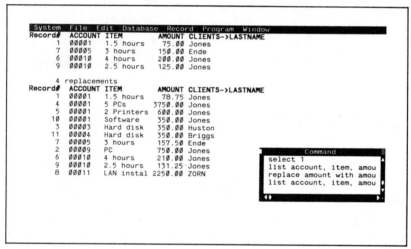

Figure 19.6: Result of a calculation with REPLACE

If you're particularly sharp-eyed, you may have noticed that "LAN instal" was not included in our search and replace operation. Even though a LAN (local area network) installation falls into the category of services, our "LAN instal" field did not include the word "hour," so this record was left out. This oversight spotlights the need for standard terminology in keeping your records: if similar items are called different things in different records, it can be very difficult to collect your data to make useful comparisons and calculations.

Locating Records with LOCATE/CONTINUE and SEEK

When you want to edit or delete records but you aren't sure where to find them, you can use LOCATE or SEEK. LOCATE, as we saw in Lesson 12, can be used with a "for" clause to find records in a non-indexed database file. SEEK, on the other hand, can be used only with indexed files, and only to search for data in the primary index field. This dictates the differences in how the two commands are used: **locate for** <**fieldname**> <**operator**> <**value**> versus **seek** <**value**>.

These are pretty abstract, of course, so let's flesh them out with a couple of examples. Here's a typical LOCATE command:

locate for amount > 50.00

Here, "amount" is the field you want to search on. The greater-than symbol (>) is an operator that shows what relation you want between the field and the value you specify—in this case, 50.00. You could just as easily use some other operator, such as equal (=), less than (<), or less than or equal to (<=). For a character field, you could use the substring operator ($), although in this case you'd have to reverse the order between the field and the value, e.g., **locate for "PC" $ item**.

Once you've located a record, you can display it, edit it, or delete it. To move to the next matching record, you type **continue** in the Command window.

With SEEK, you search for a value in the primary index field, as in **seek "00005"**, which searches for the record with "00005" in the account field. Note that even though it has numbers in it, Account is a character field. Therefore, we had to put the "00005" in quotes. If we set up the sales file with *Amount* as the primary index field, we could enter a SEEK (or LOCATE) expression without quotes, as in **seek 350.00**, because "Amount" is a numeric field.

The advantage of SEEK, as we noted in Lesson 12, is that with large databases it can be much faster than LOCATE. The drawback is that it finds only the first matching record. However, you can then use LOCATE and CONTINUE to find all the other matching records.

But why not use LOCATE in the first place? The reason is that in a large and indexed database, SEEK, which takes advantage of the index, will move the record pointer directly to the first matching record. Furthermore, because the database is indexed, all the matching records are together. If you started with LOCATE, it would have to conduct a lengthy search through the database, comparing every single record until it found the first one that matched. The advantage of using SEEK first is simply that you "get there faster," and you can then switch to LOCATE because you're already at the block of matching records.

Editing and Deleting Records

Once you've found the record you want, you can make changes in it by entering **edit**, which opens up an edit window. If you know which record you want to edit and don't need to search for it, you can simply enter **edit <recordnumber>** to go directly to that record.

DELETE, which marks records for deletion but doesn't physically remove them from the file, works the same way. You can delete the current record by simply entering **delete**, or delete a different record by entering **delete <recordnumber>**. You can even combine the DELETE command with a "for" clause, as in **delete for amount = 0.00**. If you want to mark all your records for deletion, enter **delete all**.

If you change your mind about marking a record or records for deletion, you can enter the RECALL command, as in

- **recall** to unmark the current record
- **recall all** to unmark all records
- **recall for amount > 10.00** to unmark all records where the amount is over $10.00

Once you've marked records for deletion and are sure that you want to delete them, you can enter **pack**, which will actually remove the records from your database.

The neutron bomb of database deletion is ZAP. ZAP should not be used by children under 16, Democrats, Republicans, or any other persons of dubious mental competence. (Check your local and state laws for other restrictions.) ZAP instantly deletes and packs all records in the current database, leaving it an empty shell. Once you've used ZAP, you can't recover your records. You Have Been Warned.

Using SET Commands

FoxPro's SET commands are used to set everything from data-entry screen formats to the default directory. To enter a SET command, you enter **set <parameter> to <value>**, where the <value> can be a filename, a directory, or whatever is appropriate for the thing you are setting. Normally, you can cancel a SET command by entering it without any parameters, as in

- **set index to sales** (opens sales index)
- **set index to** (closes active index files)
- **set filter to amount > 10.00** (filters out records where the amount is less than or equal to 10.00)
- **set filter to** (cancels the filter condition)

*I*mportant SET Commands

FoxPro has so many SET commands that it's impossible to show them all here. These are the SET commands that you'll use most often:

- **SET CARRY ON.** This tells FoxPro that when you're appending records, you want the values from the previous record carried forward into each new record. You use this when your records have a lot of data in common, such as when they all have the same street, city, state, and zip code.
- **SET CLOCK ON.** This causes a small clock to be displayed at the top right corner of your FoxPro screen.
- **SET DEFAULT TO <drive:directory>.** This is used to set the default directory for FoxPro's operations, as in **set default to c:\foxpro\myfiles**. If you don't use this command, FoxPro assumes that you want the FoxPro program directory (usually c:\foxpro) as the default.
- **SET FIELDS TO <field1>, <field2> ...** This selects the fields that you want displayed in a Browse window. You can include fields from linked database files by preceding the field name with the database file name, as in "clients − >lastname".
- **SET FILTER TO <field> <operator> <value>.** This sets up a filter condition so that only records matching the condition are displayed in a Browse window.

- **SET FILTER TO** <field> <operator> <value>. This sets up a filter condition so that only records matching the condition are displayed in a Browse window.
- **SET FORMAT TO** <formatname>. This sets up a screen format (that is, a ".fmt" file like the one we created in Lesson 14) for data entry.
- **SET INDEX TO** <index1>, <index2>, ... This opens index files for your database.
- **SET RELATION TO** <link field name> **INTO** <Work Area>. This sets up a link between two database files.
- **SET VIEW TO** <viewfile>. This opens a view file, which in turn automatically restores the database, index, and link setup that were in effect when you saved the view file.

LESSON 20
Using FoxPro's Text Editor

Featuring

- Entering and editing text
- Using multiple text windows

IN ADDITION TO ITS DATABASE MANAGEMENT FEATURES, FoxPro includes a surprisingly powerful text editor.

In case the term is unfamiliar, a text editor is a sort of "mini" word processor: it lets you enter text and do some editing chores, but it lacks advanced word processing features. For example, a text editor keeps its files in plain ASCII format, which leaves out all the extra codes used by word processors to pretty up their documents. (A benefit of keeping files in ASCII format, however, is that they can be used by almost any other program.)

You can use FoxPro's text editor (and, more generally, its text editing features) to enter text into memo fields and—as we'll see in this chapter—even to create your own computer programs.

Starting the Text Editor

There are two ways to start FoxPro's text editor. The quickest is to enter **modify command** <**filename.ext**> in the Command window. This starts up the text editor and opens the file you want to work with. If the file already exists, FoxPro simply opens the file for you to edit; if it doesn't exist, FoxPro creates it.

When you use MODIFY COMMAND to start the text editor, it's important to specify not only the filename but its extension. For example, the files ABC.prg, ABC.fmt, and ABC.txt are all different files because they have different extensions. If you don't specify an extension, FoxPro assumes that you want to create or open a program file, which has a *.prg* extension.

If you're trying to open a file with another extension, but forget to include it in your MODIFY COMMAND statement, FoxPro will tell you that it can't find the file. An alternative is to use MODIFY FILE, which doesn't expect a *.prg* extension.

Using the Menus

The second way to start the text editor is by selecting "New" from the File menu, then selecting either "Program" or "File" at the New File dialog box. The only difference between selecting "Program" and "File" is that a "Program" file will have a *.prg* extension, while a "File" file won't have an extension unless you specify one. In Figure 20.1, we've created a file called MYFILE.TXT.

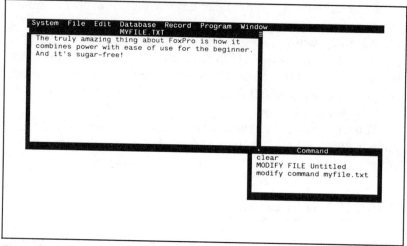

Figure 20.1: Opening a file in the text editor

As with all screen windows, you can zoom the text editor window to full-screen by pressing Ctrl-F10, or zoom it back to normal by pressing Ctrl-F10 a second time.

Because you don't name the file when you create it from the menus, you're prompted to name the file the first time you save it to disk. (This is another area in which using the menu system differs from using MODIFY COMMAND.)

The Edit Menu

When you are working in FoxPro's text editor, the Edit menu expands to offer menu options that are designed for text editing (see Figure 20.2). As usual, you open the Edit menu by either pressing Alt-E or clicking on "Edit" with the mouse.

The Edit menu offers a number of options that can make your editing work easier:

- **Undo** (speed key: Ctrl-U) allows you to "undo" or restore any changes you've made, step by step, all the way back to the beginning of the file. To undo a deletion, simply press Ctrl-U; to undo the deletion before that, press Ctrl-U again; and so on. This aspect of the "Undo" feature—that it can undo each and every change you have made in a data-entry session—is,

Using FoxPro's Text Editor

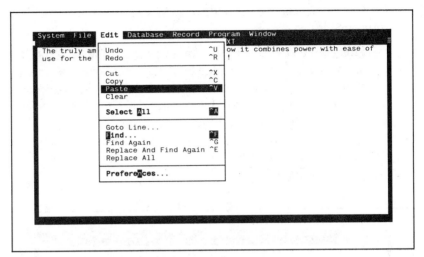

Figure 20.2: The Edit menu in the text editor

amazingly, more powerful than in the vast majority of word processing packages, many of which can undo only the most recent one or two changes.

- **Redo** (speed key: Ctrl-R) lets you "undo an undo." In other words, if you've used "Undo" to reverse an editing change, but decide that you didn't want to reverse it after all, you can use "Redo" to cancel your "Undo."

- **Cut** (speed key: Ctrl-X) deletes a block of text, but keeps the text in your PC's memory so that you can move it (using "Paste"—see below) to another location in your file. For example, you would use "Cut" together with "Paste" to move a paragraph from the start of your file to the middle.

- **Copy** (speed key: Ctrl-C), together with "Paste," copies a block of text without deleting the original block. You would use this if, for example, you needed a paragraph in both its present location and somewhere else.

- **Paste** (speed key: Ctrl-V) takes a block of text that you have "cut" or "copied" and inserts it at the current cursor position.

- **Select All** (speed key: Ctrl-A) selects all the text in your document. You can then perform a block operation on it, such as copying it to a different text file in another window.

- **Goto Line** lets you move directly to a specific line number in your file.

- **Find** (speed key: Ctrl-F) lets you search your file for a specific text string. It calls up a dialog box that asks if you just want to find the text, or if you also want to replace it with a different text string (see Figure 20.3). Options related to "Find" ("Find Again," "Replace and Find Again," and "Replace All") appear below "Find" in the Edit menu. These options, which let you repeat the search in various ways, are activated only when you first select "Find."

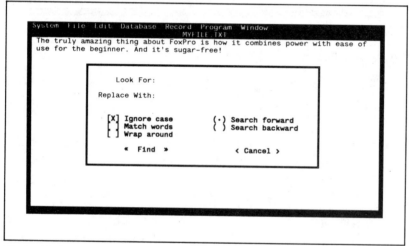

Figure 20.3: The Find Text dialog box

- **Preferences** calls up a dialog box (see Figure 20.4) that lets you set up the text editor the way you want it, including word-wrap, auto-indent, and Tab stops.

Saving and Closing Your File

No matter how you start the text editor and open your file, you save your file by selecting "Save" from the File menu. You can then close the file and exit from the text editor by pressing Escape. If you've made changes, you'll be prompted to save them before exiting. To save and exit at the same time, press Ctrl-W.

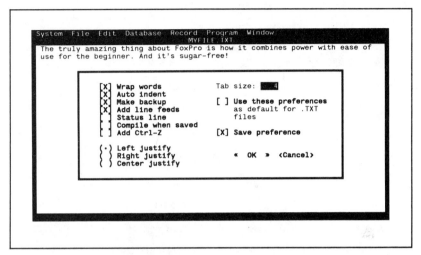

Figure 20.4: The Preferences dialog box

Moving Around in Your File

It's easy to move around in the text editor. The arrow keys move you one space or line at a time, and the right and left arrow keys combined with the Control key move you one word at a time. The keys for moving around in your text file are summarized in Table 20.1.

Selecting Text

Selecting text for block operations is easiest with a mouse, but it works fine from the keyboard. We'll go over both methods. If you have a mouse, you simply position the mouse cursor at the beginning of the text you want to select, then hold down the left mouse button and drag the mouse cursor down to the end of the desired text. Release the mouse button, and your text is selected, as shown in Figure 20.5.

To use the keyboard to select an area of text, position the cursor at the beginning of the text you want to select, then hold down the Shift key while using the arrow keys to move the cursor to the end of the desired text. When you release the Shift key, your text is selected. You can then copy, delete, move, or do other block operations with it.

Table 20.1: Text Editor Navigation Keys

PRESS	TO MOVE
Right arrow	Right one space or character
Left arrow	Left one space or character
Up arrow	Up one line
Down arrow	Down one line
PgUp	Up 21 lines (one screen)
PgDn	Down 21 lines (one screen)
Home	To left end of current line
End	To right end of current line
Control-Right arrow	One word to the right
Control-Left arrow	One word to the left
Control-Home	To beginning of file
Control-End	To end of file

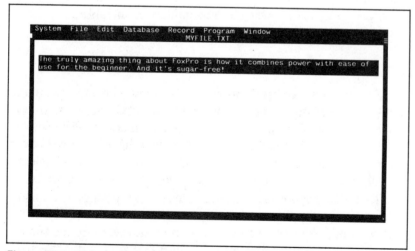

Figure 20.5: A block of text selected

FoxPro also lets you select text by the character, word, line, or file. The options are summarized in Table 20.2.

Table 20.2: Key Combinations for Selecting Text

PRESS	TO SELECT
Shift-Right arrow	Character at cursor; extends block one character at a time to the right
Shift-Left arrow	Character to left of cursor; extends block one character at a time to the left
Shift-Down arrow	Current line, from the cursor to the right end; extends block down one line at a time
Shift-Up arrow	Current line, from the left of the cursor to the line above the cursor; extends block up one line at a time
Shift-Control-End	Everything from cursor to end of file
Shift-Control-Home	Everything from cursor to beginning of file
Control-A	Entire file (selects All)

Copying Text between Files

As an exercise, let's select some text and then copy it to a different file. For the purposes of this example, we'll create two text files.

① Select "New" from the File menu and "File" in the File Type dialog box.

② Type **quantum leap** in the text editor window that opens up. Select "Save" from the File menu, and save the file as **myfile1**.

③ Open another text file by repeating Step 1. We won't name this file until we have something in it to save.

④ Open the Window menu. At the bottom of the menu, you'll see both files listed, each in its own numbered window, starting with zero. Switch to the first file (myfile1) by pressing *0* or highlighting and selecting "0 MYFILE."

⑤ Select the entire line of text by pressing Shift-Down arrow with the cursor on the *q* in *quantum*.

⑥ Select "Copy" from the Edit menu.

⑦ Switch to the second file by selecting "1 UNTITLED" from the Window menu.

⑧ Move the previously selected text ("quantum leap") to the new file by selecting "Paste" from the Edit menu. Now save this second file as **myfile2**.

⑨ Press Escape twice. This will close both files.

To copy text between already existing files, the procedure is essentially the same. You would open the files through the File menu and select each file's type (e.g., "Database") in the Open dialog box. Of course, there is no need to save an already named file until you've made changes to it, so you can skip the naming and saving operation of Step 2 above. The only file you need to save in Step 8, then, is whatever file you copy to.

Lesson Summary

- **To open a file in Foxpro's text editor,** either type **modify command** <filename> in the Command window (where <filename> is the name of the file), or select "Open" from the File menu and choose either the "Program" or "File" file type.

- **To save your file and exit from the text editor,** press Ctrl-W. To save your file but continue editing, select "Save" from the File menu.

- **FoxPro's text editor offers a wide range of editing functions,** most of which have associated speed keys—such as Undo (Crtl-U), Cut (Ctrl-X), and Paste (Crtl-V).

- **To select a block of text,** position the cursor at the beginning of the block, hold down the Shift Key, and press the down arrow key until the entire block is highlighted. With a mouse, position the mouse cursor at the beginning of the block, hold down the left mouse button, and drag the cursor downward until the entire block is highlighted.

LESSON 21
Creating Form Letters

Featuring

- How to design a database for form letters
- How to insert fields
- How to print form letters

CREATING FORM LETTERS IS EASY IN FOXPRO, THOUGH the process differs in its details from some other database packages. A form letter, in case you're not totally clear on the subject, is a standard letter that is specially set up so that each copy you print draws its name and address from a different record in the database.

Form letters give you a way to send more-or-less personalized mail to large numbers of people at a far lower cost than writing a different letter to each person. To be sure, when you get a letter from your senator that opens by saying "Dear Bill," you know that everyone else in your state is probably getting the same letter. But at least it's a cut above "Dear Occupant."

In FoxPro, a form letter is just another kind of report. Hence, you create it not in the text editor—which is where you might expect to create it—but in the Report Layout screen.

Form Letters in FoxPro

Before we create a form letter, it's worthwhile to think about what we need in a database to generate form letters.

First, if we are going to use our client database to generate form letters on a fairly regular basis, we should add a MRMS (Mister or Ms.) field to hold the person's honorific or title, whether it's "Mr.," "Ms.," "Dr.," or something else.

Likewise, we should add a SALUTATION field. The salutation is what you call someone when talking to him or her, such as "Dr. Sparrow," "Mrs. Peel," or "Fred." We can, of course, construct a salutation from the MRMS and LASTNAME fields. However, if someone has been a client and friend for 15 years, it doesn't make much sense to send him a letter that calls him "Mr. Rock" when you normally call him "Jim." Adding a salutation field takes care of this problem.

Depending on how much you want to personalize your form letters, you can even include "areas of interest" or other fields in your database. With an "interest" field, for example, the body of your letter can say things like "Knowing of your interest in <interest>, <salutation>, I have enclosed several brochures on the subject." When you print your form letter, a sentence like that might come out as "Knowing of your interest in database management, Mr. Codd, I have enclosed several brochures on the subject."

Creating a Form Letter

Let's see what kind of form letter we can produce with our database as it currently stands, that is, without the MRMS and SALUTATION fields. First, open the clients database by entering **use clients** in the Command window or by selecting "Open" from the File menu. Then do the following:

① In the Command window, type **set century on** and press Enter. This makes our work easier when it comes to inserting a "live date," that is, whatever the date is whenever the user runs the program. Make sure, however, that CENTURY is set on any time you *print* this form letter as well; otherwise, the year will still print as 91 (or whatever year it is) even though the report layout displays 1991.

② Type **create report formltr1** in the Command window and press Enter. Layout is especially important for a letter, so select "Page Layout" from the Report menu and enter the following values: top and bottom margins, **3**; Printer indent, **10**; and Right margin column, **75**. Press Ctrl-Enter to return to the Layout window.

③ In the first line of the Detail band, at R:4 C:0, press Ctrl-F to call up the Report Expression box. Press Enter to open the Expression Builder.

④ Press Ctrl-D to open the Date functions popup and select MDY( ). The function should appear in the expression box.

⑤ With the cursor between the parentheses in MDY( ), reopen the Date functions popup and select DATE( ). Your screen should now match the one shown in Figure 21.1.

⑥ Press Ctrl-Enter (or click on OK) to return to the Report Expression box. Notice, at the right, that the width is set to 12. That won't be enough to handle some dates, so tab to the "Width" box and enter **20**. Press Ctrl-Enter to return to the Layout window.

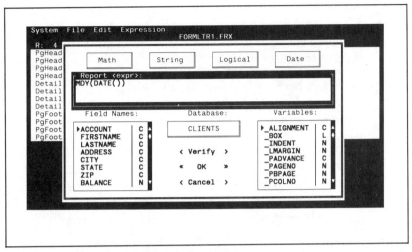

Figure 21.1: Inserting the date in a form letter

⑦ Using the arrow keys, move down to the line under the date field. The text of the letter has to fit into the Detail band of the report, so four lines aren't going to be enough. Add 15 lines to the Detail band by pressing Ctrl-N 15 times.

Inserting Name and Address Fields

Now that we have enough space to enter the text of our letter, let's put in the name and address fields:

① Move the cursor to the second line below the date field, at R:6 C:0. Press Ctrl-F and open the Expression Builder.

② With the cursor in the expression box, press Ctrl-S to open the String functions popup. Select TRIM( ) from the list.

③ With the cursor between the parentheses in TRIM( ), use Shift-Tab to move back to the field list at the lower left. Highlight FIRSTNAME and press Enter.

④ From the String functions popup, select " + " to add to what you have in the expression box.

5. Again from the String functions popup list, select "text." When the double quotes appear in the expression box, press the space bar once to insert a space. Add another " + " to the right of the quote marks.

6. Shift-Tab back to the field list and select LASTNAME (or double-click on LASTNAME with the mouse). Press Ctrl-Enter to exit from the Expression Builder.

7. In the Report Expression box, if the "Width" box is set to a value less than 25, change it (to 25) and press Ctrl-Enter to return to the Layout window. Even though only the Firstname field is shown in the Layout window, both the first and last names will be there when you print the form letters.

8. On the line below the name (R:7 C:0), press Ctrl-F to place another field. In the Expression Builder, select ADDRESS and press Ctrl-Enter twice to return to the Layout window.

9. At R:8 C:0, press Ctrl-F again. This time, in the expression box, enter the following by typing it or constructing it from the popup lists:

trim(clients.city) + ", " + clients.state + " " + clients.zip

Press Ctrl-Enter to exit. In the Report Expression box, the width is set to 18, which might be too short; change it to 20. Press Ctrl-Enter again to return to the Layout window.

10. At R:10 C:0, type "Dear" and press Enter.

11. Using the arrow keys, move over one space to R:10 C:5 and press Ctrl-F to place a field there. Because most of our clients are old friends, we're going to skip the amenities (e.g., an honorific field) and use their first names.

12. Open the Expression Builder box and select "trim" from the String functions list. Then, with the cursor between the parentheses in "trim( )", select the firstname field. Press Ctrl-Enter twice to return to the report layout screen.

⑬ Use the right arrow key to move the cursor so that it is just to the right of the field on-screen. Then type a colon and press Enter.

⑭ Move the cursor so that it's two lines below the *D* in *Dear* and type the rest of the letter.

Note that unless you're in the FoxPro editor (and you're not), FoxPro considers each new line you type to be a text object. This means you have to press Enter at the end of each line simply to confirm the object's position; further, you have to use the down arrow key to move down to each new line.

It's been our pleasure to help with your computer needs for the past five years. We are expanding our operation with new offices in Chicago, Phoenix, and Santa Barbara. If you need faster service in the future, please call the office nearest to you.

Sincerely,

Pete de Fermat
Senior Consultant

Unfortunately, FoxPro can't sign the letter for you. Your screen should look like Figure 21.2.

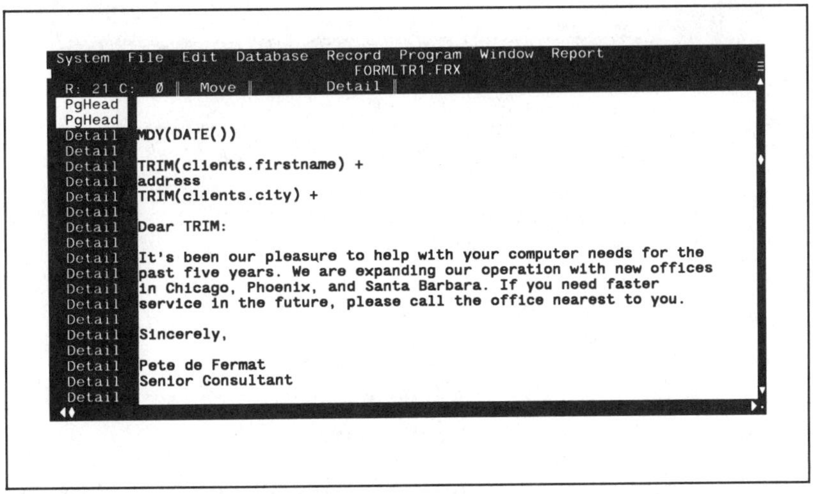

Figure 21.2: Form letter with body text added

*F*inal Formatting

There are only two more major steps to get our letter ready to print. To print a separate record—that is, a separate letter—on each page, we need to put a forced page break in a summary band at the bottom of the letter. We also need to group the records by account number. Do the following:

① From the Report menu, select "Title/Summary." When the dialog box opens up, select "Summary Band" and check the "New Page" checkbox as in Figure 21.3. Press Ctrl-Enter.

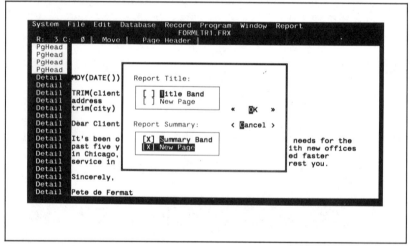

Figure 21.3: Inserting a Summary band with a forced page break

② Select "Data Grouping" from the Report menu and select the "Add" button in the Group dialog box.

③ At the Group Info dialog box, press Enter to open the Expression Builder.

④ Shift-Tab back to the field list, then highlight and select ACCOUNT. Press Ctrl-Enter to exit.

⑤ When you return to the Group Info dialog box, select the "New Page" checkbox by pressing *N*. Press Ctrl-Enter twice to return to the Layout screen.

And we're done! Take a look at how your letter will print out by pressing Ctrl-I to call up Page Preview, as in Figure 21.4. Then, save your work by selecting "Save" from the File menu.

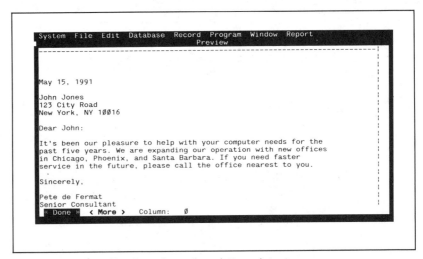

Figure 21.4: Page Preview of your form letter printout

Printing Your Form Letters

Printing your form letters is accomplished just like printing any other type of report. Simply do the following:

① Choose "Report" from the Database menu.

② When the dialog box opens, simply press *P* to select the "To Print" checkbox.

③ Make sure that your printer is turned on, is on-line, and has plenty of the right kind of paper. Then press Ctrl-Enter to start printing your form letters.

You'll probably need to go back to the Report Layout window to adjust the top, bottom, and side margins in your form letter. These vary from one printer model to another, and it's really just a matter of experimenting until your form letters look the way you want them to.

LESSON 22
Creating Mailing Labels

Featuring

- How to select a label format
- How to print labels

◊ ◊ ◊ ◊ ◊

THE METHOD FOR CREATING A MAILING LABEL FORMAT will seem very familiar; in fact, it's almost identical to creating a report format. The one big difference is that instead of working in the Report Layout screen, you're working in the Label Layout screen.

Creating a Label Format

Before you can create a label format, you have to define the size of the label. FoxPro's default setting is for labels that are 3½ inches wide and 5 lines high, printed one across. However, you can design a different size label by choosing the "Layout" option of FoxPro's Label menu, as shown in Figure 22.1.

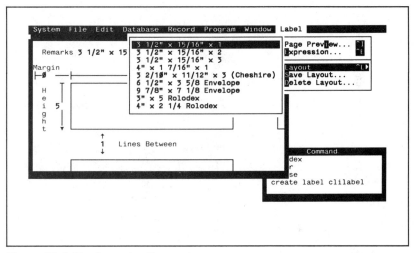

Figure 22.1: The Layout options submenu

The Layout options submenu not only lets you pick different label sizes, but also gives you options for printing on different sizes of envelopes and index cards. FoxPro also has menu options that let you print labels two or three across. If you have a wide-carriage printer (very, very wide!), FoxPro lets you define a custom layout that will print up to 120 labels across.

Setting Up Your Database

If you have a small number of items to mail, then it may not matter very much what order the labels are printed in. On the other hand, if you have a large database and many items to mail, you'll probably want to have your records indexed by zip code so that the labels will print out in zip code order.

There are two benefits of using zip code order. First, you can sometimes get a lower mailing rate from the U.S. Postal Service if your letters are presorted by zip code, because this reduces the amount of work that has to be done by the Postal Service itself. Second, if you're using the items as a marketing tool, you may want to target your mailing on a specific city or state.

Of course, you may have other criteria that influence your decision about the order in which you print your labels, but for now, we'll just use zip code order. In Lesson 11, we left creating a zip code index as an exercise. If you didn't do it then, you should do it now. Open your "clients" database file and enter **index on zip to zipcode**.

If you did create the zip code index in Lesson 11, simply open your "clients" database file and enter **reindex** in the Command window.

Setting Up a Label Format

Open the Label Layout screen by typing **create label clilabel** in the Command window and pressing Enter. (If you prefer, you can also do it by selecting "New" from the File menu and choosing the "Label" file type. You will be prompted to name the label file the first time you save it to disk.) Then, when the Label Layout window opens, do the following:

① Press Ctrl-E to open the Expression Builder. (Note that this differs from the Report Layout screen, where you press Ctrl-F to call up the Expression Builder.)

② In the expression box, type or construct the expression

   trim(firstname) + " " + lastname

   Select the "Verify" button to make sure that the expression is valid; then press Ctrl-Enter to return to the Layout window.

③ Use the arrow key to move down to the beginning of the second line. Press Ctrl-E again. In the expression window, type **address** and press Ctrl-Enter to exit.

④ At the beginning of the third line, press Ctrl-E again. In the Expression Builder, enter

   trim(city) + ", " + state + " " + zip

and verify the expression by selecting the "Verify" button. Then press Ctrl-Enter to return to the Layout window. Your screen should look like Figure 22.2.

⑤ And that's it! Save your work by selecting "Save" from the File menu.

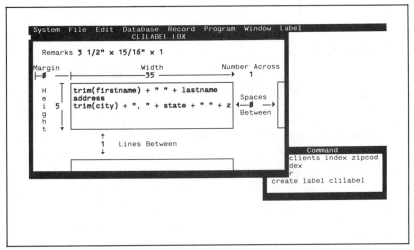

Figure 22.2: The completed label layout

⑥ Call up Page Preview by pressing Ctrl-I to see how your labels will look when printed, as in Figure 22.3. Notice that the labels are in zip code order.

Creating an Envelope Format

In addition to labels, you can also design envelope address formats in FoxPro. This feature is intended for continuous-feed envelopes, which come lightly glued onto continuous-feed computer paper. While it can be used for addressing single envelopes, it's really not practical to do so.

Creating an envelope format is a little more complicated than creating a label, but is still quite similar. To create an envelope format,

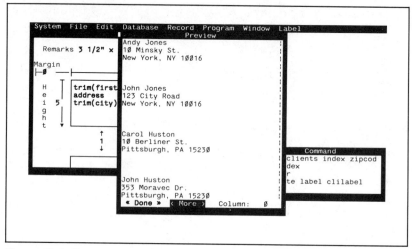

Figure 22.3: Page preview of printed labels

first exit from the CLILABEL Layout screen by pressing Escape. Then do the following:

① In the Command window, type **create label clienv** and press Enter.

② Select "Layout" from the Label menu and choose "6 1/2 × 3 5/8 Envelope" from the Layout submenu. Your Envelope Layout screen will open as shown in Figure 22.4.

③ Tap the Down arrow key six times to move to line number seven. Press Ctrl-E to call up the Expression Builder.

④ In the Expression Builder, type

trim(firstname) + " " + lastname

and select the "Verify" button to make sure the expression is valid. Press Ctrl-Enter to return to the Layout window.

⑤ Move the cursor to the beginning of the next line and press Ctrl-E. In the Expression Builder, type **address** and press Ctrl-Enter to return to the Layout window.

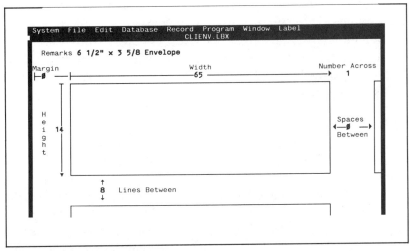

Figure 22.4: The Envelope Layout screen

⑥ With the cursor on the next line, press Ctrl-E to call up the Expression Builder. Type or construct the expression

trim(city) + ", " + state + "   " + zip

Verify that the expression is valid by selecting the "Verify" button, and then press Ctrl-Enter to return to the Layout window. Your screen should look like Figure 22.5.

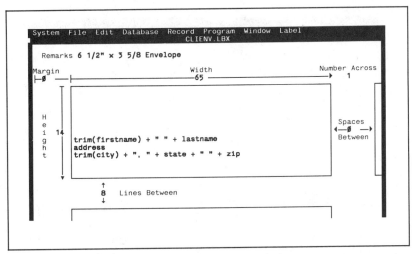

Figure 22.5: Entering expressions in the Layout window

If you press Ctrl-I now, you'll see that the address is aligned with the envelope's left margin. Normally, of course, you want the address to print more toward the right side of the envelope.

This is where the Label Layout window differs slightly from the Report Layout window. In the Report Layout window, you moved fields in the window to their approximate positions in the report. If you try this in the Label Layout window, however, nothing will happen: the address will still be left-aligned.

The trick is to realize that the printer indent for a label (simply called "Margin" in the Label Layout window, as you can see on the upper left) has a default setting of zero. Though you might try to get around this by entering a few blank spaces before each line of the address, you won't meet with any success: the label generator ignores such leading spaces. However, all the numbers in the Layout screen can be changed—even the ones outside the envelope box. To move your address information toward the right side of the envelope, press the Tab key twice (or use the mouse) to move the highlight to the "Margin" setting, which by default is 0. Change the margin by typing **35** and pressing Enter.

If you need to, you can move to any of the other numbers in the screen and change them. Now, if you call up Page Preview, you'll see that the address is positioned correctly on the envelope, as in Figure 22.6.

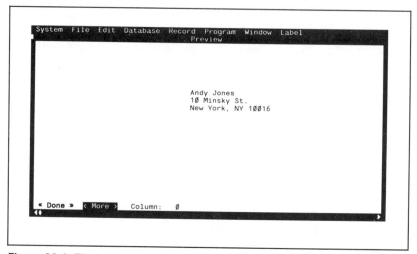

Figure 22.6: The address positioned on the envelope

There's one other surprise that you need to be aware of. If you try to save your envelope format by selecting "Save" from the File menu, an error message pops up and says

Warning: Error in line 1 of label definition

This error message is nothing to worry about. The "error" that Fox-Pro is warning you about is that there's nothing on the first line of your envelope format definition. Unlike a person, to whom it's quite obvious, FoxPro has no way of knowing that this is the way you intended your format to be; hence, the warning. Simply ignore the error message and press Enter to save your envelope format.

Printing Labels and Envelopes

Printing labels and envelopes works just like printing a report. First, make sure that your database file is open along with the correct index files, and that your printer is on-line and properly loaded with labels or envelopes. Then, do the following:

① Select "Label" from the Database menu.

② In the Label dialog box (shown in Figure 22.7), press Enter to select the label (or envelope) format you want to use.

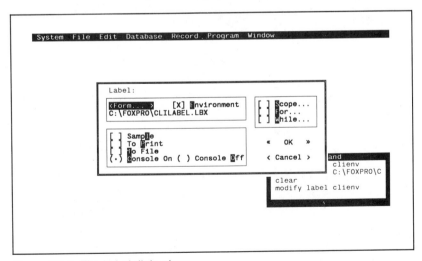

Figure 22.7: The Label dialog box

③ Press *P* to select the "To Print" checkbox. If you wish, use the Scope, For, and While checkboxes to dictate which records will be included in the label printout.

④ Press Ctrl-Enter to start printing.

As with reports, the specific settings that you should use will vary from one printer model to another. You should experiment until the labels or envelopes print just the way you want.

LESSON 23
Using Macros to Speed Up Your Work

Featuring

- What's a macro?
- How to record a macro
- Making a macro pause for user input

EVEN IF YOU PRIMARILY USE THE MENUS, FOXPRO STILL requires you to do a certain amount of typing. One way to speed up your work is by creating *macros*.

A macro is a predefined series of keystrokes and commands that you call into action with a single key combination. You can create macros to do anything from opening FoxPro menus and selecting menu choices to typing several paragraphs into the text editor. If you find yourself repeatedly typing the same things or making the same menu choices, then macros can save you a lot of time and effort.

In some software packages, you have to write each macro as a simple computer program. FoxPro, however, lets you record keystrokes as you type them. You just turn on the macro recorder, pick a key combination for the macro, and type the keystrokes you want. The next time you press the key combination, FoxPro enters the keystrokes for you.

Creating Some Useful Macros

Let's start by creating a macro to clear the screen and start the TESTFILE program—all in response to a single keypress by you.

To record our first macro, do the following:

① Choose "Macros" from the System menu to open the Keyboard Macros dialog box shown in Figure 23.1. Select the New button.

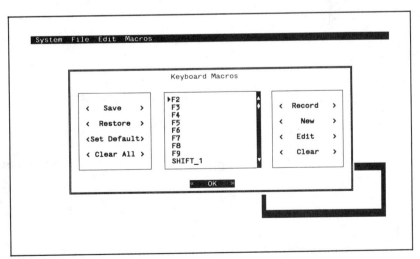

Figure 23.1: The Keyboard Macros dialog box

② At the Macro Key Definition dialog box (Figure 23.2), press Alt-M to select that key combination for the macro.

③ Tab to the "Macro Name" blank and type **run_testfile_app**.

④ Select OK in the dialog box.

⑤ A message box will appear in the upper right corner of your screen to let you know that a macro is being recorded for Alt-M and that you press Shift-F10 again to stop recording.

⑥ In the Command window, type **clear** and press Enter.

⑦ Type

   do testfile

   and press Enter.

⑧ When your TESTFILE Main Menu appears, press Shift-F10 to stop recording.

⑨ A dialog box will open, asking if you want to stop recording the macro. Select OK.

⑩ Exit from your CLIMENU program by selecting the "Quit" button.

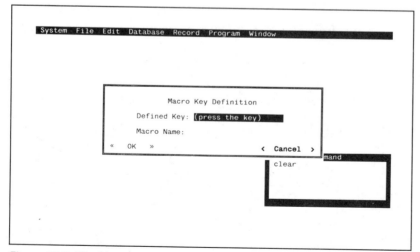

Figure 23.2: The Macro Key Definition dialog box

Testing the Macro

Now, let's test the macro to see if it works properly. Once you're back in the Command window, press Alt-M (the key we chose for the macro). The following actions should take place:

- The screen is cleared.
- The TESTFILE program is started.

If your macro doesn't work properly, try recording it again, taking care to follow each step exactly as it appears in this lesson.

Saving Your New Macro

After you've verified that your macro works properly, you should save it for future use; FoxPro does not do this automatically.

Before you save your macros, however, remember one important fact: FoxPro deposits all new files in the current default directory. If the current default directory is not c:\foxpro (the main FoxPro program directory) then FoxPro won't be able to find them in the future. To save your macros, do the following:

① Just to be safe, type **set default to c:\foxpro** in the Command window and press Enter. (If your FoxPro directory is named something other than C:\foxpro, use that directory name instead.)

② Open the Keyboard Macros dialog box by selecting "Macros" from the System menu.

③ Highlight "Save" and press Enter to save your current macros.

④ In the "Save current macros to file" dialog box, type **default.fky**, press Enter, and select "Save." This saves your macros in the default macro file that FoxPro loads automatically.

⑤ If the dialog box asks if you want to overwrite the existing default macro file (DEFAULT.FKY), answer Yes. The default macro file is not really overwritten; your macros are appended to the file and will automatically be available to FoxPro.

Creating a More Sophisticated Macro

Now let's create a more sophisticated macro. This macro will not only clear the screen and switch directories, but will then pause to let the user specify which database file and index to use, after which the macro will open a Browse window for that database file. Do the following:

1. Press Shift-F10 to call up the Macro Key Definition box.

2. Press Alt-N for the Defined Key and enter **USEFILE** for the macro name. Select OK to start recording the macro.

3. The **Recording** message should appear in the upper right corner of the screen. Type **clear** in the Command window and press Enter.

4. Type **use** and press the space bar. Don't press Enter. (This is where the procedure begins to differ from our previous exercise.)

5. Press Shift-F10 to open the Stop Recording dialog box. Press *P* to select the Insert Pause button as in Figure 23.3.

6. When the **Recording** message reappears, press Enter.

7. On the next line in the Command window, type **browse** and press Enter. (Ignore the Select File dialog box that opens up.)

8. Press Shift-F10 to stop recording the macro. In the dialog box, select OK. (Ignore the error message that warns you that no database is in use.)

Testing the Macro

Now, let's verify that the macro works correctly. In the Command window, press Alt-N to activate the macro.

The macro should play back, first clearing the screen, then switching the default directory to c:\foxpro\menus. After typing **use** in the

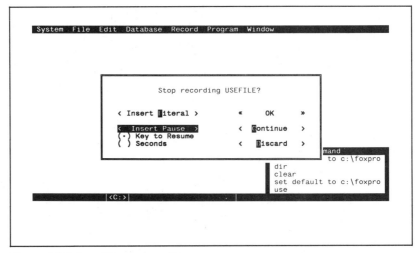

Figure 23.3: Inserting a pause in a macro

Command window, the macro will pause. At this point, the user can enter the name of the database file that he or she wants to work with.

Type **clients** and press Shift-F10 to resume playback of the macro. The macro will open your CLIENTS database file and then open a Browse window, as shown in Figure 23.4. You could have

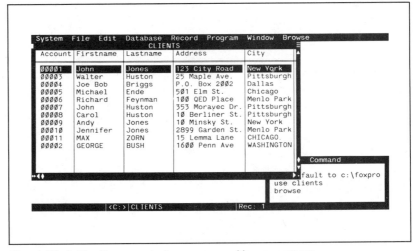

Figure 23.4: The Browse window as opened by your macro

specified any database file in the current directory, along with any index files to be opened at the same time.

Save the current macro setup as DEFAULT.FKY.

LESSON 24
Using FoxPro's Desk Accessories

Featuring

- FoxPro's File Manager
- Calculator
- Calendar/Diary

OCCASIONALLY YOU MAY FIND THAT YOU NEED TO perform other computer tasks while you're working in a database management program. Perhaps you need to copy some files from one directory to another, do a quick math calculation, write a note to yourself about an idea for a new database, or put some special characters into a program file.

You can do all these things within FoxPro by using its built-in "desk accessories." Available from the System menu, the accessories consist of a file manager, a calculator, a calendar/diary, a special-characters insertion box, an ASCII table, a cut-and-paste feature, and a game. We'll discuss only the first three.

While the last four accessories are mainly for use by programmers (except the game, of course), the first three can be extremely valuable for anyone who uses FoxPro. We can only give you a sampling of their capabilities in this lesson, but as you continue to use FoxPro, you will find many more ways to put them to use.

It may seem obvious, but it's worth noting that the FoxPro desk accessories are available *only while you're working in FoxPro*—unlike memory-resident desk accessory programs such as SideKick, which are available no matter what program you're running.

FoxPro's Filer

FoxPro has a surprisingly capable file manager called the "Filer" (shown in Figure 24.1). It lets you perform a wide range of file and directory management chores.

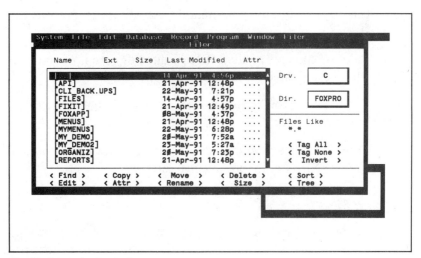

Figure 24.1: *FoxPro's Filer*

These chores include tagging files for mass copying, moving, or deleting; listing your files in different orders; searching for particular files by filename content; and showing a tree diagram of your disk directories, a feature which is normally found only in stand-alone file management software products.

*F*iler Operations

On the left side of the Filer window, FoxPro lists the files and directories that are in your current directory. You can scroll up and down in the list by using the PgUp and PgDn keys on your keyboard; the Home and End keys take you directly to the top and bottom of the list. You can switch to a different directory by highlighting it and pressing Enter or by double-clicking on it with the mouse.

The very first item in the files list may look puzzling: [..]. This is FoxPro's (and the PC's) way of showing the next higher level of directory—or the "parent directory"—that contains the directory you're currently in. The current directory is shown in the rectangular "Dir" button to the right. Let's do a quick directory-switching exercise:

① Move the highlight down to [MENUS] in the file and directory list. (If you don't have a MENUS directory, just follow the instructions but use your main FOXPRO directory instead.)

② Press Enter. The name in the Dir button changes to MENUS, and the contents of the MENUS directory are now shown in the file and directory list.

③ Note that the top line of the list is again [..]. Highlight this line and press Enter.

④ You're now back in the "c:\foxpro" directory that contains the MENUS (c:\foxpro\menus) directory.

Tagging Files

The ability to "tag" files is a particularly useful feature of the Filer. There are many times when you want to copy, move, or delete a group of files. If all the file names have something in common—the same extension, perhaps, or some of the same characters in the name—then it's very easy to perform mass operations. In MS-DOS, for example, you can enter the command

copy congr*.*   \foxpro\menus

and all the files whose names start with "congr" will be copied to the c:\foxpro\menus directory. However, if the file names have nothing in common, mass operations are impossible—except with FoxPro's Filer.

Whether you're tagging one file or several, the Filer makes it easy. To tag a file, just move the highlight to the file name and press the space bar or single-click with the mouse. To untag a file, highlight it again and press Shift-space.

Let's tag a group of files and copy them to another directory. With c:\foxpro as the default directory, select "Filer" from the System menu. Then do the following:

① Move the highlight down to SALES.DBF and press Shift-space.

② Move the highlight to TESTFILE.APP and press Shift-space again.

③ In the same way, highlight and select DEFAULT.FKY and CSALES.VUE. All four files should now have little arrows on their left, indicating that they have been tagged for a mass operation.

④ Open the Filer menu by pressing Alt-L and select the "Copy" menu choice. (You can do the same thing by selecting the "Copy" button in the Filer window or by pressing Ctrl-C.)

⑤ In the Copy File dialog box, type in

c:\foxpro\menus

as the target directory, as shown in Figure 24.2. Press Ctrl-Enter to start copying.

⑥ When the copying is finished, press the Home key to return to the top of the Filer's directory list. Move the highlight down

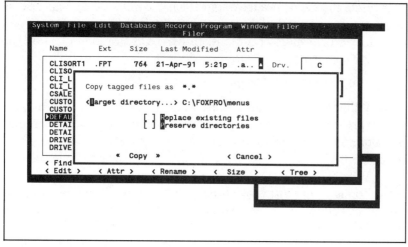

Figure 24.2: The Copy File dialog box

to the MENUS directory and press Enter to list files in that directory. By paging down through the file list, you can verify that your files were copied.

Instead of copying the tagged files, you could just as easily have deleted them or moved them to a different directory. Moving files copies them to the new directory and then deletes the original files in the current directory.

Using the "Files Like" Box

If the file names you want all have some feature in common—e.g., they all have the same extension (like .dbf) or start with the same letter—you don't have to tag them individually. Simply tab to the "Files Like" box on the right and type in the file specification by using the asterisk wildcard character.

The default is to display all files (using *.*), but you can change it to display only database files (*.**dbf**), for example, or files whose names start with C (**c***.*). By using the ? wildcard, which stands in for single letters, you can tag all files whose names (for example) start with *my,* then a number, then *file,* such as MY1FILE, MY2FILE,

MY3FILE (**my?file.***). Figure 24.3 shows the Filer with the "Files Like" box set to show only database files.

As you can see, the "Files Like" box works exactly like a database filter condition. Once you have limited the display to the files you want, you can select the Tag All button for copying, moving, deleting, etc. To untag them, select the Tag None button.

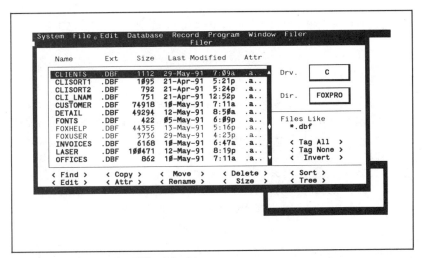

Figure 24.3: Using the "Files Like" box

Finally, to restore the full directory list, enter *.* to change the "Files Like" box back to its original setting. (Don't forget to do this, or else ten minutes down the road you'll be wondering where your other files went!)

Searching for Files

One of the Filer's most amazing features is its ability to find files in your current directory—either by searching for the files' names or by searching for what the files contain. For instance, if you're looking for a file that has the word "Rosebud" in it, but you don't remember the file name, searching by content is about the only way you're going to find it.

Let's try a simple search. You may recall several of our screen and report format files include the string "My Computer Company." Since this is an unusual string to find in a database directory, it provides us with a good method to search for just that file. Do the following:

① With the FOXPRO directory shown in the Dir button at the right, open the Filer menu by pressing Alt-L.

② Select the "Find" menu option.

③ When the Find File dialog box opens (Figure 24.4), press Enter to accept *.* as the file-name search condition. This means we are putting no restrictions on what the file name must be; we want to search all the files.

④ Check the "Specify text to search for" checkbox. In the dialog box, you are asked to specify whether you want to tag files that contain *any* or only those that contain *all* of the strings you are searching for. In this case we will be searching for only one phrase, so it doesn't really matter which button we choose; you may press Ctrl-Enter to accept the default button ("Any"). Then type **My Computer Company.**

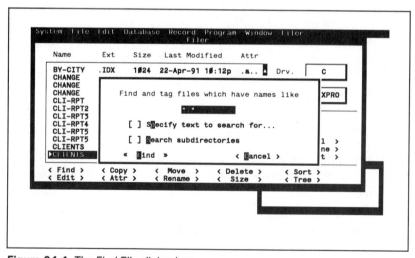

Figure 24.4: *The Find File dialog box*

⑤ Press Ctrl-Enter again to begin the search. FoxPro will scan through the current directory looking for files that contain the search string "My Computer Company."

⑥ If you now use the PgDn key to scroll down through the directory list, you'll find that all the appropriate files have been tagged by the search.

Sorting Files

The Filer also lets you display files in a different order than the normal order, i.e., alphabetical by file name. If you want to see your files in order by the date they were created, for example, simply select "Sort" from the Filer menu, and when the dialog box opens (shown in Figure 24.5), select the Date button and press Ctrl-Enter. The files will be listed in date order.

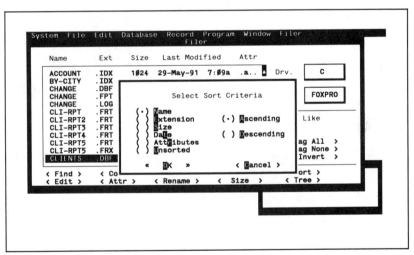

Figure 24.5: *The Filer Sort dialog box*

The Directory Tree Panel

The Filer will also display a tree diagram of your disk directories, as shown in Figure 24.6. You call up the Tree Panel by selecting the "Tree" button at the lower right of the Filer.

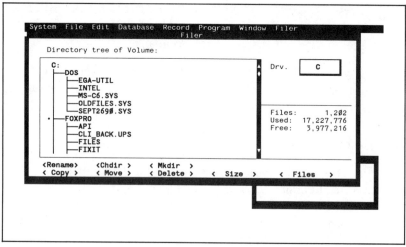

Figure 24.6: The Tree Panel

In the Tree Panel, you can perform a variety of directory management tasks, such as renaming, copying, creating, and deleting directories. You should be very careful when using this panel. If you delete a directory, all the files in it (if any) will be lost. Even simply renaming a directory can cause problems: if a program expects to find its files in directory X, but you've renamed it directory Y, the program won't be able to function.

FoxPro's Calculator

The calculator accessory in the System menu displays an on-screen picture of a calculator that you can use very much like a real calculator (see Figure 24.7). You *can* use the mouse to click on the on-screen keys, but for the most part it is easier to use your PC's keyboard to enter the numbers and select operations.

To add 100 + 75, for example, you type **100** on your keyboard, then the plus (+) sign, then **75**, and press Enter. If you then want to take the square root of 2, you first clear the previous entry from the calculator by pressing *C*. Then, type **2** and **Q**. (The *Q* stands for the square-root symbol, which does not appear on a PC keyboard.)

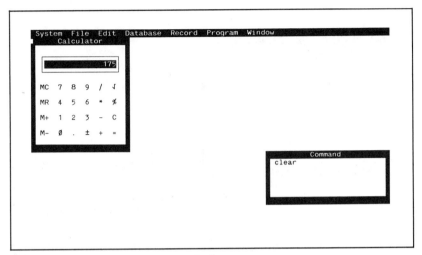

Figure 24.7: *FoxPro's on-screen calculator*

You can enter the numbers with either the numeric keypad on the right of your keyboard or with the row of number keys above the letters. The numeric keypad also provides the keys for addition (+), subtraction (−), multiplication (*), and division (/). The calculator will automatically retain the result of your last calculation until you clear it by pressing *C*—even if you quit FoxPro and turn off your PC! You can also change the number of decimal places used by your calculator while it is displayed onscreen, by selecting the "Preferences" option from the Edit menu.

FoxPro's Calendar/Diary

The calendar/diary desk accessory (shown in Figure 24.8) lets you keep track of appointments and activities as you work.

The calendar/diary starts with the highlight on the current date in the calendar section on the left. To enter text in the diary, press Tab and then just type yourself a note; to switch back to the calendar, press Shift-Tab. The new Diary menu, displayed at the top of the PC screen when you first select "Calendar/Diary" from the System menu, allows you to move backward and forward a month or a year at a

Lesson 24

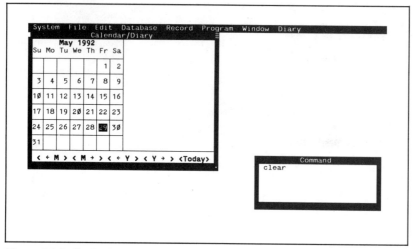

Figure 24.8: FoxPro's calendar/diary

time. The corresponding speed keys are PgUp (to go back a month), PgDn (to go forward a month), Shift-PgUp (to go back a year), and Shift-PgDn (to go forward a year).

The "Delete" menu option lets you delete all diary entries prior to a date that you specify. Unless you periodically delete your diary entries, they are kept forever in the FOXUSER resource file in your C:\FOXPRO directory.

LESSON 25
Introducing FoxPro 2's Advanced Features

Featuring

- Relational Query-by-Example (RQBQ)
- New Index File Types
- Project Files
- External Routine API
- Rushmore Technology

IN THE PREVIOUS LESSONS, WE COVERED ALL THE features you need to perform fairly sophisticated database management tasks in FoxPro. You might be surprised to learn, therefore, that we have only scratched the surface of what FoxPro can do. FoxPro 2, in particular, has many advanced features that are beyond the scope of this book. In this lesson, we'll simply look at a "preview" of those features. If you want more in-depth knowledge of how to use these powerful features, you should see your FoxPro manuals or *Mastering FoxPro 2*, from SYBEX.

Different Versions of FoxPro

The box you got when you purchased FoxPro 2 (whether you bought the single-user or the LAN version) actually contains two *different* versions of FoxPro. Each version is specially designed to get the best performance out of a particular PC or local area network. The version you should use depends on the type of PC or network equipment you have.

The different versions of FoxPro 2 are:

- *Standard FoxPro:* This version is designed for single-user installation on a PC with an 8088/8086 or 80286 processor (a standard PC or PC/AT-class machine).

- *Extended FoxPro:* This is a "32 bit" version of FoxPro that uses all available extended memory as well as the advanced capabilities of the 80386 and 80486 microprocessors. It requires a PC with at least an 80386 microprocessor, and Fox Software recommends at least three megabytes of random-access memory (RAM).

- *Standard FoxPro/LAN:* This is the standard version of FoxPro for local area networks with workstations using the 8086/8088 or 80286 processors.

- *Extended FoxPro/LAN:* This is the extended version of FoxPro for local area networks in which *both the network file server and the workstations using FoxPro* have (a) at least an 80386 microprocessor, and (b) at least three megabytes of RAM.

Lesson 25

Relational Query-By-Example

FoxPro 2's Relational Query-by-Example (RQBE) capability makes it easy for you to get information out of multiple data files with a common field, such as our sales and client data files. Behind the scenes, RQBE manages FoxPro 2's implementation of the "select" command that is part of SQL (Structured Query Language, the standard language for relational database management systems). However, you don't need to worry about that in order to use the RQBE facility. Let's run through a simple example just to show you how easy it is. (For more detailed information, see *Mastering FoxPro 2*).

In the FoxPro command window, type **set view to csales** and press Enter. If you set up the "csales" view file in Lesson 11, this command should open both the sales and client data files, with each file indexed on the account field and a link going from the sales to the client file. Then do the following:

① Select "New" from the File menu. In the File Type dialog box, press *Q* for "Query" and press Ctrl-Enter. The RQBE window will open up, as shown in Figure 25.1.

② The initial data file displayed is SALES because it is open in Work Area A. Select the "Add" button to add a new data file to the query: when the dialog box opens up, select the CLIENTS data file.

③ The RQBE Join Condition dialog box will open. With the highlight on the left button, press Enter or click the mouse. A field list will open, as shown in Figure 25.2.

④ From the field list, select CLIENTS.ACCOUNT as the link field. (The highlight should already be on that field.) Then press Tab twice to move to the "Like" button and press Enter.

⑤ Highlight and select "Exactly Like" in the list that pops open. Then press Tab once more to move to the right button.

⑥ Highlight and select SALES.ACCOUNT. Then press Ctrl-Enter to return to the RQBE window, which should look like Figure 25.3.

Introducing FoxPro 2's Advanced Features   293

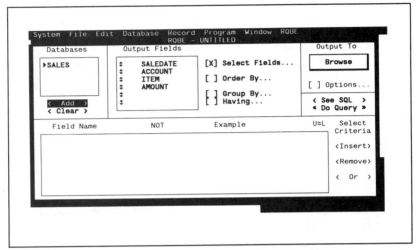

Figure 25.1: The Relational Query-By-Example (RQBE) window

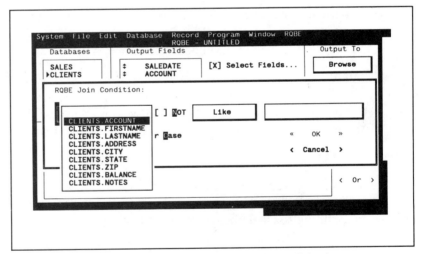

Figure 25.2: Selecting a link field in the Join Condition dialog box

In the box at the top labeled "Output Fields" is a list of the fields that will be included in the answer to your query. Right now, it contains only fields from the SALES data file. Let's add two more fields to the list.

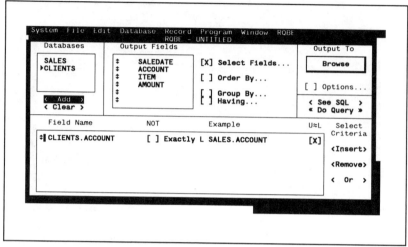

Figure 25.3: *The RQBE window with Join conditions added*

⑦ Tab to the "Select Fields" checkbox and press Enter; if you're using a mouse, simply click inside the square brackets. The Select Fields dialog box will open, as shown in Figure 25.4.

⑧ Highlight and select the CLIENTS.FIRSTNAME and CLIENTS.LASTNAME fields in the Database Fields box, just as you would in any other Field Picker window. The two fields should now appear in the Group by fields box on the right.

⑨ Press Ctrl-Enter to return to the RQBE window.

⑩ We want the records to be in order by account number, so select the "Order By" checkbox and pick the SALES.ACCOUNT field in the dialog box that opens up. Press Ctrl-Enter to return to the RQBE window.

⑪ Finally, select the "Output To" button at the top right to see the different types of output that the RQBE window can generate. After our query finds the data we want in our two data files, we can display it in a Browse window, print it in a report, or send it to a new data file. Right now, we'll just open a Browse window, so press Esc to exit from the list.

⑫ Press Ctrl-Enter to carry out the query. FoxPro will work for a few seconds and then display a Browse window with data from both files, as shown in Figure 25.5. Select "Save" from the File menu and save your query as **myquery**. Now, you can re-run the same query by re-loading the query file—you never need to construct the same query twice!

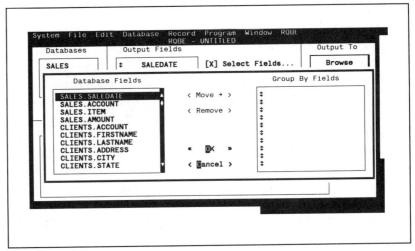

Figure 25.4: The Select Fields dialog box

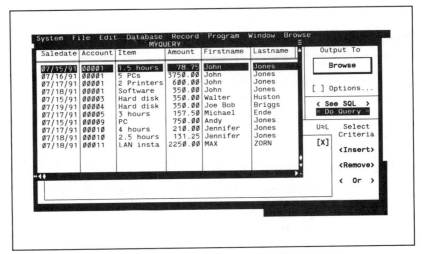

Figure 25.5: Browse window with data from an RQBE query

New Index File Types

FoxPro 2 also has two new types of index files. One type saves disk space, while the other simply makes things easier for the user. Both, however, are incompatible with earlier versions of FoxPro as well as with other database management systems that use the dBASE file format, so you should use them with caution if you are upgrading old FoxPro applications.

Standard index files (.IDX files in FoxPro and FoxBase+) can take up considerable disk space when you index a large data file. FoxPro 2 lets you create "compact" index files that can save up to 83 percent of the disk space required for standard .IDX index files.

Another problem with standard index files is that you have to remember to open them each time you change the data in a file. If you forget to open one of the index files associated with a data file, then that index will be out of date. Creating view files helps to combat this problem somewhat, but FoxPro 2's "compound" index files are a more complete solution. Similar to the .MDX index files in dBASE IV, a FoxPro compound index file (which has a .CDX filename extension) keeps track of all of the indexed fields of a data file in a single index file.

Projects

A project file is very much like a database view file (like those we created in Lesson 17). While a view file keeps track of all the data files and index files that must be open in a particular application, a project file keeps track of data files, index files, screens, menus, report formats, queries, label formats, and other files needed in a particular database application.

From a project file, you can create either an application to run inside FoxPro or a stand-alone executable (.EXE) program.

External Routine API

While FoxPro's programming language is very powerful, it is designed for database applications and is therefore not suitable for all programming tasks—particularly for tasks that involve low-level system programming. FoxPro 2's External Routine API (Application Programming Interface) allows you to link programs written in the C programming language or PC assembly language to FoxPro applications—thereby giving you the best of both worlds.

Obviously, this capability can really only be used by C and assembly language programmers, but it puts FoxPro at the forefront of PC database technology.

Rushmore Technology

FoxPro's patent-pending "Rushmore" technology allows large databases to be searched hundreds of times faster than with conventional approaches. You shouldn't worry too much about using Rushmore unless your database has at least 10,000 records: with small databases, the speed difference is barely noticeable.

Rushmore requires the "extended" version of FoxPro to handle very large databases (over 500,000 records), but if your database is that large, you're probably already using at least an 80386-based PC with several megabytes of RAM, so running the extended version presents no problem.

APPENDIX
Installing FoxPro

INSTALLING FOXPRO IS AN EASY PROCEDURE, BUT there are a few things that you should be careful about. First of all, make sure that you have enough space on your hard disk (about 8 megabytes) before you begin to install FoxPro. If you don't have enough space, make copies of those files that you can do without and then delete them from your hard disk.

Before beginning the installation process, you should create a directory to hold your FoxPro program files. You can name this directory anything, but FOXPRO makes the most sense. Do the following:

① Turn on your PC. When the "C:" prompt appears, type **verify on** and press Enter. This will provide some simple error-checking to make sure that when your files are copied to the hard disk, the copies are correct.

② Type **md\foxpro** and press Enter. This will create the FOXPRO directory.

③ Type **cd\foxpro** and press Enter. This will move you to the FOXPRO directory, from which you can start the installation process.

Warning: Be *absolutely sure* that you have switched to the FOXPRO directory. (To check this, type **dir** at the "C:" prompt; the name at the top of the empty directory list should be C:\FOXPRO.) The installation procedure copies the FoxPro program files to whatever the current directory is on your hard disk. If it is not FOXPRO (or whatever directory you've chosen), then you'll end up with program files in the wrong directory.

The Installation Process

To start the installation process, make sure that you are in the C:\FOXPRO directory, and that you have your FoxPro serial number and activation code at hand. Then do the following:

① Insert FoxPro System Disk #1 in the "A:" drive.

② At the "C:" prompt, type

   a:install c:

   and press Enter. (This assumes that you are installing FoxPro in the C:\FOXPRO directory. If the directory or drive is different, you should make the appropriate changes in the install command.)

Appendix

③ Follow the on-screen prompts and help messages to install FoxPro.

Modifying FoxPro's Start-up with CONFIG.FP

Once you've become familiar with FoxPro's commands, you may want to create a CONFIG.FP file so that your favorite FoxPro settings are automatically invoked whenever you start the program. Each time you start FoxPro, it searches the current directory for the CONFIG.FP file; if it's not in the current directory, then FoxPro searches your entire directory path (as specified in your AUTOEXEC.BAT file). If CONFIG.FP is not available, FoxPro uses its built-in default settings.

A typical CONFIG.FP file might contain the following settings:

status = on
scoreboard = on
escape = on
talk = off

Similarly, placing a DO statement in the file will automatically run any FoxPro programs you have written.

You may use DOS's EDLIN or any other plain text editor to create CONFIG.FP. (If you use a word processor, be sure to save the file as an ASCII plain text file.) You can even create several CONFIG.FP files, placing each in a different work directory. Then, when you start FoxPro from that directory (assuming that the main FoxPro program directory is in your DOS PATH), the settings in the work directory's CONFIG.FP file will be used.

INDEX

A

A picture code, 214–215
action buttons, 51–52
addition, 286–287
ALLTRIM( ) function, 221
Alpha Only formatting option, 215
Alt key, 7
.AND. operator, 117
API (Application Programming Interface), 297
APPEND command, 228
appending records, 24–25, 43–44, 217–218, 228
Application menu with FoxApp, 194
arrow keys, 4, 7, 25, 35, 247
ascending sorts, 93
asterisks (*)
    for file displays, 230–231, 282–283
    for multiplication, 287
    in programs, 197
at sign (@) as picture code, 153, 215
attributes, field, 152–157

B

Backspace key, 25
.BAK (backup) files, 61–62
Bottom button in menus, 192–193
boxes
    for data-entry screens, 150–151
    printing, 86–87, 139–140
    for report titles, 81–82
BROWSE command, 27–29, 55
    with linked files, 232–233
    with searches, 123–124
Browse window, 27–29, 55
    modifying, 68–73
    splitting, 38–40
bugs with memo fields, 74

buttons
    action, 51–52
    on data entry screens, 158–161
    default, 32

C

calculations, fields for, 57
calculator desk accessory, 286–287
calendar/diary, 287–288
caret (^), 35
CARRY ON (SET command), 225, 239
case-sensitivity
    with indexing, 111
    with searches, 116
    with sorts, 93
CASE statements, 196–197
CDOW( ) (character day of the week) function, 131, 221
.CDX files, 296
CENTURY ON (SET command), 219, 254
character fields, 14, 57, 64
CLEAR command, 227
CLOCK ON (SET command), 239
closing files, 30, 106, 246
CMONTH( ) function, 132
columns
    moving, 68–70
    resizing, 70–71
    selecting, 71–72
Command window, 12
    for creating database files, 227–238
    for indexes, 111–112
comments in programs, 197
conditional statements, 196–197
conditions, search, 115, 117–118

CONFIG.FP file, 300
CONTINUE command, 121, 237
Control key, 6-7
converting field types, 221
Copy text editor option, 245
copying
 files, 280-282
 text, 249-250
CREATE command, 228
CREATE LABEL command, 262, 264
CREATE REPORT command, 254
Currency format, 152-153
current date in reports, 129-130
cursor keys, 7
Cut text editor option, 245

D

data-entry screens
 boxes for, 150-151
 field arrangement on, 148-150
 formats and data validation for, 151-158
 push buttons on, 158-161
 screen painter for, 145-151
 testing, 157-158
DATE( ) function, 129-131, 133, 221, 254
dates
 fields for, 58
 in form letters, 254
 formatting, 130-133, 221-222
 in reports, 79-80, 129-133, 219
DAY( ) function, 132
day of the week (CDW( )) function, 131
dBASE-compatible menus, 197-204
decimal places, 15
default buttons, 32
DEFAULT TO (SET command), 111, 239
default windows, 39-40
DELETE command, 238

Delete key, 25
deleting
 fields, 62-63
 records, 46-48, 194-195, 238
descending sorts, 93
desk accessories, 278
 calculator, 286-287
 calendar/diary, 287-288
 Filer, 279-286
Detail report band, 79, 181
dialog boxes, 12-13
DIR command, 230-231
directories
 for database files, 15-16
 displaying, 231-232, 285-286
 for FoxPro, 299
 in prompt, 18
 with sorting, 97-98
disk, saving reports to, 138
DISPLAY STRUCTURE command, 231
displaying
 columns, 71-72
 database structure, 58-59, 231
 directories, 231-232, 285-286
 files, 230-231, 282-283
 records, 27-30, 201
division, 287
DO WHILE...ENDDO command, 200
dollar sign ($) function, 125, 235
double angle brackets (<< >>), 32
double-clicking of mouse, 18
double lines, drawing, 200
drop-down menus, 204-206
DTOC( ) function, 224
DTOS( ) function, 221, 224

E

EDIT command, 238
Edit menus
 with FoxApp, 193
 with text editor, 244-246

Index

editing records, 44–46, 194, 238
    program for, 201–202
    and searches, 119
    with text editor, 244–246
EJECT command, 118
ELSE statements, 196
End key, 7
ENDCASE command, 196–197
ENDDO command, 200
ENDIF command, 196
enhanced keyboard, 4–5
Enter key, 5
envelopes
    format for, 263–267
    printing, 267–268
equals operator (=), 117–118, 237
Escape key, 6
exclamation marks (!), as picture code, 153, 214
expressions
    with formatting fields, 216–217
    index, 101–105
Extended FoxPro, 291
External Routine API, 297

F

fields, 11
    adding, 59–62
    attributes of, 152–157
    creating, 14–15
    on data-entry screens, 148–150
    deleting, 62–63
    entering data into, 24–25
    formatting, 136–137, 211–216
    functions for, 218–224
    for linking, 166
    maximum number of, 30
    memo. *See* memo fields
    in RQBE queries, 293–294
    types of, 14, 57–58, 64, 221
FIELDS TO (SET command), 239
Filer desk accessory, 279–286
files, 11
    backup, 61–62
    closing, 30, 106, 246
    copying, 280–282

displaying, 230–231, 282–283
index. *See* index files
linking, 54, 163–171, 175–176, 232–233
moving within, 247–250
opening, 23–27, 105–106, 228–229
project, 296
saving, 8, 246
searching for, 283–285
sorting, 91–97, 194, 285
tagging, 280–282
unlinking, 171–172
view, 109–110, 172
FILTER TO (SET command), 123–124, 239
filtering
    for browsing, 123–124, 239
    for reports, 137–138
Find option (text editor), 246
flatfile databases, 164
float fields, 57
"for" clauses in commands, 234–236
forced page breaks, 258
form letters, 252–253
    creating, 254–259
    printing, 259
form reports, 83–86
form views, 27–28, 45–46
FORMAT TO (SET command), 228, 240
formatting
    data-entry screens, 152–158
    dates, 130–133, 221–222
    envelopes, 263–267
    fields, 136–137, 211–216
    reports, 136–137, 219–222
FoxApp for menus, 189–195
FoxView, 145
.fpt files, 58
function keys, 4, 7
functions, 130–131, 218–224

G

Generate button for applications, 191
Generate dialog box, 154
GO command, 232

GO BOTTOM command, 232
GO TOP command, 231–232
Goto Line option, 246
greater-than sign (>), 118, 176, 237
group bands, 183
grouping records, 134–136

H

help, 12, 193
Home key, 7

I

IF statements, 196
"included in" ($) operator, 125, 235
indentation, printer, 128
index files
    creating, 101–107, 194
    expressions for, 101–105
    with field functions, 222–224
    for linking files, 166
    multiple, 107–110
    new types of, 296
    ordering, 53–54, 108–109
    and searches, 121–123
    updating, 105–107
INDEX ON command, 262
INDEX TO (SET command), 107, 230, 240
input, programming commands for, 198–200
installing FoxPro, 298–300
interpreters, 195

K

keyboard, 4–7, 35–39
keystrokes, macros for, 270–276

L

labels. *See* mailing labels
LAN versions of FoxPro, 291
Layout Window, 78–80

layouts for reports, 78–80, 127–138. *See also* data-entry screens
less-than sign (<), 118, 237
letters. *See also* form letters
    picture code for, 214–215
    sorting on, 96–97
lines, drawing, 200
linking files, 54, 163–171
    and browsing, 232–233
    for reports, 175–186
LIST command, 232
    for linked reports, 176–177
    with searches, 115–117
LOCATE command, 119–121, 236–237
logical fields, 58
logical operators
    with LOCATE, 237
    with searches, 117–118
loops, programming, 200
LOWER( ) function, 116
LTRIM( ) function, 220–221

M

machine language, 195
macros, 270–276
mailing labels, 260
    envelope format for, 263–267
    label format for, 261–263
    printing, 267–268
many-to-one reports, 175, 234
margins, 128, 266
marking records, 46–47, 238
master files for linking, 166
MDY( ) function, 222, 254
memo fields, 58
    bug with, 74
    entering data into, 67–68
    searching in, 125
menu bars, 12
menus, 188
    creating, 189–195
    dBASE-compatible, 197–204
    drop-down, 204–206
    for text editor, 243–247
microprocessors, 3

minus sign (-)
   with file linking, 176
   for subtraction, 287
MODIFY STRUCTURE command, 63, 231
modifying
   Browse window, 68-73
   form reports, 84-86
   Quick Reports, 80-83
month function, 132
mouse, 8, 36-37, 39
moving
   columns, 68-70
   in files, 247-250
   windows, 35-38
multicolumn tables, editing records in, 44-45
multiple fields
   indexing on, 223-224
   sorting on, 94-96, 223-224
multiple files
   for indexes, 107-110
   opening, 229
   for reports, 175-186
multiple search conditions, 117-118
multiplication, 287

N

names
   for applications, 191-192
   for databases, 14
   for fields, 149-150
Next button in menus, 192-193
9 for numbers in fields, 216
non-indexed files, searching, 119-121
non-linking approach to databases, 163-164
not equal operator (< >), 118
numbers
   in character fields, 64
   picture code for, 216
numeric fields, 15, 57
   for reports, 136-137
   sorting on, 96-97, 223
numeric keypad, 4
NumLock key, 7

O

On/Off panel, 224-225
one-to-many reports, 175-176, 234
Open button, 52
opening files, 23-27, 105-106, 228-229
.OR. operator, 117
ordering index files, 53-54, 108-109

P

PACK command, 238
packing databases, 48, 195, 238
page breaks, 258
Page Layout dialog box, 127-128
page numbering in reports, 79-80, 129-130, 219-221
_PAGENO function, 130, 220-221
parameters, 229-230
Paste text editor option, 245
pauses in macros, 274
permanent characters in formatting fields, 216
PgDn key, 7, 49
PgFoot report band, 79, 128
PgHead report band, 79, 128, 180-181
PgUp key, 7, 49
PICTURE option for fields, 153, 212-216
plus sign (+)
   for addition, 286-287
   with index expressions, 102
   with strings, 255-256
predefined report field formats, 136
Preferences text editor option, 246-247
primary files for linking, 166
printing
   boxes, 86-87, 139-140
   form letters, 259
   labels and envelopes, 267-268
   reports, 83, 138, 177
   search results, 118
Prior button in menus, 192-193
programming, 195-206

project files, 296
prompt pg command (DOS), 18
protecting data, menus for, 189
push buttons on data entry screens, 158-161

Q

question marks (?) with file listings, 282-283
Quick Reports
    creating, 77-80
    linked, 178-180
    modifying, 80-83

R

RAM (random-access memory), 8
range restrictions for fields, 216-217
records, 11
    appending, 24-25, 43-44, 217-218, 228
    deleting, 46-48, 194-195, 238
    displaying, 27-30, 201
    editing, 44-46, 119, 194, 201-202, 238, 244-246
    filtering, for reports, 137-138
    grouping, 134-136
    linking, 166
    locating, 236-237
    maximum number of, 30
    searching for. *See* searches
    in table view, 29
Redo text editor option, 245
REINDEX command, 262
RELATION TO (SET command), 240
relational databases, 165-166
Relational Query-by-Example, 292-295
relations, 54
REPLACE command, 235-236
reports. *See also* Quick Reports
    dates in, 79-80, 129-133, 219
    form, 83-86
    formatting, 136-137, 219-222
    layouts for, 78-80, 127-138
    multifile, 175-186
    page numbering in, 79-80, 129-130, 219-221
    printing, 83, 138, 177
    program for, 203
    saving, 82-83
resizing
    columns, 70-71
    windows, 36-38
Return key, 5
RQBE (Relational Query-by-Example), 292-295
Rushmore technology, 297

S

saving
    databases, 16
    envelope formats, 267
    files, 8, 246
    macros, 273-276
    memo fields, 67
    reports, 82-83
    RQBE queries, 295
@...SAY...GET...READ command, 198-200
screen painter, 146-147
    boxes with, 150-151
    fields with, 148-150
    formats and data validation with, 151-158
    push buttons with, 158-161
screens. *See* data-entry screens; windows
Search button in menus, 192-193
searches
    conditions for, 115, 117-118
    dollar sign ($) for, 125
    for files, 283-285
    with LIST, 115-117
    with LOCATE and SEEK, 119-123
    with RQBE, 292
    with SET FILTER, 123-124
    with text editor, 246
secondary files for linking, 166

Index

SEEK command, 121-123, 236-237
Select All text editor option, 245
SELECT command, 229
selecting
    columns, 71-72
    text, 247-249
    work areas, 229
SET CARRY ON command, 225, 239
SET CENTURY ON command, 219, 254
SET CLOCK ON command, 239
SET DEFAULT TO command, 111, 239
SET FIELDS TO command, 239
SET FILTER TO command, 123-124, 239
SET FORMAT TO command, 228, 240
SET INDEX TO command, 107, 230, 240
SET RELATION TO command, 240
SET VIEW TO command, 240
Setup window, 53-54
single fields, sorting on, 92-94
SKIP command, 232
slashes (/) for division, 287
sorting
    with field functions, 222-224
    files, 91-98, 194, 285
spaces, trimming, 139, 220-221, 255-256
speed keys, 6
splitting windows, 38-40
SQL (Structured Query Language), 292
square roots, 286
Standard FoxPro, 291
status line, 78-79
STR( ) function, 220-221
structure, database, 14
    changing, 58-63, 231
    viewing, 231
subtotaling in reports, 184-186
subtraction, 287
summary report functions, 184-186, 258
System menu with FoxApp, 193

T

Tab key, 6-7
table views, 27-29, 44-45
tagging files, 280-282
testing
    data entry screens, 157-158
    macros, 273
text and text editor, 242
    copying, 249-250
    menus for, 243-247
    searching for, 283-285
    selecting, 247-249
Title report band, 180
titles for reports, 80-82, 128-129, 179-181
To Upper Case formatting option, 215
toggles, 47
Top button in menus, 192-193
totaling in reports, 184-186
transaction files, 163-169
Tree Panel, 285-286
TRIM( ) function, 139, 221, 255-256
types of fields, 14, 57-58, 64, 221

U

Undo text editor option, 244-245
undoing commands, 229-230, 244-245
unlinking files, 171-172
updating index files, 105-107
UPPER( ) function, 111, 116
USE command, 228-230
Utility menu with FoxApp, 194-195

V

Valid dialog box, 159
validation of field data, 151-157, 216-217
variables, programming, 200
versions, 291
view files, 109-110, 172
VIEW TO (SET command), 240
View window, 51-54

viewing database structures, 231
views, 27–29, 44–45

W

width of fields, 14
wildcards for file displays, 230–231, 282–283
windows
    Browse, 27–29, 55
    Command, 12, 111–112, 227–238
    Layout, 78–80
    moving, 35–38
    resizing, 36–38
    Setup, 53–54
    splitting, 38–40
    View, 51–54
word wrapping in memo fields, 67–68
work areas, 54, 229

Y

YEAR( ) function, 133

Z

ZAP command, 238
zooming windows, 39

Selections from The SYBEX Library

DATABASES

The ABC's of dBASE III PLUS
Robert Cowart
264pp. Ref. 379-1

The most efficient way to get beginners up and running with dBASE. Every 'how' and 'why' of database management is demonstrated through tutorials and practical dBASE III PLUS applications.

The ABC's of dBASE IV 1.1
Robert Cowart
350pp, Ref. 632-4

The latest version of dBASE IV is featured in this hands-on introduction. It assumes no previous experience with computers or database management, and uses easy-to-follow lessons to introduce the concepts, build basic skills, and set up some practical applications. Includes report writing and Query by Example.

The ABC's of Paradox 3.5 (Second Edition)
Charles Siegel
334pp, Ref. 785-1

This easy-to-follow, hands-on tutorial is a must for beginning users of Paradox 3.0 and 3.5. Even if you've never used a computer before, you'll be doing useful work in just a few short lessons. A clear introduction to database management and valuable business examples make this a "right-to-work" guide for the practical-minded.

Advanced Techniques in dBASE III PLUS
Alan Simpson
454pp. Ref. 369-4

A full course in database design and structured programming, with routines for inventory control, accounts receivable, system management, and integrated databases.

dBASE Instant Reference
SYBEX Prompter Series
Alan Simpson
471pp. Ref. 484-4; 4 ¾" × 8"

Comprehensive information at a glance: a brief explanation of syntax and usage for every dBASE command, with step-by-step instructions and exact keystroke sequences. Commands are grouped by function in twenty precise categories.

dBASE III PLUS Programmer's Reference Guide
SYBEX Ready Reference Series
Alan Simpson
1056pp. Ref. 508-5

Programmers will save untold hours and effort using this comprehensive, well-organized dBASE encyclopedia. Complete technical details on commands and functions, plus scores of often-needed algorithms.

dBASE IV 1.1 Programmer's Instant Reference (Second Edition)
Alan Simpson
555pp, Ref. 764-9

Enjoy fast, easy access to information often hidden in cumbersome documentation. This handy pocket-sized reference presents information on each command and function in the dBASE IV programming language. Commands are grouped according to their purpose, so readers can locate the correct command for any task—quickly and easily.

FREE CATALOG!

Mail us this form today, and we'll send you a full-color catalog of Sybex books.

Name _____
Street _____
City/State/Zip _____
Phone _____

Please supply the name of the Sybex book purchased.

_____

How would you rate it?

____ Excellent   ____ Very Good   ____ Average   ____ Poor

Why did you select this particular book?

____ Recommended to me by a friend
____ Recommended to me by store personnel
____ Saw an advertisement in _____
____ Author's reputation
____ Saw in Sybex catalog
____ Required textbook
____ Sybex reputation
____ Read book review in _____
____ In-store display
____ Other _____

Where did you buy it?

____ Bookstore
____ Computer Store or Software Store
____ Catalog (name: _____)
____ Direct from Sybex
____ Other: _____

Did you buy this book with your personal funds?

____ Yes   ____ No

About how many computer books do you buy each year?

____ 1-3   ____ 3-5   ____ 5-7   ____ 7-9   ____ 10+

About how many Sybex books do you own?

____ 1-3   ____ 3-5   ____ 5-7   ____ 7-9   ____ 10+

Please indicate your level of experience with the software covered in this book:

____ Beginner   ____ Intermediate   ____ Advanced

Which types of software packages do you use regularly?

_____ Accounting	_____ Databases	_____ Networks
_____ Amiga	_____ Desktop Publishing	_____ Operating Systems
_____ Apple/Mac	_____ File Utilities	_____ Spreadsheets
_____ CAD	_____ Money Management	_____ Word Processing
_____ Communications	_____ Languages	_____ Other _____
		(please specify)

Which of the following best describes your job title?

_____ Administrative/Secretarial	_____ President/CEO
_____ Director	_____ Manager/Supervisor
_____ Engineer/Technician	_____ Other _____
	(please specify)

Comments on the weaknesses/strengths of this book: _____

_____
_____
_____
_____

PLEASE FOLD, SEAL, AND MAIL TO SYBEX

– –

SYBEX, INC.
Department M
2021 CHALLENGER DR.
ALAMEDA, CALIFORNIA USA
94501

SYBEX ®

SEAL

Function Keys in FoxPro 2

KEY	ACTION
F1	Opens context-sensitive "help screen" that explains your current task. The help screen also includes an index so that you can get explanations of most FoxPro features.
F2	Opens the FoxPro View window, from which you can open data and index files, create multifile links, and do many other FoxPro tasks.
F3	Issues FoxPro LIST command. This shows the data in the currently selected database.
F4	Issues FoxPro DIR command. This shows a list of available database files.
F5	Issues FoxPro DISPLAY STRUCTURE command. This shows the structure of the currently selected database file.
F6	Issues FoxPro DISPLAY STATUS command. Displays information about current database files and FoxPro settings.
F7	Issues FoxPro DISPLAY MEMORY command. Mostly useful in writing programs in FoxPro. Displays a list of currently defined memory variables, windows, menus, and popup lists.
F8	Issues FoxPro DISPLAY command. Similar to LIST, this shows data from the current database.
F9	Issues FoxPro APPEND command. This enables you to add new data to the current database.
F10	Activates FoxPro's drop-down menus across the top of the PC screen.